Beginning IntelliJ IDEA

Integrated Development Environment for Java Programming

Ted Hagos

Apress®

Beginning IntelliJ IDEA: Integrated Development Environment for Java Programming

Ted Hagos
Makati, Philippines

ISBN-13 (pbk): 978-1-4842-7445-3
https://doi.org/10.1007/978-1-4842-7446-0

ISBN-13 (electronic): 978-1-4842-7446-0

Managing Director, Apress Media LLC: Welmoed Spahr
Acquisitions Editor: Steve Anglin
Development Editor: Matthew Moodie
Coordinating Editor: Mark Powers

Cover designed by eStudioCalamar

Cover image by Pixabay (www.pixabay.com)

Distributed to the book trade worldwide by Apress Media, LLC, 1 New York Plaza, New York, NY 10004, U.S.A. Phone 1-800-SPRINGER, fax (201) 348-4505, e-mail orders-ny@springer-sbm.com, or visit www. springeronline.com. Apress Media, LLC is a California LLC and the sole member (owner) is Springer Science + Business Media Finance Inc (SSBM Finance Inc). SSBM Finance Inc is a **Delaware** corporation.

For information on translations, please e-mail booktranslations@springernature.com; for reprint, paperback, or audio rights, please e-mail bookpermissions@springernature.com.

Apress titles may be purchased in bulk for academic, corporate, or promotional use. eBook versions and licenses are also available for most titles. For more information, reference our Print and eBook Bulk Sales web page at http://www.apress.com/bulk-sales.

Any source code or other supplementary material referenced by the author in this book is available to readers on GitHub via the book's product page, located at www.apress.com/9781484274453. For more detailed information, please visit http://www.apress.com/source-code.

Printed on acid-free paper

For Adrianne, Stephanie, JB, and Charlie.

Table of Contents

About the Author xi

About the Technical Reviewer xiii

Acknowledgments xv

Introduction xvii

Chapter 1: Getting Started 1

Which Version to Use 1

Getting the Java Development Kit... 6

    Installing on macOS... 7

    Installing on Windows.. 7

    Installing on Linux 7

Getting and installing IntelliJ IDEA.. 8

    Installing IntelliJ IDEA.. 8

Configuring IntelliJ... 10

Key Takeaways... 12

Chapter 2: Creating and Running a Project 13

Building a Basic Java Project... 13

Building a Large Project... 27

Key Takeaways... 30

Chapter 3: Project Files **31**

The iml File 31

The .idea Folder 32

The SRC Folder 33

The Out Folder... 34

External Libraries 36

Key Takeaways 37

Chapter 4: IDE Tools... **39**

The IDE.. 39

The Project Tool Window 41

Structure Tool Window 44

Navigation Bar.. 45

Scratch File 46

TODO 49

Problems 50

Terminal 51

The Main Editor Windows 53

Key Takeaways.. 56

Chapter 5: Code Navigation and Generation **57**

Navigation 57

Search Everywhere 58

Finding Actions 60

Opening Files.. 61

Opening Classes 64

Go to Symbol 65

Recent Changes and Files 66

Open Target Type 68

Peek to Definition 72

Show Members 73

View Class Hierarchy... 74

Code Generation... 75

Key Takeaways.. 80

Chapter 6: Inspections and Intentions.. 81

Code Inspections... 81

Addressing Inspections 82

Inspecting Code.. 86

Inspecting the Whole Project.. 93

Intention Actions 95

Key Takeaways.. 99

Chapter 7: Refactoring.. 101

Refactoring.. 102

When to Refactor 104

Refactoring in IntelliJ 105

Some More Refactorings in IntelliJ.. 111

Extract Method 111

Move Members.. 113

Change Signature 117

Key Takeaways.. 121

Chapter 8: Live Templates 123

So What Are Live Templates?... 123

Parameterized Templates.. 126

Showing All Available Templates.. 128

Surround Live Templates... 130

Creating Your Own Templates 135

Share Templates 143

Key Takeaways.. 145

Chapter 9: Debugging **147**

Types of Errors 147

    Syntax Errors 147

    Runtime Errors 148

    Logic Errors 150

Debugger 151

    Step Actions... 160

Breakpoints 161

Key Takeaways 163

Chapter 10: Source Control **165**

Git.. 165

Create Git As a Local Repository 168

    Adding and Committing Changes 174

    Branches 177

    Changes in the Changelist 178

    Ignore Files 181

GitHub Integration 187

    Committing and Pushing to a Remote Repo.............................. 194

    Creating Gist 195

Key Takeaways 198

Chapter 11: Testing **199**

Types of Testing 199

Unit Testing 201

    Why You Should Do Unit Testing 202

    When to Write Tests 202

    When to Run Tests 203

JUnit in IntelliJ 203

    Testing an Actual Class.. 210

More Examples 220

Key Takeaways.. 233

Chapter 12: JavaFX...**235**

A Brief History.. 235

Setup.. 237

Stages, Scenes, and Nodes... 249

Hello World.. 251

    Life Cycle of a JavaFX App 253

    Main.java 254

Scene Builder... 255

    Building FXML Files 258

    Configure IntelliJ for Scene Builder... 264

    Opening Files in Scene Builder.. 266

Key Takeaways... 268

Index...**269**

About the Author

Ted Hagos has been a professional developer since the late 1990s. Right now, he's chief technology officer and data protection officer of RenditionDigital International, a software development company based out of Dublin. In his more than 20 years in software development, Ted wore many hats, for example, team lead, project manager, architect, and director for development. He worked with quite a few languages and tech stacks through the years, like C#, C++, JavaScript, NodeJS, and Java — most of it in Java. He also spent time as a trainer at IBM Advanced Career Education, Ateneo ITI, and Asia Pacific College.

About the Technical Reviewer

Andres Sacco has been a professional developer since 2007, working with a variety of languages, including Java, Scala, PHP, NodeJs, and Kotlin. Most of his background is in Java and the libraries or frameworks associated with it, but since 2016, he has utilized Scala as well, depending on the situation. He is focused on researching new technologies to improve the performance, stability, and quality of the applications he develops.

Acknowledgments

Loads of thanks to those who made this book possible. Special thanks to Steve Anglin and Mark Powers. Not to forget Andres Sacco, who reviewed the book and gave me many tips for improving it.

Introduction

Welcome to *Beginning IntelliJ IDEA*. You've already downloaded IntelliJ IDEA, played around with it a bit, and maybe even used it in a small project. Now, you want to understand it a bit more so you can take advantage of the productivity tools the evangelists at JetBrains are harping about — that's why you bought this book (thank you, by the way). Well, the book aims to do just that – to get you more productive.

IDEA is a big and robust IDE. There's more than one way to get something done — sometimes it's in the toolbar, other times it's in the context menu or the main menu bar, and lots of times, the task has a keyboard shortcut. The keyboard shortcut is always the fastest. Whenever possible, I included the keyboard shortcuts for the tasks presented in the chapters — so you can improve your *keyboard-fu*.

Who This Book Is For

IntelliJ supports various programming languages, but the book is Java-centric, so it's aimed squarely at Java devs. IntelliJ is a commercial IDE, but there is a community edition that you can download and use (free of charge). I used the community edition for most parts of the book. Whenever I performed a task that required the Ultimate Edition (paid version), I indicated it in the book.

Chapter Overviews

Chapter 1 – We'll walk through the installation and setup of IntelliJ for macOS, Linux, and Windows folks.

Chapter 2 – We'll create a small project, edit our codes a bit, compile the project, and run it as well so you'll get into the programming groove.

Chapter 3 – After building a small project, we will look closer at the project structure in IntelliJ. We get to examine what's inside the **.idea** folder.

Chapter 4 – We get to see the IDE up close and personal. In this chapter, we'll explore the various Tool Windows of IntelliJ.

Chapter 5 – We start exploring some of the productivity boosters in IntelliJ. We'll look at code generators and some important keyboard shortcuts so you can get to where you need to be (quickly).

Chapter 6 – This chapter deals with one of IntelliJ's special sauces — code inspections and intentions. If you're like me — can't be bothered to remember the correct syntax — this chapter is especially for you. You'll learn how to quickly fix syntactical problems using the quick fix shortcut.

Chapter 7 – IntelliJ has great support for code refactoring; this chapter walks us through it.

Chapter 8 – This chapter discusses more on IntelliJ's productivity boosters. This chapter discusses live templates. If you're a fan of expanding code snippets, this chapter has got your back.

Chapter 9 – You've got to deal with errors sometimes. IntelliJ's debugging facilities are top-notch, which is what this chapter is about.

Chapter 10 – IntelliJ supports a variety of source control systems. Git is very popular among devs. This chapter talks about that.

Chapter 11 – If you're a fan of unit testing — and why shouldn't you be? — this is for you. We'll walk through the steps on how to write and run unit tests using JUnit5.

Chapter 12 – JavaFX is a popular desktop UI library for Java. This chapter provides an overview on how to get started with JavaFX in IntelliJ.

Additionally, the following online-only appendixes will be available as part of the source code, which can be accessed at `github.com/apress/beginning-intellij-idea`.

Appendix A (JakartaEE apps) – If back-end dev is more your thing, this is for you. We'll walk through how to build some simple JakartaEE apps. This is available online.

Appendix B (Customizing IntelliJ) – IntelliJ works great out of the box. Most of the time, you don't need to mess around with it; but if you'd like to customize it to suit your taste (or some coding standards), then this appendix is for you. This is available online.

Appendix C (Tips and Tricks) – Some more developer productivity tips for you. This is available online.

CHAPTER 1

Getting Started

In this chapter, we will cover the following:

- Which version to use
- Download
- Install and configure

Which Version to Use

IDEA comes in two flavors, Ultimate and Community editions.

The Community edition (CE hereafter) is the free and open source edition of IntelliJ IDEA. This edition is probably best for you if you're a beginner programmer or coding as a weekend warrior. You can use IntelliJ without any cost. IDEA CE supports some programming languages like Java, Groovy, Kotlin, Scala, Python, Dart, HTML, etc.

The CE is not a crippled version, not by a long shot; it's a competent editor; there's also no angle nor strings attached. There are no expiration dates. You can use it for free. Forever.

The Ultimate edition is the paid option for IDEA. It does everything the CE does (of course), plus a lot more. It supports more languages, more frameworks, a lot more tools, etc. It's a lot easier to compare the two editions on a table, so let's do that now. Table 1-1 compares the features and support for Community and Ultimate editions.

1

© Ted Hagos 2022
T. Hagos, *Beginning IntelliJ IDEA*, https://doi.org/10.1007/978-1-4842-7446-0_1

Table 1-1. *IDEA Community vs. Ultimate Editions*

		Ultimate edition	Community edition
Language support	Java	✓	✓
	Groovy	✓	✓
	Kotlin	✓	✓
	Scala (via plugin)	✓	✓
	Python and Jython (via plugin)	✓	✓
	Dart (via plugin)	✓	✓
	Rust (via plugin)	✓	✓
	HTML, XML, JSON, YAML	✓	✓
	XSL, XPath	✓	✓
	Markdown	✓	✓
	JavaScript, TypeScript	✓	
	CoffeeScript, ActionScript	✓	
	SQL	✓	
	CSS, Saas, SCSS, Less, Stylus	✓	
	Ruby and JRuby	✓	
	PHP	✓	
	Go	✓	

(*continued*)

Table 1-1. (*continued*)

		Ultimate edition	Community edition
Framework support	Android	✓	✓
	Swing	✓	✓
	JavaFX	✓	✓
	Spring (Spring MVC, Spring Boot, Spring Integration, Spring Security, etc.)	✓	
	Spring Cloud	✓	
	Java EE/Jakarta EE (JSF, JAX-RS, CDI, JPA, etc.)	✓	
	Hibernate	✓	
	Micronaut	✓	
	Grails	✓	
	GWT	✓	
	Play (via plugin)	✓	
	Thymeleaf, FreeMarker, Velocity	✓	
	AspectJ, OSGi	✓	
	Akka, SSP, Play2	✓	
	Selenium	✓	
	React, React Native	✓	
	Angular, AngularJS	✓	
	Vue.js	✓	
	Ruby on Rails	✓	
	Django, Flask, Pyramid	✓	
	Drupal, WordPress, Laravel, Symfony	✓	

(*continued*)

Table 1-1. (*continued*)

		Ultimate edition	Community edition
Build tools	Maven	✓	✓
	Gradle	✓	✓
	Ant	✓	✓
	sbt, Bllop, Fury	✓	✓
	npm	✓	
	Webpack	✓	
	Gulp, Grunt	✓	
Integrated developer tools	Debugger	✓	✓
	Decompiler	✓	✓
	Bytecode Viewer	✓	✓
	Test Coverage	✓	✓
	Test runners (JUnit, TestNG, Spock, Cucumber, ScalaTest, spec2, etc.)	✓	✓
	Embedded Terminal	✓	✓
	Database tools/SQL	✓	
	HTTPClient	✓	
	Profiling Tools	✓	
Version control	Git, GitHub	✓	✓
	Subversion	✓	✓
	Mercurial	✓	✓
	Team Foundation Server (via plugin)	✓	✓
	Perforce	✓	

(*continued*)

Table 1-1. (*continued*)

		Ultimate edition	Community edition
Deployment	Docker, Docker Compose	✓	✓
	Tomcat	✓	
	TomEE	✓	
	GlassFish	✓	
	Resin	✓	
	Jetty	✓	
	Virgo	✓	
	JBoss, WildFly	✓	
	Weblogic	✓	
	WebSphere, Liberty	✓	
	Kubernetes	✓	
Others	Custom Themes (via plugin)	✓	✓
	Issue tracker integration (YouTrack, JIRA, GitHub, TFS, Lighthouse, Pivotal Tracker, Redmine, Trac, etc.)	✓	✓
	Diagrams (UML, Dependencies)	✓	
	Dependency Structure Matrix	✓	
	Detecting Duplicates	✓	
	Settings synchronization via JetBrains account	✓	
Customer support	Resources	Issue tracker and Community Forums	Issue tracker and Community Forums
	Support	Guaranteed	Possible
License		Commercial	Opensource, Apache 2.0

The pricing information for the IDEA Ultimate edition is at www.jetbrains.com/store.

Getting the Java Development Kit

It's best to install the Java Development Kit (JDK henceforth) Standard Edition before installing IDEA. When you do this, IDEA detects the JDK installation automatically — that will save you some time on configuration work.

You have a couple of options on which JDK to use, but the two more popular choices are

- **Oracle JDK** – You can download the installers from here: `www.oracle.com/java/technologies/javase-downloads.html`.

- **OpenJDK** – You can find the download link and installation instructions here: `https://openjdk.java.net/install/`.

For this book, I used the Oracle JDK. You don't have to do the same. You can use OpenJDK if that's what you prefer.

Get the appropriate installer for your OS from the preceding links I provided. Figure 1-1 shows the Oracle page for the JDK download — at the time of this writing, JDK is version 15.

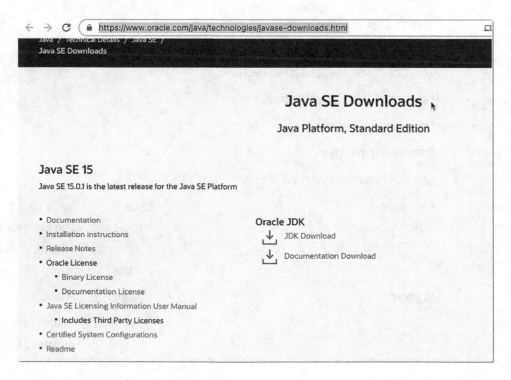

Figure 1-1. *Java SE download page*

You'd want to click the "JDK Download" link. It's best to download the Documentation too. That will come in handy later.

Oracle will ask you to agree to a license agreement before you can proceed.

Installing on macOS

Installing JDK on macOS is very straightforward: simply double-click the downloaded DMG file, and then follow the prompts until completion. The installer takes care of updating the system path, so you don't need to perform any further action after the installation.

Installing on Windows

On Windows, double-click the downloaded installer file, and then follow the prompts until completion, just like in macOS; but unlike in macOS, you'll need to include the JDK tools and binaries in the system PATH. You will need to know how to do the following on Windows:

1. Include **Java/bin** in your OS system path

2. Add a CLASSPATH definition in the **System Path**

Note that you only need to do the preceding steps if you want to use the JDK tools from the Windows command line. You don't need to do it if you will use the JDK exclusively from an IDE like IDEA.

Installing on Linux

There is a tarball option to install Java on Linux. There's also an RPM option if you're on RHEL, Fedora, or CentOS. These are all available from the Oracle link I mentioned earlier.

Alternatively, you may install the JDK using PPA. This instruction applies to Debian and its derivatives, for example, Ubuntu, Mint, etc.

On a terminal window, type the following command:

```
sudo add-apt-repository ppa:linuxuprising/java
```

Enter your user password, as usual. Then, check for updates and install the script

```
sudo apt update
sudo apt install oracle-java15-installer oracle-java15-set-default
```

When the script finishes, you'd have JDK 15 on your system.

Getting and installing IntelliJ IDEA

Before you install IDEA, ensure that your machine meets recommended requirements — let's skip the minimum hardware requirements because, who are we kidding, it's next to impossible working on a machine that barely meets minimum requirements. The recommended hardware specs to install IDEA are as follows:

- **RAM** – 8GB RAM (more is better).

- **Disk** – SSD drive with plenty of room to spare.

- **Monitor resolution** – Full HD (1920x1080); go 4K if at all possible. The more screen real-estate you can afford, the better.

- **OS** – Latest 64-bit versions of Windows, macOS, or Linux (e.g., Debian, Ubuntu, or RHEL).

JetBrains recommends that you use the ToolBox app to install IntelliJ IDEA, but that's not what we will use here. For our purposes, we'll use the stand-alone method of installation.

Let's get the IDEA CE installer from `www.jetbrains.com/idea/download/`. Download the appropriate installer for your platform. You can install IDEA on Windows, macOS, and Linux.

Installing IntelliJ IDEA
On Windows

Download the installer. Double-click the installer to run it, and then follow the wizard to completion. During the installation, you can configure the following:

- Create a desktop shortcut.

- Add the IDEA command-line launchers to the system path. This can be handy, and I suggest you tick this box.

- Add an item **Open Folder as Project** to the system context menu (when you right-click a folder).

- Associate specific file extensions with IntelliJ IDEA to open them with a double-click.

Figure 1-2 shows the setup options.

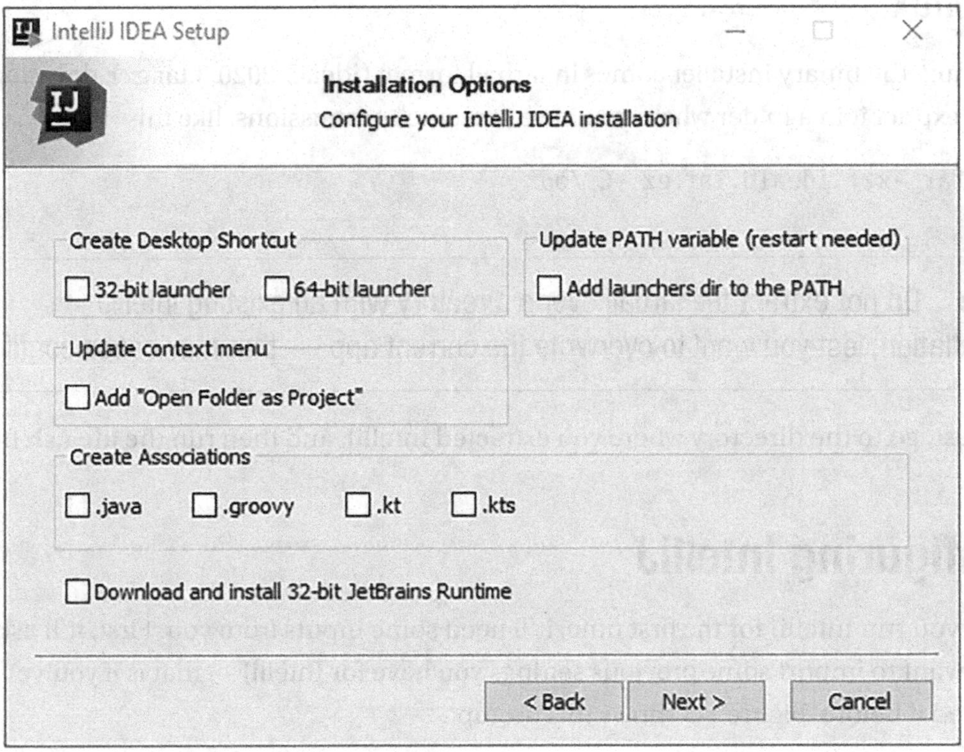

Figure 1-2. *IntelliJ installation options*

When the setup finishes, launch IntelliJ.

On macOS

Follow these steps for macOS:

1. Download the DMG installer.

2. Double-click the installer to mount it.

3. Drag and drop the IntelliJ IDEA app to the /**Applications** folder.

4. In Finder, go to the /**Applications** folder, right-click IntelliJ IDEA, and then choose "Open"; macOS may ask you if you want to open the application. This may happen the first time you launch IntelliJ in macOS.

On Linux

On Linux, the binary installer comes in tarball format (ideaC-2020.3.tar.gz); download it. Then, extract it in a folder where you have "execute" permissions, like this

```
sudo tar -xzf ideaIU.tar.gz -C /opt
```

Note   Do not extract the tarball over a directory with an existing IntelliJ installation, lest you want to overwrite the current app — that may cause conflicts.

Next, go to the directory where you extracted IntelliJ, and then run the **idea.sh** file.

Configuring IntelliJ

When you run IntelliJ for the first time, it'll need some inputs from you. First, it'll ask if you want to import some previous settings you have for IntelliJ — that is if you've installed it before. Figure 1-3 shows this prompt.

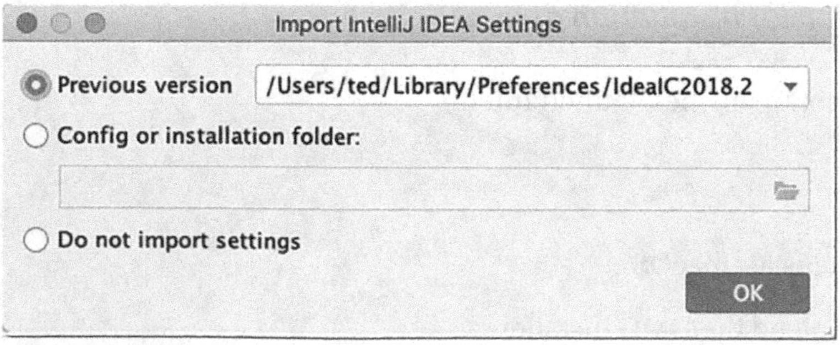

Figure 1-3. *Import IntelliJ IDEA Settings*

You can choose a dark or light theme in the window that follows, as shown in Figure 1-4.

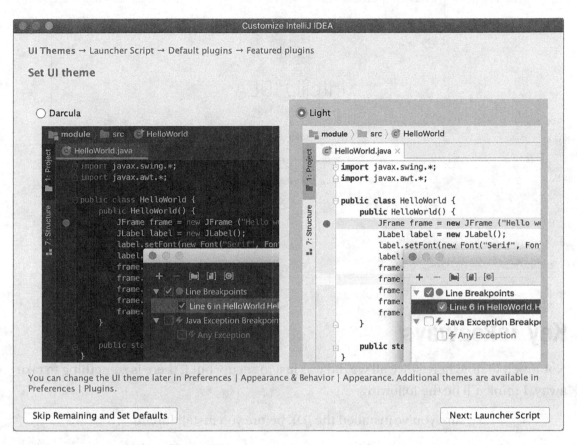

Figure 1-4. *Customize IntelliJ*

You may continue to explore the first-time launch configuration options, or you may skip — which is what I did.

After that, you'll see IntelliJ's welcome screen, as shown in the following:

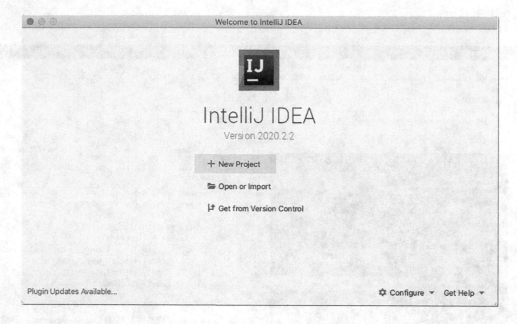

Key Takeaways

Not much to note here since all we did was just to set up; but if there is something to take away, I think it'll be the following:

- Make sure you've installed the JDK before you install IntelliJ.

- Ensure that your machine meets the requirements of IntelliJ before installing it. It's not a very heavy IDE (relatively, compared to its peers like Eclipse or NetBeans), but it's also not exactly light like a program editor (think of Sublime).

- In Linux, make sure to install IntelliJ in a folder where you have "execute" permissions. Installing it in the /opt folder is recommended by JetBrains, but you can install it anywhere you like.

## CHAPTER 2

Creating and Running a Project

What we'll cover in this chapter is as follows:

- Creating a project

- Building it

- Running it

The essential task you need to know is creating, building, and running projects in IntelliJ. That's what we will do in this chapter.

When working with IntelliJ, you need to get used to the concept of a project because you can't do much in IntelliJ without a project structure. If you want to build an application, you need to create a project and add the source codes (and other assets) to that project.

Building a Basic Java Project

If you haven't launched IntelliJ yet, now is a good time to do so; when it's opened, you'll see the Welcome window (shown in Figure 2-1).

© Ted Hagos 2022
T. Hagos, *Beginning IntelliJ IDEA*, https://doi.org/10.1007/978-1-4842-7446-0_2

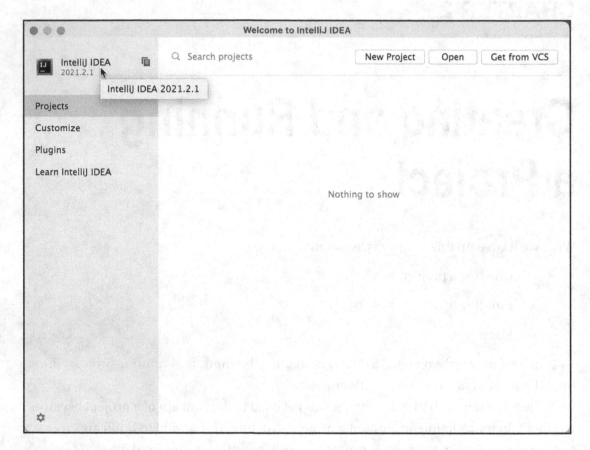

Figure 2-1. *Welcome to IntelliJ IDEA*

The four options that are prominently displayed allow us to work on a project:

- **New Project** – This option is quite simple and obvious. It will let you create a project from scratch.

- **Open or Import** – This will let us point to an existing project and have IntelliJ bring in all the artifacts from that folder. In the process, IntelliJ will create a new project configuration file as it loads the project.

- **Get from VCS** – If you've set up version control (which we haven't), you can use this option to load a project from repos like GitHub, Bitbucket, or a local repo.

- **Search Projects** – There would be a long list in this opening screen when you've created several projects. You can use the "Search Projects" function to launch a project quickly.

Let's create a new project. Choose **New Project**.

You'll see the **New Project** dialog (shown in Figure 2-2).

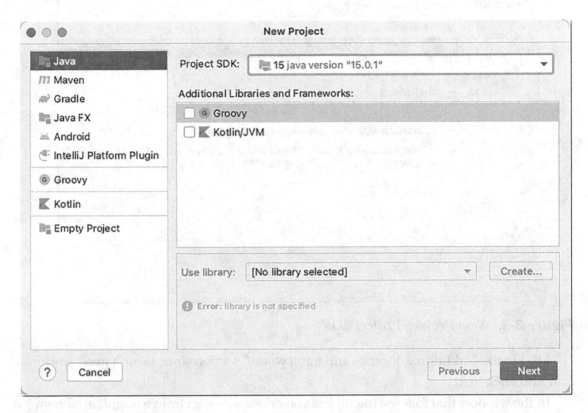

Figure 2-2. *New Project*

As you can see, IntelliJ lets us work with various projects using a couple of programming languages like Kotlin, Groovy, and Java. We'll use Java.

As you can see in Figure 2-2, IntelliJ has detected my installed JDK; in my case, it's JDK 15. If you have several JDK versions in your machine, you can click the Project SDK dropdown button (shown in Figure 2-3) to select which JDK you want to use.

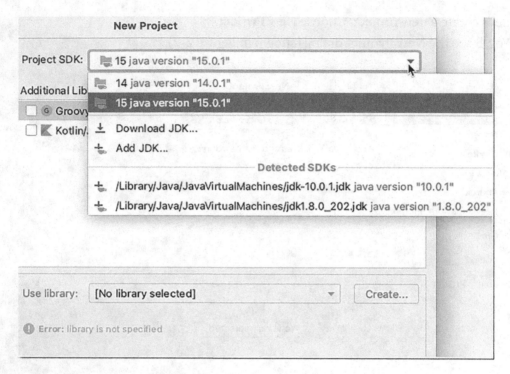

Figure 2-3. *New Project, Project SDK*

I'll skip the "Additional libraries and frameworks" section since I won't need any for now and click **Next**.

In the window that follows, IntelliJ lets you create a project from a template (shown in Figure 2-4).

Figure 2-4. *New Project, Template*

I'll choose a **Command Line App**, and then click **Next**.

In the next window, we'll enter the project's name, package, and location, as shown in Figure 2-5.

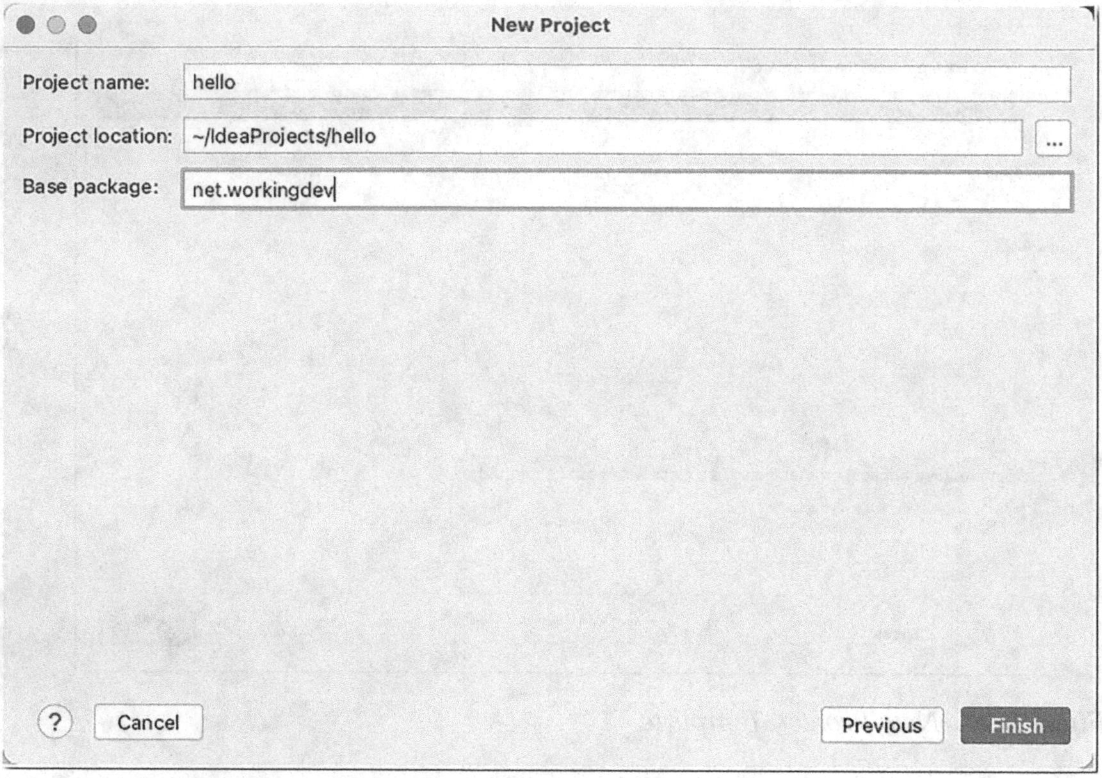

Figure 2-5. Project name, location, and package

This is a "Hello World" project, so I'll use "hello" as the **Project Name**.

The **Project Location** shows where IntelliJ will store the project files. IntelliJ shows the project files' default location, but you can change it if you prefer to store it in a different location — click the ellipsis (the button with the three dots) if you want to do so.

The **Base Package** will dictate the namespace of the classes you'll create within the project.

Once you're happy with the name, location, and package, click **Next** to proceed.

IntelliJ kicks into high gear to create your shiny new project, and in the window that follows, it shows the **Main.java** file (shown in Figure 2-6).

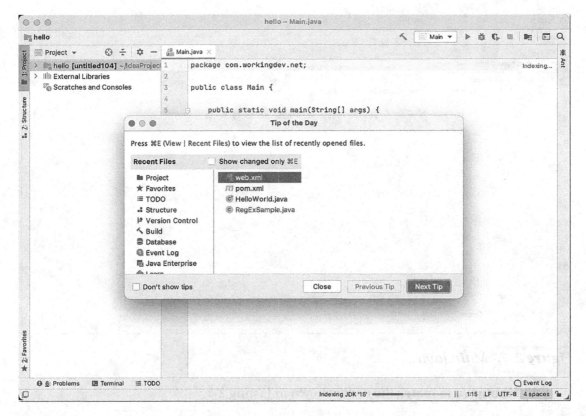

Figure 2-6. *Main.java, with "Tip of the Day"*

The very first time you create a project in IntelliJ, the TOD (tip of the day) dialog pops up, and it'll keep on showing up every time you launch the IDE unless you tick the **Don't show tips** checkbox. I just keep the TOD there — because the tips are excellent. You can click the **Close** button to dismiss the dialog.

Now we can see our main program (Figure 2-7).

Figure 2-7. *Main.java*

Edit **Main.java** to match the codes shown in Listing 2-1.

Listing 2-1. Main.java

```java
package com.workingdev.net;

public class Main {

    public static void main(String[] args) {
        System.out.println("Hello World");
    }
}
```

When you're done, you can save the changes by going to the main menu bar and then to **File ➤ Save All**, as shown in Figure 2-8. Alternatively, you can use the keyboard shortcuts for saving files:

- **cmd + S** (macOS)

- **CTRL + S** (Linux and Windows)

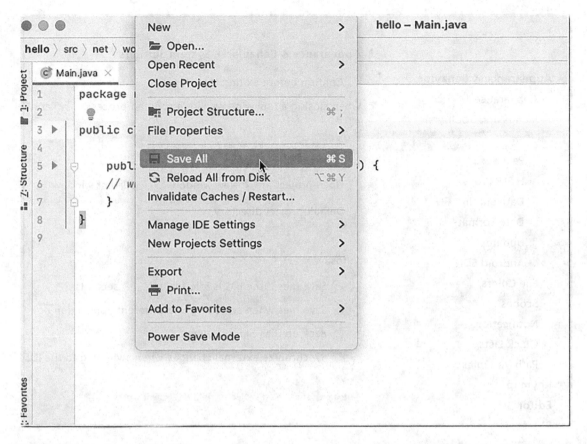

Figure 2-8. *Save All*

An excellent time-saver in IntelliJ — which isn't available in Eclipse — is the option to turn "Autosave" on. You can turn this feature on in the Preferences (macOS) or Settings (Linux/Windows), and then go to **Appearance and Behavior ➤ System Settings ➤ Autosave** (as shown in Figure 2-9).

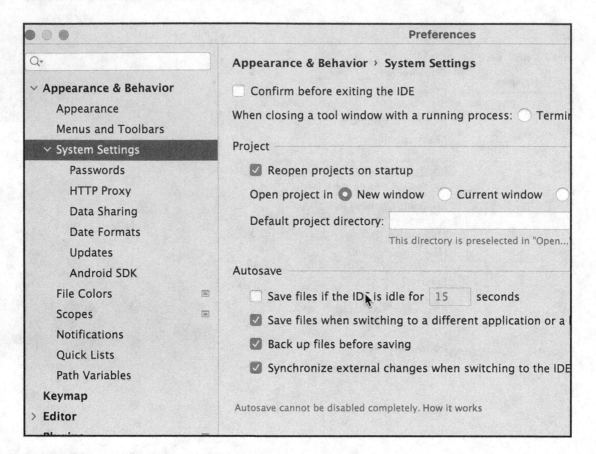

Figure 2-9. *Preferences | Autosave*

The next step is to build the project. You can do that from the main menu bar, and then choose **Build ➤ Build Project**, as shown in Figure 2-10.

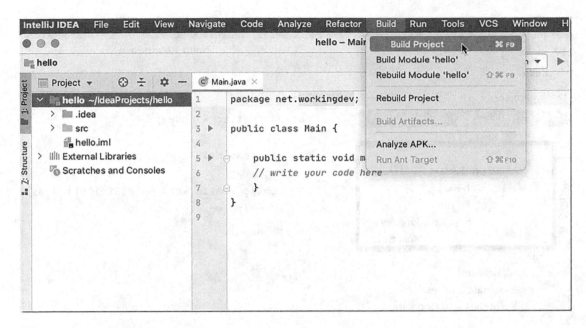

Figure 2-10. *Build project*

When the build finishes, you'll notice that there will be a new orange folder named **out** within the **Project Tool** window (shown in Figure 2-11).

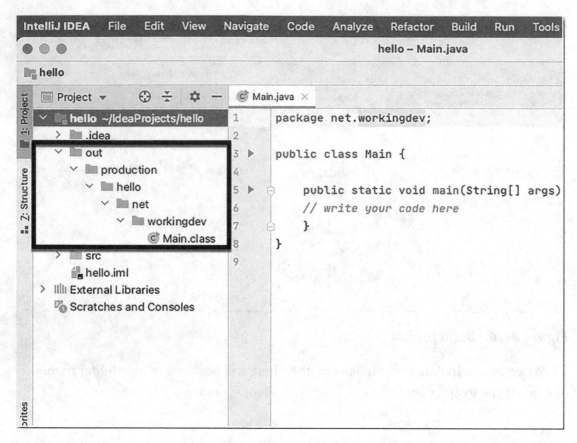

Figure 2-11. out folder in the Project Tool window

The **out** folder contains the generated class files. The **out** folder is marked as orange because it's excluded from the project — it's generated code after all, so it makes sense.

You can mark folders in different ways. If you want to explore it a bit more, try to use the context menu on the **out** folder, and then choose Mark Directory (as shown in Figure 2-12).

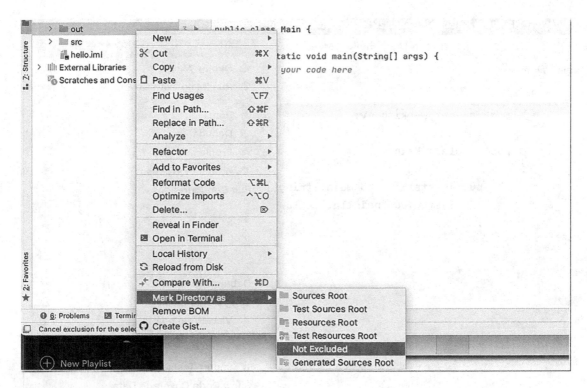

Figure 2-12. *Mark Directory as*

You don't need to change anything right now. I just wanted to point out what IntelliJ can do about marking folders. This can be handy if you add some temporary resources to the project but aren't necessarily part of the project — like the output directory — or when you're creating test root folders (when unit testing).

The next step is to run the program. Go to the main menu bar, and then go to **Run ➤ Run Main**, as you can see in Figure 2-13.

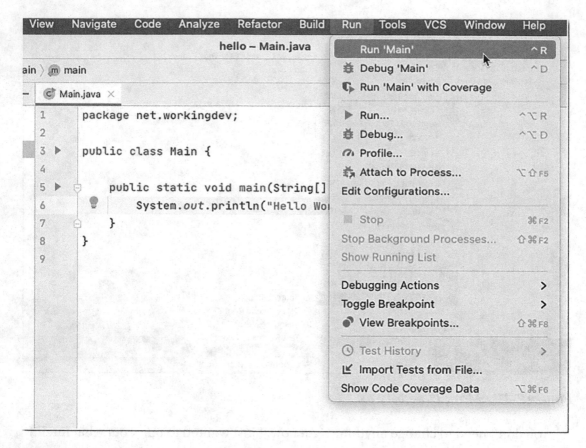

Figure 2-13. *Run*

The output window pops out in the bottom part of the IDE (shown in Figure 2-14) and prints our program's result.

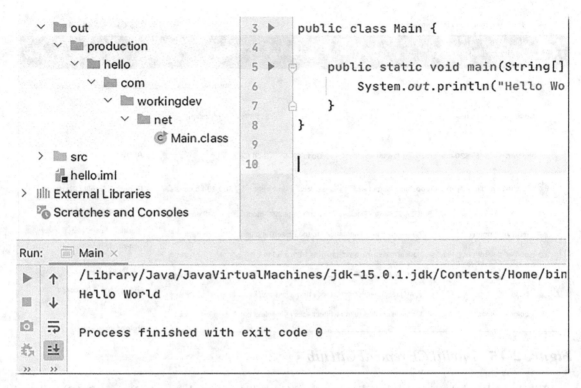

Figure 2-14. *Hello World output*

There you go. That's how to create, build, and run a Java project in IntelliJ.

Building a Large Project

In this section, I'd like to show you how IntelliJ handles a large project. You don't have to follow along here. In fact, I advise you not to because we're not yet equipped to troubleshoot problems attendant to importing nontrivial projects.

What I'll do is to download the source for IntelliJ IDEA CE from its GitHub home repo (shown in Figure 2-15) `https://github.com/JetBrains/intellij-community`. This project is huge. It's been forked 3.8 thousand times; it has 320 branches and 614 contributors. This isn't a trivial project.

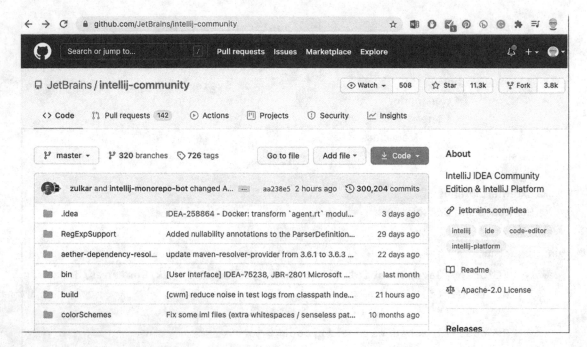

Figure 2-15.   IntelliJ CE repo at GitHub

I'll download the project by clicking the "Code" button (shown in Figure 2-16). I'll get the zipped file.

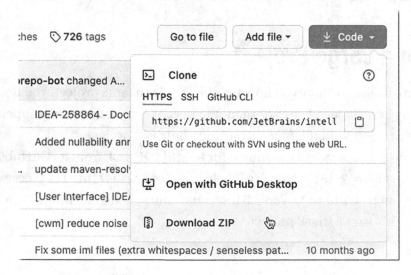

Figure 2-16.   Download ZIP

I'll extract the zipped file, and then open it in IntelliJ. The "Hello World" project is still open in my machine, so I'll go to the main menu bar, then **File ➤ Open**, and then point to the directory where I extracted the zipped file.

IntelliJ will load all the artifacts of the project and create new configurations. In the process, I'll need to resolve some conflicts like Gradle version, SDK settings, etc.; but once that's done, the IntelliJ project from GitHub will be loaded.

I'll build the project, just like how we built the "Hello World" project. IntelliJ gets busy building the project (shown in Figure 2-17).

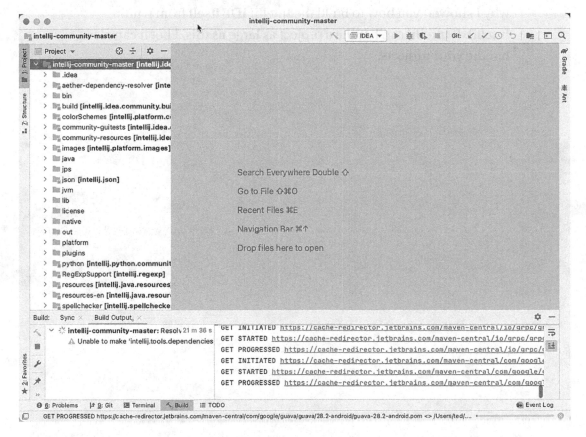

Figure 2-17. *IntelliJ project loaded within IntelliJ*

This won't be a short process. It'll take a while — more than enough time for me to grab some coffee and a quick snack.

When it's finally done, I'll run the project, *et voila*, I'll see the Welcome window of IntelliJ again — which I won't show you anymore because you've already seen it.

Key Takeaways

- It's straightforward to create a project from scratch. You can do that from the Welcome window.

- You can load existing projects into IntelliJ; just use the Open option from the Welcome window and point to the folder of the existing project.

- IntelliJ is a very capable IDE; it can handle huge projects — this is why I showed you how to build the IntelliJ IDE itself from within IntelliJ. If IntelliJ can handle a project as large as this, I bet it can also handle your projects.

CHAPTER 3

Project Files

What we'll cover in this chapter is as follows:

- The IntelliJ module

- The .idea folder

- The out folder

- The external libraries

In the previous chapter, we created a small project. It isn't much, but it gave us a taste of project creation, compilation, and execution in IntelliJ. In this chapter, we'll look closer at the files that make up an IntelliJ project.

Most IDEs that are advanced enough to do things beyond simple editing of source files will generate proprietary files that hold configuration, state, preferences, etc. IntelliJ isn't an exception.

This chapter will look at some of the files that IntelliJ generates as part of the project.

The iml File

This contains basic module information. A module in IntelliJ isn't the same as a Java module (introduced in Java 9). The IntelliJ module is a discreet chunk of functionality that you can run, test, and debug independently within the IDE. A project may contain more than one module, and it may contain things such as source code, build scripts, unit tests, deployment descriptors, etc. The **iml** file describes a module.

Figure 3-1 shows the content of an example **iml** file.

© Ted Hagos 2022

T. Hagos, *Beginning IntelliJ IDEA*, https://doi.org/10.1007/978-1-4842-7446-0_3

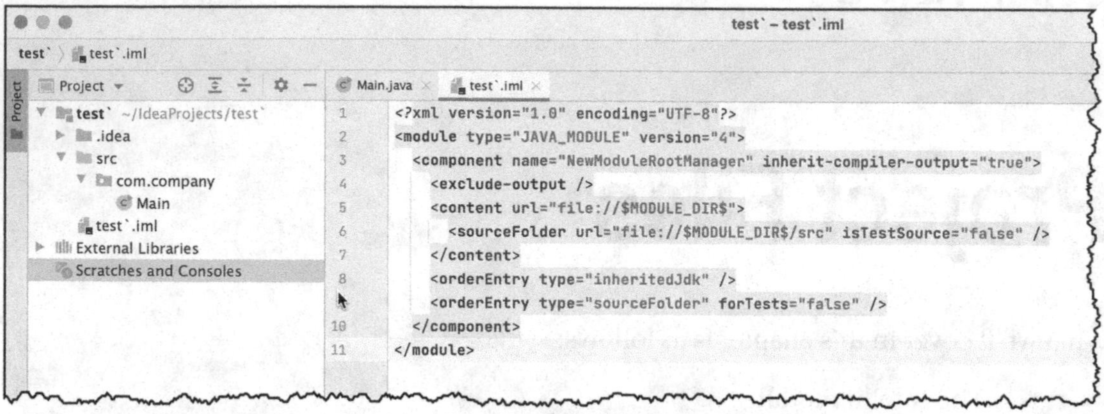

Figure 3-1. *A small project showing the iml file*

As you can see, there's only one module in this project. It's the one that got automatically created with the project. You can add modules (as needed) to your project.

Each module in the project may use a specific SDK or even inherit an SDK based on project settings. Listing 3-1 shows the content of our (default) iml file.

Listing 3-1. test.iml

```xml
<?xml version="1.0" encoding="UTF-8"?>
<module type="JAVA_MODULE" version="4">
  <component name="NewModuleRootManager" inherit-compiler-output="true">
    <exclude-output />
    <content url="file://$MODULE_DIR$">
      <sourceFolder url="file://$MODULE_DIR$/src" isTestSource="false" />
    </content>
    <orderEntry type="inheritedJdk" />
    <orderEntry type="sourceFolder" forTests="false" />
  </component>
</module>
```

The .idea Folder

The **.idea** folder is a collection of configuration files that applies to the entire project, no matter how many modules it contains. It's at the root of every project. Figure 3-2 shows a project with the **.idea** folder expanded in the Project Tool window.

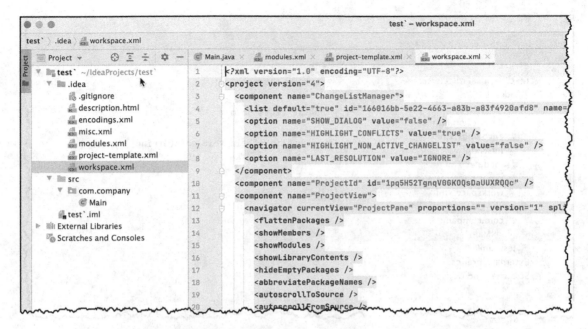

Figure 3-2. *Contents of the .idea folder*

When you change something in the settings of the project or settings of the IDE, those changes will reflect in one of the many files inside the **.idea** folder. If you changed the JDK settings, added a module to the project, changed the encoding, etc., those changes make it into one of these files. It's best not to edit these files manually.

If this is the first time you're using IntelliJ, you might wonder whether you should include the contents of the .idea folder in source control. JetBrains advises that all the contents of the .idea folder, save for one, be put in source control. The one thing you should not check in is the **workspace.xml** because it contains your personal preferences for the project; it's just for you.

The SRC Folder

The src folder is where we do most of our work. As you might have guessed, src is short for the source, as in the source code. Figure 3-3 shows a source code displayed in editing window.

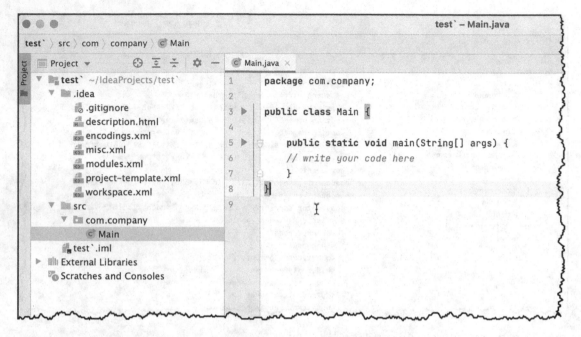

Figure 3-3. *Main.java is shown in the main editing window.*

Our small sample project only has a single Java source file, and it's under the **com. company** folder, as shown in Figure 3-3. IntelliJ puts the source file under a folder with the same name as the package declaration.

As you add code (on the same package), you'll see them under the same folder name. When you add a code, not on the same package, a new folder (with the name of the new package declaration) will be added to the **src** folder.

The Out Folder

When you run or build your code, another folder will be added to the project's root. That's the **out** folder (shown in Figure 3-4).

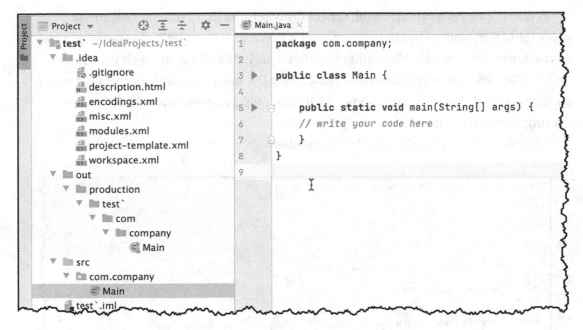

Figure 3-4. *The contents of the out folder*

The out folder contains the executable Java files (byte codes). If you click the **Main. class** file to try and view its contents, IntelliJ won't open the contents of the class file; instead, it will prompt you if you want to decompile it (as shown in Figure 3-5).

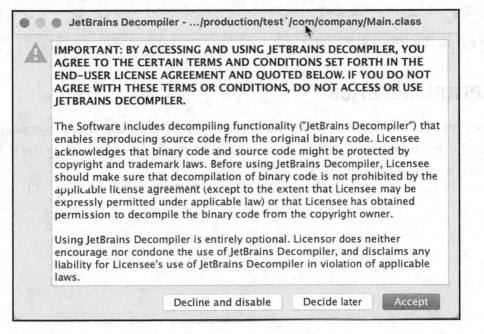

Figure 3-5. *JetBrains decompiler*

A decompiler is a valuable tool, especially when you don't have access to the executable file's source program. There's a bit of warning from JetBrains here because, as you know, the use of a decompiler is rather a gray area. There are legit uses for a decompiler, and there are also shady reasons for the same. Anyway, for the sake of our curiosity, let's decompile away, shall we? It's our own program, after all. To use the decompiler, you must click "Accept" (Figure 3-5).

Figure 3-6 shows the decompiled **Main.class**.

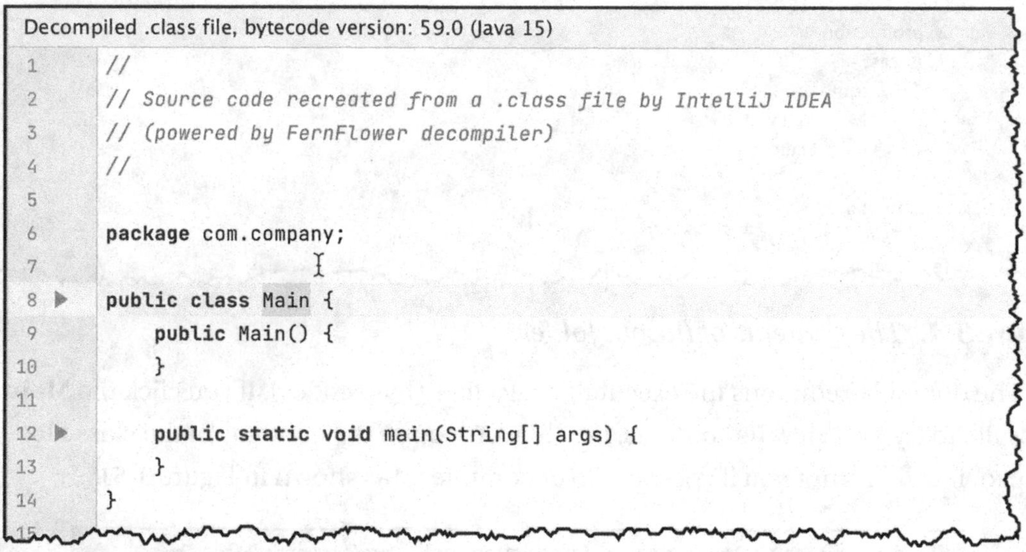

```
Decompiled .class file, bytecode version: 59.0 (Java 15)
1    //
2    // Source code recreated from a .class file by IntelliJ IDEA
3    // (powered by FernFlower decompiler)
4    //
5
6    package com.company;
7
8  ▶ public class Main {
9        public Main() {
10       }
11
12 ▶     public static void main(String[] args) {
13       }
14   }
15
```

Figure 3-6. *Decompiled Main.class*

External Libraries

The external libraries folder is where you'll see all the libraries that your project depends on. We created a simple project, so there's not much to see right now except the JDK libraries (as shown in Figure 3-7).

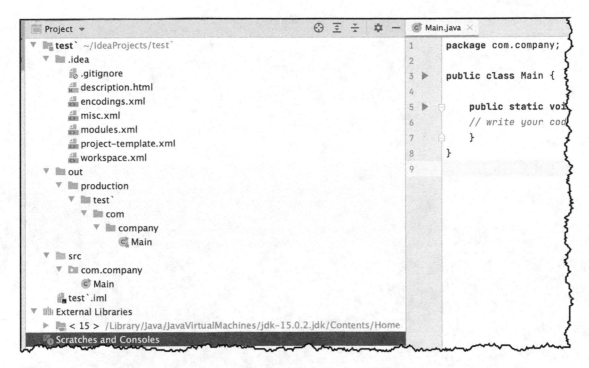

Figure 3-7. *Contents of external libraries folder*

Key Takeaways

- IntelliJ keeps its projects and IDE settings in the XML files inside the **.idea** folder. When you make changes to the project, the IDE, or your environment, those changes are persisted in the files within the **.idea** folder.

- JetBrains advises us to keep the contents of the .idea folder within source control, except for **workspace.xml**. That one you should put in **.gitignore** file (if you're using Git).

- IntelliJ has a built-in decompiler that you can use to view the source code of a decompiled class.

CHAPTER 4

IDE Tools

In this chapter, we will cover the following:

- Project Tool Window
- Navigation Bar
- Structure Tool Window
- Scratch file
- TODO
- Problem Tool Window
- Terminal
- The main editor

IntelliJ is a robust IDE. Although it's fast, it isn't exactly lightweight – and for good reasons. It's packed with features. In this chapter, we'll look at some of the most used tools of IntelliJ.

The IDE

Let's get acquainted with the IDE first. Figure 4-1 shows some parts of the IDE you'll likely deal with the most.

© Ted Hagos 2022
T. Hagos, *Beginning IntelliJ IDEA*, https://doi.org/10.1007/978-1-4842-7446-0_4

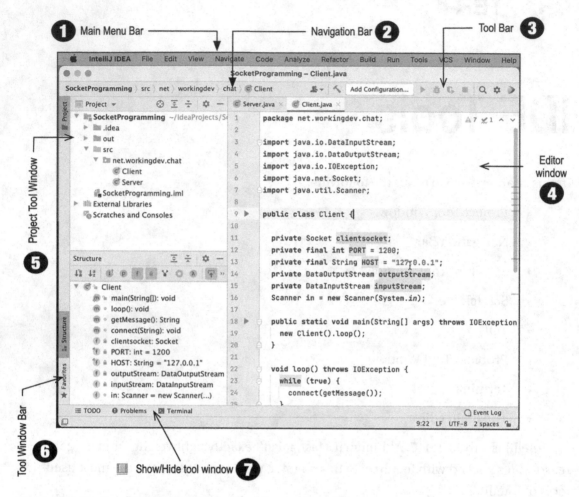

Figure 4-1. *IntelliJ IDEA (with a project opened)*

❶ **Main Menu Bar** – This is the primary way to navigate IntelliJ, but most of the items here have keyboard shortcuts, so it pays to know those shortcuts, especially for commands you will use often. JetBrains maintains a page on their website that lists the most commonly used keyboard shortcuts; you should bookmark it – or better yet, print it and stick it in your notebook, pin it in your corkboard, etc. Here's the link: www.jetbrains.com/help/idea/mastering-keyboard-shortcuts.html.

❷ **Navigation Bar** – This bar is dynamic. It leaves your footprints in here as you perform an operation, just like bread crumbs on some websites. This is very useful if you'd like to retrace your steps.

(*continued*)

❸ **Toolbar** – This is where you'll find the most common tasks for development, for example, running an app, debugging an app, search, settings, etc.

❹ **Editor Window** – The star of the show. This is where you do your coding work. When you launch a file (from the Project Tool Window), IntelliJ opens it here for editing.

❺ **Project Tool Window** – This is where you can navigate your project. You can launch any project file from this window.

❻ **Tool Window Bar** – This runs along the perimeter of the IDE. As you can see, it contains the individual buttons you need to launch specific tool windows like Favorites, Structure, Problems, TODO, Terminal, etc.

❼ **Show/Hide Tool Windows** – It shows or hides the Tool Window Bar. It's a toggle.

The Project Tool Window

Next to the Main Editor Window, the Project Tool Window is likely where you'll spend a lot of your time. This window exposes various views of the project. It also lets you add, remove, or relocate items in the project. The Project Tool Window is the primary way to launch project files into the Main Editor Window; double-click it, and out it pops for editing.

Figure 4-2 shows the Project Tool Window with the default Project View.

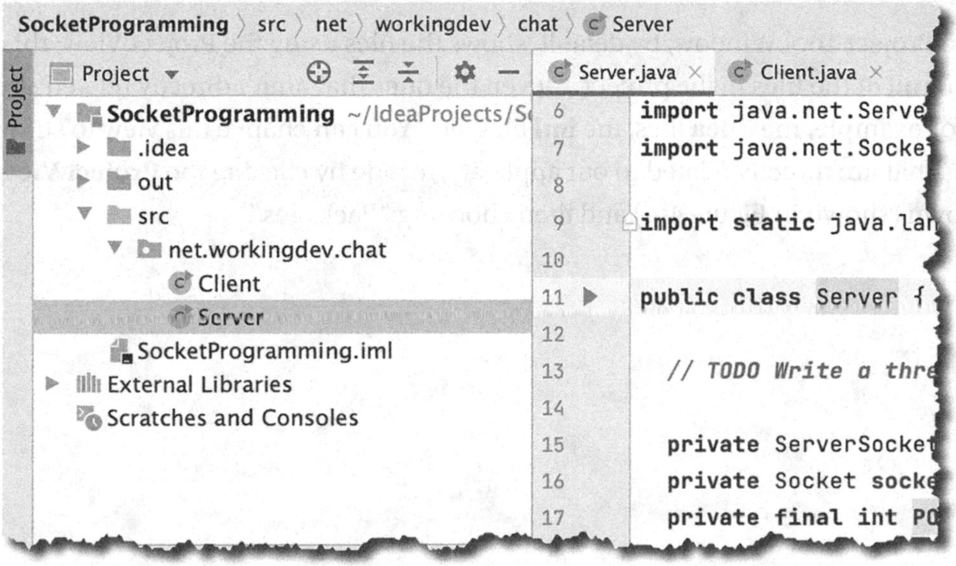

Figure 4-2. *The Project Tool Window*

If you need more screen space for the Main Editor Window, you can hide the Project Tool Window by clicking its button on Tool Window Bar (shown in Figure 4-3).

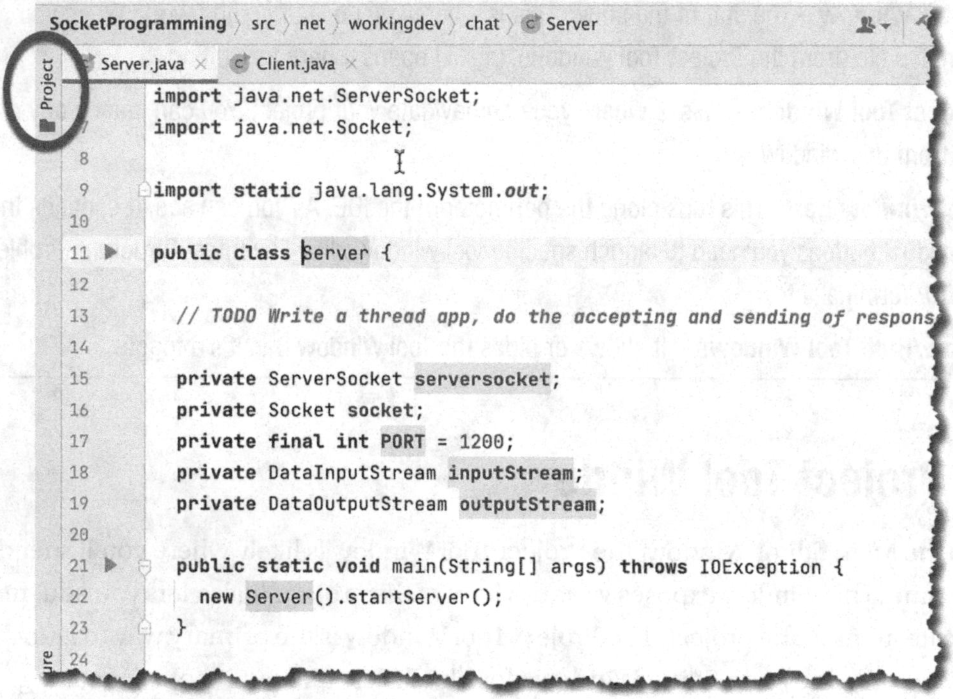

```
SocketProgramming  src  net  workingdev  chat  C Server

  Server.java ×    C Client.java ×
         import java.net.ServerSocket;
         import java.net.Socket;
    8                            I
    9    import static java.lang.System.out;
   10
   11  ▶  public class Server {
   12
   13       // TODO Write a thread app, do the accepting and sending of respons
   14
   15       private ServerSocket serversocket;
   16       private Socket socket;
   17       private final int PORT = 1200;
   18       private DataInputStream inputStream;
   19       private DataOutputStream outputStream;
   20
   21  ▶    public static void main(String[] args) throws IOException {
   22         new Server().startServer();
   23       }
   24
```

Figure 4-3. *The Project Tool Window, Hidden*

The Project Tool Window, by default, shows the files using the Project View; this view shows us all of the files in the project — even the ones that aren't directly related to our code, for example, the **.idea** files, the **iml** files, etc. You can change this view to show only the files that are directly related to our application code by clicking the **Project View** dropdown (shown in Figure 4-4) and then choosing "Packages."

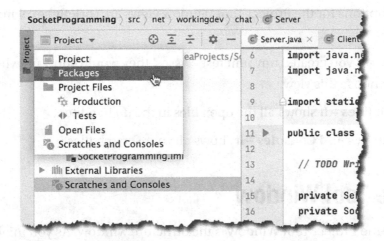

Figure 4-4. *Switch to Packages view*

Figure 4-5 shows the Project Tool Window on "Packages" view. Now we can only see the codes within our code packages — nothing else.

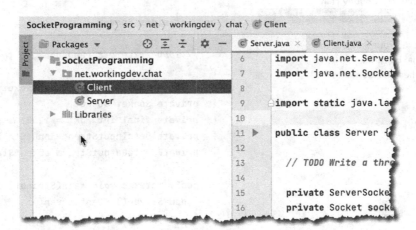

Figure 4-5. *Project Tool Window, in Packages view*

When you clicked the dropdown to change the perspective of the Project Tool Window, you may have noticed that there were other options like Open Files, Tests, and Scratches and Consoles.

The other options for the Project Tool Window views are (briefly) explained in the following:

- **Tests** – If you created any unit test classes, they would show up when you choose this view.

- **Open Files** – It shows all the open files in the main editor.

- **Scratches and Consoles** – It shows all your scratch files.

Structure Tool Window

Directly below the Project Tool Window is the Structure window. As you might have guessed from its name, it shows the structure of classes (and interfaces).

The contents of the Structure window reflect the structure of the currently selected class or interface in the Project Tool Window, as you can see in Figure 4-6.

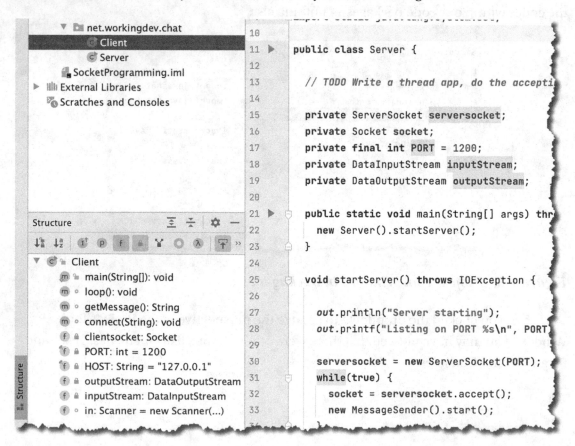

Figure 4-6. *Structure Tool Window*

The Structure window shows all fields (member variables), methods, lambdas, and properties of the selected class; it will even tell you if the class members are inherited or not.

The Structure window is a helpful tool to navigate your classes, especially when your classes become more complex.

Navigation Bar

The Navigation Bar is underappreciated. Many programmers dismiss this tool as a glorified bread crumb — well, it really is some kind of bread crumb mechanism, but it's more. You can really navigate the whole project via the Navigation Bar, just like how you would navigate using the Project Tool Window.

Each item in the bread crumb is navigable; as can be seen in Figure 4-7, when we click the bread crumb on "Socket Programming" (the name of the project), it shows the other files and folders on the project — just like in the Project Tool Window.

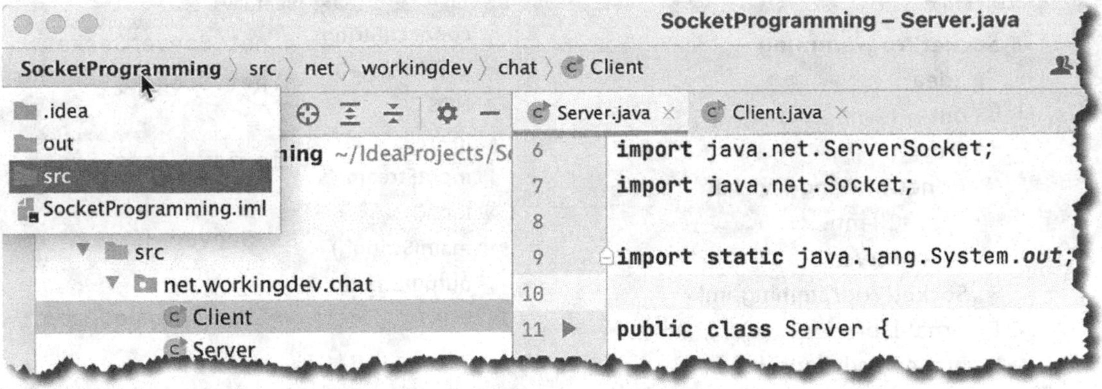

Figure 4-7. *Navigation Bar showing the dropdown on the project level.*

Figure 4-8 shows the Navigation Bar showing the contents of the package.

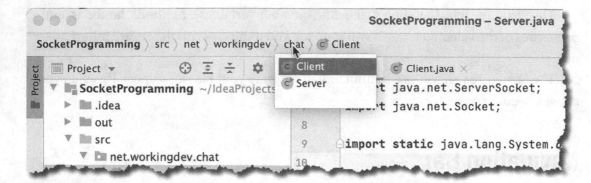

Figure 4-8. *Navigation Bar showing the dropdown on the package level*

Figure 4-9 shows the Navigation Bar showing the class members, just like in the Structure window.

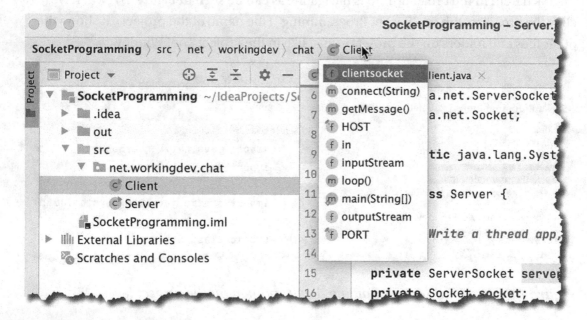

Figure 4-9. *Navigation Bar showing dropdown on the class level*

Scratch File

The name is a dead giveaway. Scratch files let you create scratches for your project. It's a handy way to write things down or keep track of things, but you aren't sure if you want these codes to be part of the project.

You can create a scratch file by using the context menu on the "Scratches and Consoles" (it's in the Project Tool Window); click **New ➤ Scratch File** (as shown in Figure 4-10).

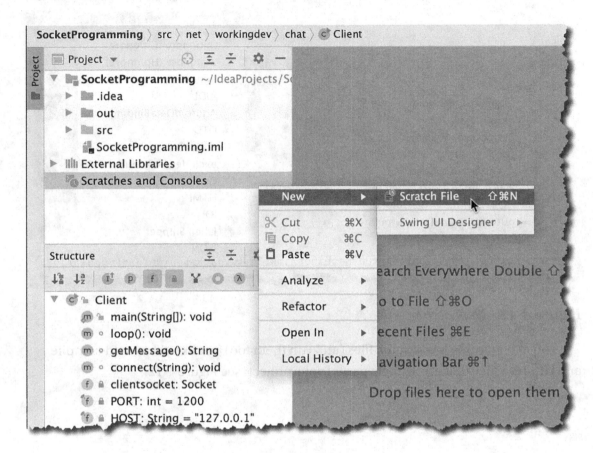

Figure 4-10. *Create a new scratch file*

In the popup that follows, choose what kind of scratch file you want to create; you can choose from a variety of types, for example, Java file, HTML, JSON, etc. (shown in Figure 4-11).

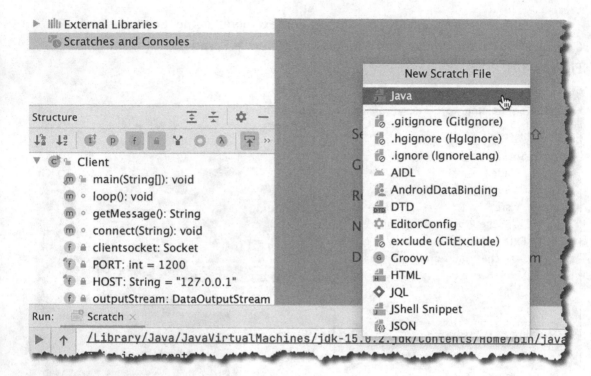

Figure 4-11. *New Scratch File*

You can compile Java scratch files (and run them too) just like you would compile and run Java files that are actually part of your project; see Figure 4-12.

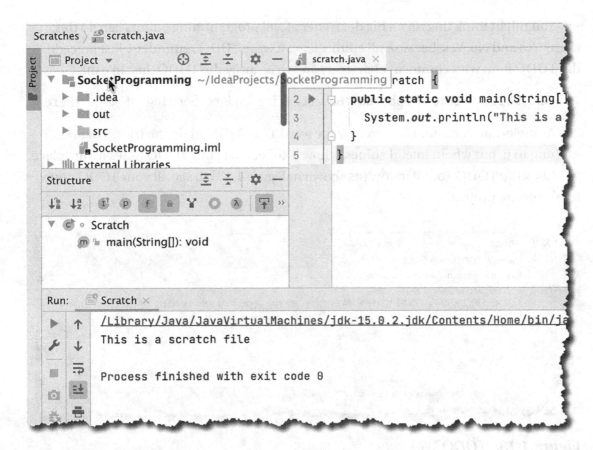

Figure 4-12. *Scratch file, compiled and ran*

You can change the file format of the scratch file quite easily; just right-click the scratch file, choose "Override File Type," and then select the new file type.

TODO

TODO items are instructions for yourself (or other members of the team). It's a note that serves as a reminder to do particular things or implement specific features on very specific classes.

You might think this isn't a big deal; after all, all programming editors can do this, right? Yes and No. Yes, because all editors let you write TODO reminders. Just precede the TODO item with comment characters and write away the TODO. Just like this:

```
// TODO Write a thread app, do the accepting and responding of msgs there
```

A single-line comment followed by the word TODO should do the trick. There's nothing to it, but where IntelliJ shines is how it collects all your TODO notes in one place.

Click the TODO Tool Window (as shown in Figure 4-13) to see all your TODO notes for the entire project.

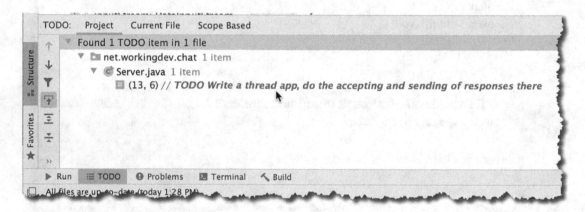

Figure 4-13. *TODO Window*

The TODO Window shows all the TODO notes that you scattered throughout the project files. What's more, if you double-click any TODO item, IntelliJ will open the file that contains the TODO note in the main editor.

Problems

The Problem Tool Window shows all the problems and warning items in the entire project. You might not see the value of the Problem Tool Window at first because IntelliJ does an excellent job of telling you (in your face, quite it seems) whenever you mess up a syntax — you'll see in red curly lines. But where this window really shines is in the area of warnings. Warnings don't make a big fuss in IntelliJ. You only become aware of them when your mouse hovers a line of code (which IntelliJ thinks it can improve), and then you'll see a yellow bulb — like the one shown in Figure 4-14.

```
// TODO Write a thread app, do the accepting and sending of resp

private ServerSocket serverSocket;
private Socket socket;                Field can be converted to a local variable
private final int PORT = 1
private DataInputStream in            Convert field to local variable in method 'start
```

Figure 4-14. *IntelliJ warning*

Otherwise, you won't even be aware of these warnings.

The Problem Tool Window shows you all the errors and warnings in the project. So, if you want to see them all, just click the "Problems" button in the Tool Window Bar (as shown in Figure 4-15).

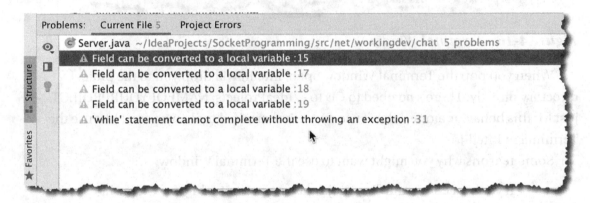

Figure 4-15. *Problem Tool Window*

Clicking any warning (or problem) item in the Problem Tool Window brings up the concerned file in the Main Editor Window.

Terminal

The Terminal Tool Window, when opened, is an actual terminal that you can use within IntelliJ. Many programmers use this tool because typing on the keyboard is still faster than hunting and pecking with the mouse. If you're pretty handy with CLI commands, you'll enjoy the Terminal Window. It pops up (and hides) at the bottom part of the IDE, as shown in Figure 4-16.

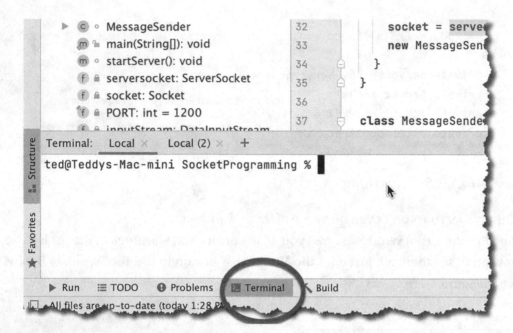

Figure 4-16. *Terminal Window*

When you pop the Terminal Window open, IntelliJ will drop you to the project directory directly. There's no need to CD to ~/IdeaProjects/NAMEOFYOURPROJECT — just for this behavior alone, I don't use my native terminal tool anymore. I just use the Terminal in IntelliJ.

Some reasons why you might want to use the Terminal Window:

- If you're a command-line ninja and you prefer to do your Git push, stash, commit, add, etc., via the command line, yet you don't want to leave the IDE, then the Terminal is perfect for you.

- You might need to run some commands on Maven or Gradle.

- You're running MongoDB (mongod and mongo). You can create multiple Terminal sessions in the IDE, which is perfect for these tasks.

The Main Editor Windows

The Main Editor Window occupies the largest screen space, and for good reasons, this is where you create and edit code.

You probably don't need instructions on using the Main Editor Window; after all, it is very intuitive. You can figure out its capabilities as you use it, but I'd still like to point out a few things. Firstly, the Main Editor lets you fold sections of the code. When you click the house-shaped pentagon (shown in Figure 4-17), sections of the code will fold. If you click the same pentagon, it will unfold. It's a great tool to use when your auditing your code.

```
1       package net.workingdev.chat;
2
3       import java.io.DataInputStream;
4       import java.io.DataOutputStream;
5       import java.io.IOException;
6       import java.net.ServerSocket;
7       import java.net.Socket;
8
9       import static java.lang.System.out;
10
```

Figure 4-17. *Code folding*

Next, the Run button on the editor gutter shows up when you're editing a class that has a runnable main method (shown in Figure 4-18). Clicking this button will let you run your class, just like clicking the Run button on the Toolbar.

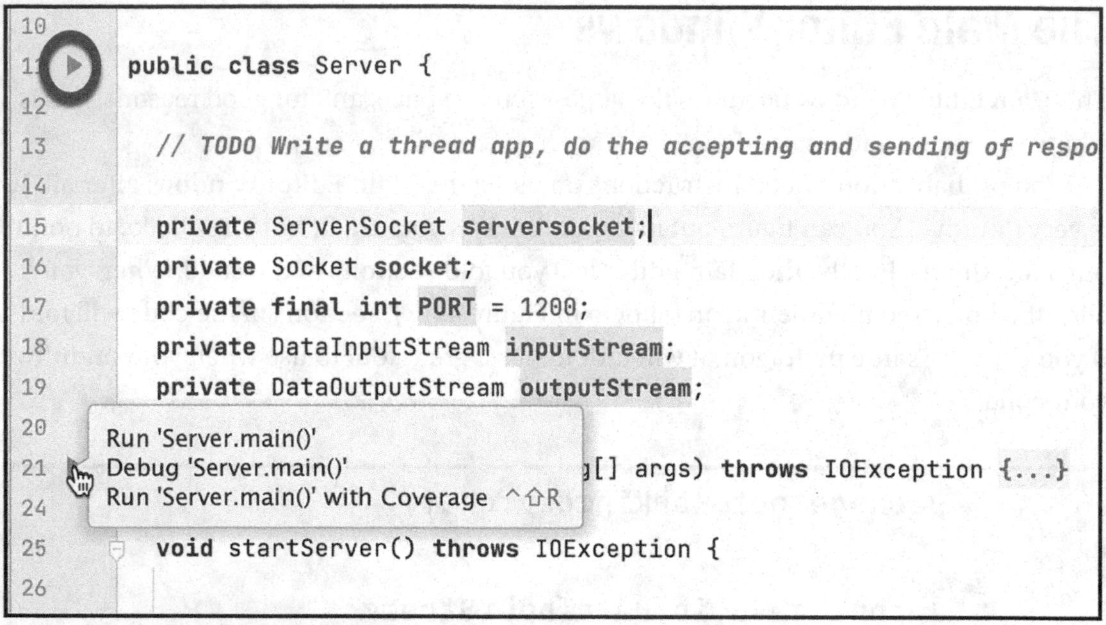

```
10
11 ▶  public class Server {
12
13      // TODO Write a thread app, do the accepting and sending of respo
14
15      private ServerSocket serversocket;|
16      private Socket socket;
17      private final int PORT = 1200;
18      private DataInputStream inputStream;
19      private DataOutputStream outputStream;
20
    ┌─────────────────────────────────┐
21  │ Run 'Server.main()'              │
    🖑│ Debug 'Server.main()'           │[] args) throws IOException {...}
24  │ Run 'Server.main()' with Coverage  ^⇧R │
25  └─ void startServer() throws IOException {
26
```

Figure 4-18. *The Run button on the editor gutter*

Next are the warning icons on the top-right corner of the editing window (shown in Figure 4-19). IntelliJ shows the summary of all the problems found in the project. Clicking the warning summary brings up the Problem Tool Window.

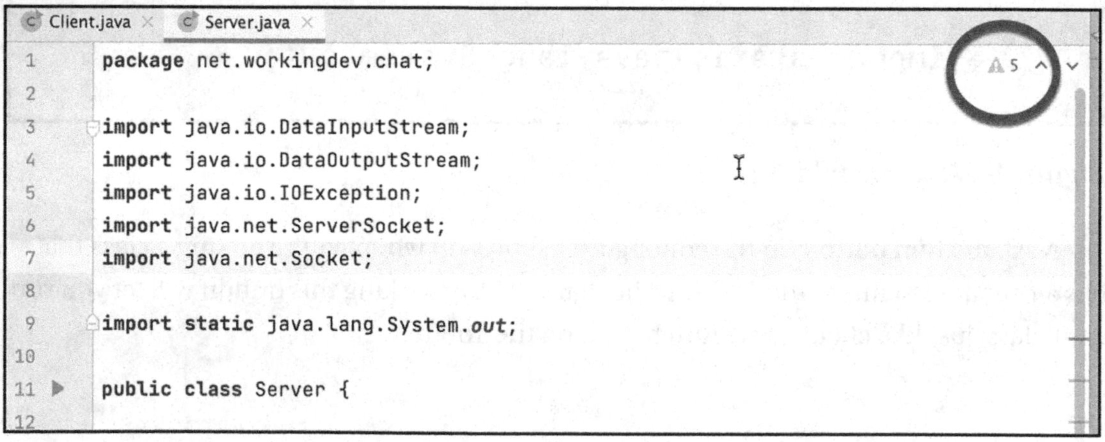

```
 Client.java ×    Server.java ×
 1      package net.workingdev.chat;                          A 5 ^ ⌄
 2
 3   ⊡import java.io.DataInputStream;
 4    import java.io.DataOutputStream;                    Ị
 5    import java.io.IOException;
 6    import java.net.ServerSocket;
 7    import java.net.Socket;
 8
 9   ⊡import static java.lang.System.out;
10
11 ▶  public class Server {
12
```

Figure 4-19. *Warning icons on the top-right corner*

Next is the GUI editor. You might work on projects with a GUI component, an Android app (shown in Figure 4-20), or a JavaFX application (shown in Figure 4-21). Whatever the case may be, IntelliJ has you covered. It has WYSIWYG capabilities to get the job done.

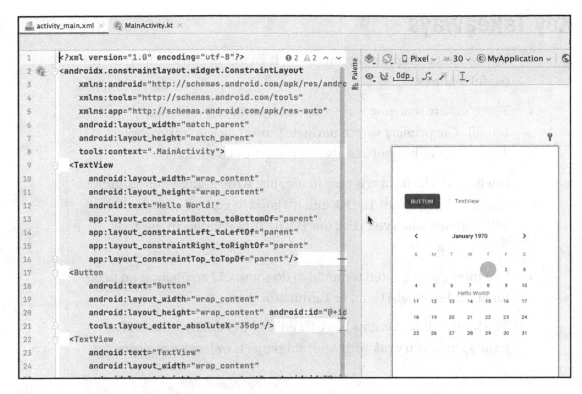

Figure 4-20. *Android project*

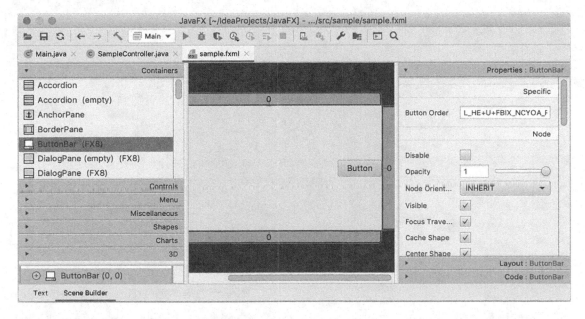

Figure 4-21. *JavaFX Scene Builder*

Key Takeaways

- IntelliJ isn't a simple program editor. It's a full-blown IDE loaded with useful features.

- There's more than one way to navigate your project files in IntelliJ. The primary way to navigate project files is via the Project Tool Window, but you can also do it via the Navigation Bar.

- IntelliJ's TODO feature is easy to use; just write a single-line comment followed by the word TODO, and it's good to go. You can see all the TODO items when you click the TODO Tool Window in the Tool Window Bar.

- Use IntelliJ's integrated terminal to do some CLI acrobatics; no need for cmd, Terminal, iTerm, or Terminator here.

- The Main Editor Window has GUI editing capabilities; this will be handy when you work with Android projects or JavaFX projects.

## CHAPTER 5

Code Navigation and Generation

In this chapter, we will cover the following:

- How to use the search everywhere feature in IntelliJ

- How to get to any IDE action using keyboard shortcuts

- How to look for files without hunting and pecking

- How to generate boilerplate codes

Have you met anyone who swears by Vim as the best editor of all? You have? Do you know why they say that? One of the reasons, I think, is because with Vim, you don't use the mouse to navigate. It's all keyboard. Your hands will never leave the keyboard — and for some people, this gets them in a state of flow.

You can do something like that with IntelliJ. If you'd like to try a workflow where your hands will (almost) never leave the keyboard, this chapter is for you.

Navigation

You might be wondering why we're devoting a chapter just for code navigation. "Sure, I know how to navigate my code," you tell yourself. "How difficult can it be to open the Project Tool Window, drill down the package and hierarchy, and then double-click to open — *et voila!*"

You might get by hunting and pecking files, classes, variables, and methods if it's a small project or when speed of coding isn't really important — anybody who's coding for a living will never tell you that speed isn't important. It's always important — but when you're no longer coding "hello world" projects, evolving your coding habits will be a big deal.

© Ted Hagos 2022
T. Hagos, *Beginning IntelliJ IDEA*, https://doi.org/10.1007/978-1-4842-7446-0_5

When you examine your coding process (your own personal coding process, I mean), you'll find that at least half of the time, you aren't really typing something – you're actually doing more navigation rather than typing code.

If you're hunting and pecking, you're losing valuable time. There are quicker ways to get to your code, and this section is all about that.

Search Everywhere

The most important keyboard shortcuts you'll ever need in IntelliJ is actually on the background start screen of the IDE (shown in Figure 5-1); however, it's also the most ignored. Most people don't pay attention to the start screen; we're so eager to open that source file and start typing.

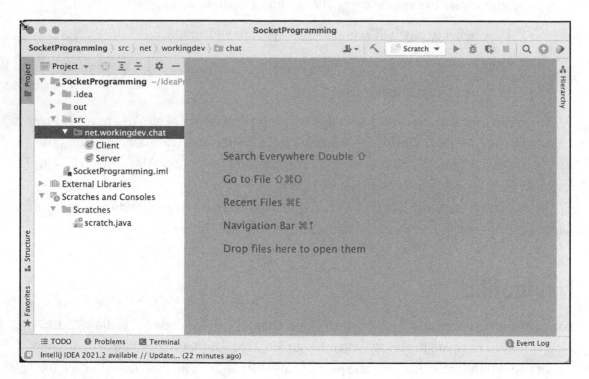

Figure 5-1. *Start screen of IntelliJ*

The starting screen tips have a few nifty keyboard shortcuts for us, but let's start with the *search everywhere* shortcut.

You can activate the *search everywhere* dialog by pressing the **Shift** key twice in quick succession (Figure 5-2 shows the search everywhere dialog).

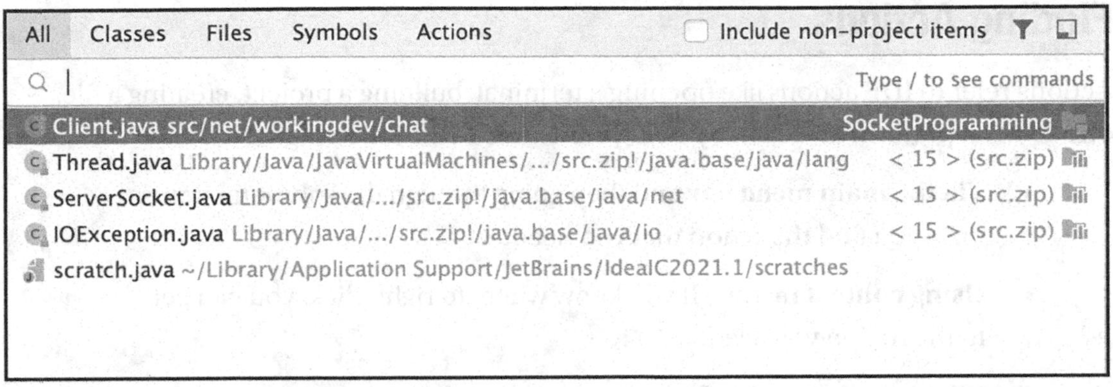

Figure 5-2. Search everywhere

You can begin typing in the search field to start seeing some results. You can find any item in the project or outside of it by its name. You can search for files, actions, classes, symbols, settings, UI elements, and anything in Git from a single entry point. If you can still remember your RegEx, you can use them to find items in the **Search Everywhere** dialog.

There are a couple of tabs on the dialog (Classes, Files, Symbols, Actions, and All). You're placed on the *All* tab by default, but you can switch tabs by selecting them with the mouse.

As you can probably tell by now, you use the *Classes* tab when you'd like to search for Classes, *Files* when you're looking for files within your solution, *Actions* when you're searching for IDE actions, and *Symbols* when you're looking for class names, variables, constants, and method names.

The *All* tab is more useful when you're looking for files within your solution rather than action. As you play around with this search tool, pay attention to how the dialog is partitioned so you can get the hang of it.

By the way, you must have noticed the tick box in the search everywhere dialog that says "Include non-project items." When you check that, you can search for non-project items like classes in the Java documentation (if you downloaded it). The quickest way to get search for non-project items is to use the double Shift keyboard shortcut and then press the double Shift again to extend the search to non-project items.

Finding Actions

Actions refer to IDE actions like opening a terminal, building a project, creating a file, etc. You can perform an action by doing either one of the following:

- **Via the main menu bar** and then going through the submenu items until you find the action that you need.

- **Using context menu** – If you know where to right-click, you can get to the Action you need.

- **Clicking a button on the toolbar** – Some of the most common actions are displayed on the toolbar(s) like Run, Debug, Stop, etc.

- **Using a keyboard shortcut** – This is the fastest, but this also means you need to commit the shortcut to your memory. You might be able to do this for those actions that you always use, but you can't do this for all actions.

- **Using the *search everywhere* dialog** and then going to Action. Start typing the name of the Action, and then press ENTER. This is the second fastest way to get to an action.

For example, if you want to launch a terminal session (within IntelliJ), you can use the **option + F12** (on macOS) or **Alt + F12** (on Linux and Windows). If you can't remember the keyboard shortcut, you can use the search everywhere dialog, and then select *Action*. Alternatively, if you don't want your fingers to leave the keyboard, you can also use the **Shift + cmd + A** shortcut (for macOS) or **Shift + CTRL + A** (for Linux and Windows) to launch the *search everywhere* dialog and go directly to the Actions tab.

Figure 5-3 shows the Actions dialog as we search for the Terminal action.

All	Classes	Files	Symbols	Actions		Include disabled actions
Q terminal						Press ⌥↵ to assign a shortcut
Terminal ⌥F12						View | Tool Windows
Terminal						Preferences > Plugins
Terminal notifications						Preferences > Notifications
Terminal//Command to run using IDE						Preferences > Console Colors
Open in Terminal						
Configure terminal keybindings						Preferences > Terminal
Emulates the behavior when Subversion commands are executed directly...						Preferences > Subversion
Plugins: Terminal						ON
Terminate process						Preferences > System Settings
msg live template						Preferences
Replace return with 'if' expression						Preferences > Intentions
Replace return with 'when' expression						Preferences > Intentions

Figure 5-3. *Actions*

The dialog shows us a bit of information about the Terminal action. We can see its keyboard shortcut, and we can also see where this action is on the main menu bar. At this point, you can simply press the ENTER key to launch the action.

Opening Files

If you've always opened files using the Project Tool Window, you'll be glad to know there are quicker ways to get to your files.

The project shown in Figure 5-4 is a small one, but it's enough to demonstrate how to search for files using the Project Tool Window. Position your mouse right beside the down-arrow in the Project Tool Window (as shown in Figure 5-4), and then start typing (as shown in Figure 5-5).

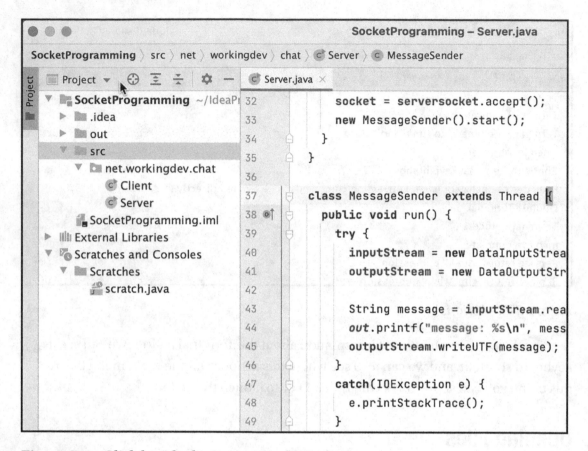

Figure 5-4. *Click beside the Project Tool Window*

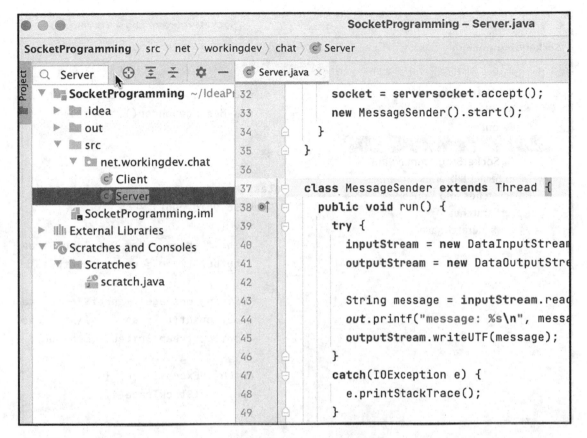

Figure 5-5. *Searching for files in the Project Tool Window*

However, this technique is only effective if the file is visible within the Project Tool Window. If it isn't — like when the src folder is collapsed, for example — this method of searching fails (as shown in Figure 5-6). Well, you can always use the *search everywhere* dialog to look for files anyway.

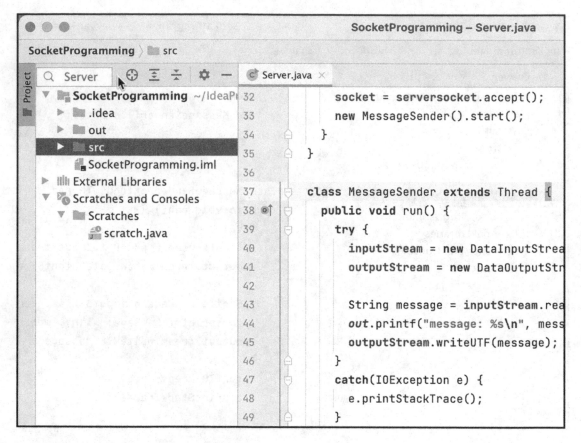

Figure 5-6. *Project Tool Window with collapsed src folder*

Opening Classes

When naming Java source files, it's a good idea to name the file the same as the name of the class. That way, when you look at the Project Tool Window, you can tell where the class files are just by looking at the actual source files. If you followed this advice, then good for you. If you did not, it's a good thing that IntelliJ's got your back. It's quite easy to search for class definitions in IntelliJ; just press **cmd + O** (capital letter O, not zero) if you're on macOS and **CTRL + N** if on Windows and Linux, and then start typing.

Figure 5-7 shows the search class dialog.

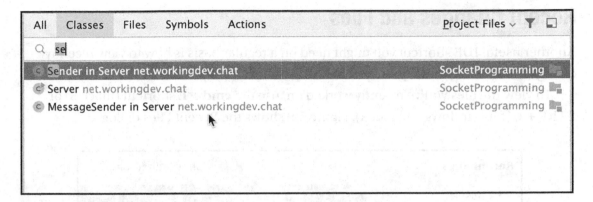

Figure 5-7. Search for a class

Go to Symbol

To complete our rounds on the tabs of the *search everywhere* dialog, let's look at *Symbols*. When you're looking for variables, method names, and constants, the Symbols tab of the search everywhere dialog is the way to go.

The keyboard shortcut for *go to Symbols* is **option + cmd + O** (capital letter O) on macOS and **Shift + CTRL + Alt + N** on Windows and Linux.

Figure 5-8 shows the *go to Symbols* dialog in action.

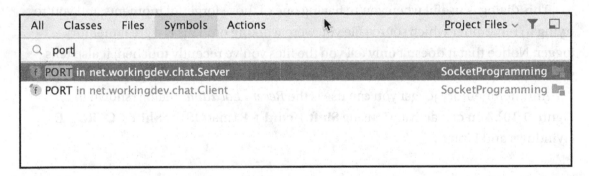

Figure 5-8. Symbols

Recent Changes and Files

Another useful IDE shortcut you might need on a regular basis is how to view recently changed files and, generally, the recent changes in your project.

To view the files you've recently worked on, use the **cmd + E** shortcut (macOS) or **CTRL + E** (for Windows and Linux). Figure 5-9 shows the Recent Files dialog.

Recent Files   ☐ Show edited only ⌘E

🗀 Project ⌘1	© Server.java
★ Favorites ⌘2	MD README.md
❶ Problems ⌘6	© Thread.java
▪ Structure ⌘7	© ServerSocket.java
↖ Build	© IOException.java
◯ Event Log	scratch.java
☰ TODO	
▣ Terminal ⌥F12	
Recent Locations ⇧⌘E	

~/IdeaProjects/SocketProgramming/src/net/workingdev/chat

Figure 5-9. *Recent Files*

This dialog is useful when you're having one of those forgetful moments and you're trying to remember which source file you were working on. This is a great memory jogger. Notice that it doesn't only tell you the files you've recently touched; it also tells you some of your recent actions (it's on the left-hand side of the dialog).

Another memory jogger you can use is the *Recent Locations* dialog (shown in Figure 5-10). You can activate it using **Shift + cmd + E** (macOS) or **Shift + CTRL + E** (Windows and Linux).

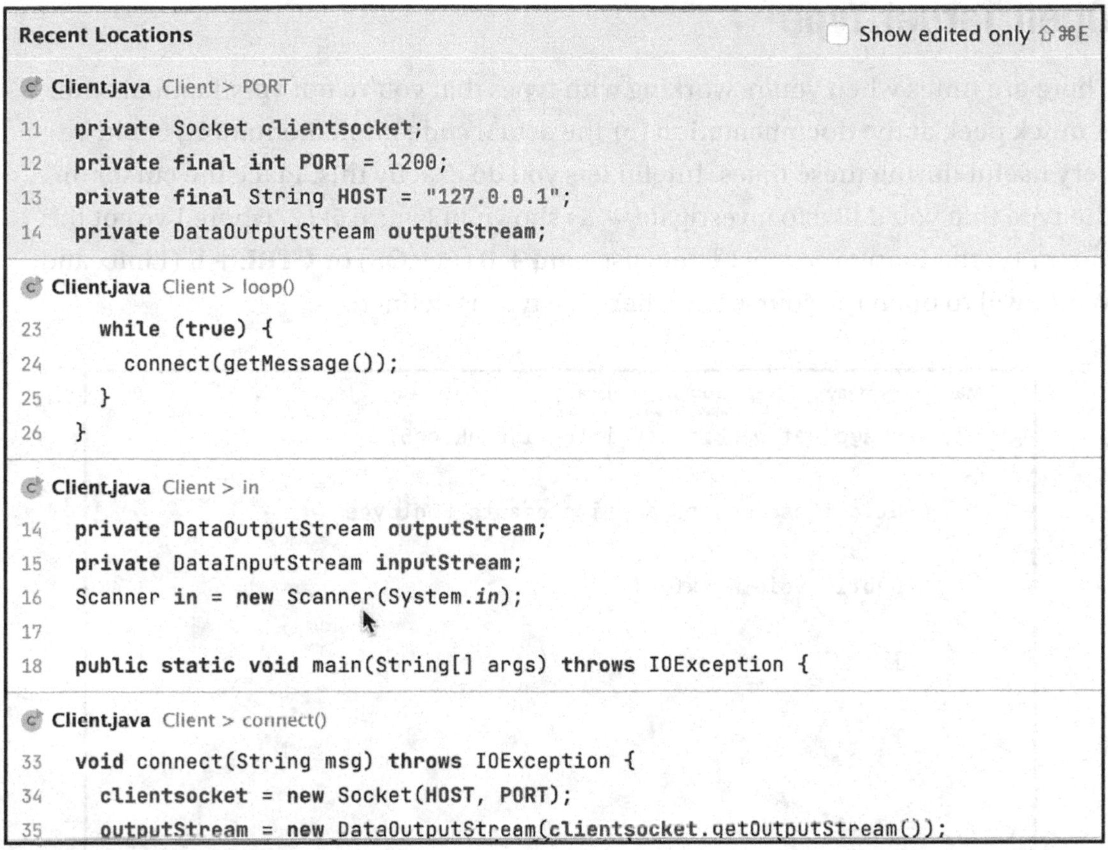

```
Recent Locations                                      ☐ Show edited only ⇧⌘E

Ⓒ Client.java Client > PORT

11   private Socket clientsocket;
12   private final int PORT = 1200;
13   private final String HOST = "127.0.0.1";
14   private DataOutputStream outputStream;

Ⓒ Client.java Client > loop()

23     while (true) {
24       connect(getMessage());
25     }
26   }

Ⓒ Client.java Client > in

14   private DataOutputStream outputStream;
15   private DataInputStream inputStream;
16   Scanner in = new Scanner(System.in);
17
18   public static void main(String[] args) throws IOException {

Ⓒ Client.java Client > connect()

33   void connect(String msg) throws IOException {
34     clientsocket = new Socket(HOST, PORT);
35     outputStream = new DataOutputStream(clientsocket.getOutputStream());
```

Figure 5-10. *Recent Locations*

If you'd like to see a list of all the recent changes you've made in the project, for example, creation of a new file, use the shortcut **Shift + cmd + C** (macOS) or **Shift + Alt + C** (Windows and Linux). Figure 5-11 shows the list of Recent Changes dialog.

The dialog shows you what the change was (creating a file, in this case) and when the change was made. The items on the list are clickable. It acts like hyperlinks to the changed files, so you can view or edit them quickly by simply clicking them.

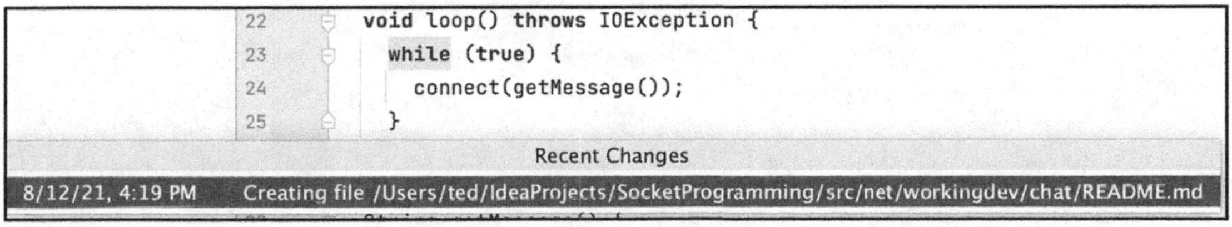

```
22     void loop() throws IOException {
23       while (true) {
24         connect(getMessage());
25       }
                        Recent Changes
8/12/21, 4:19 PM   Creating file /Users/ted/IdeaProjects/SocketProgramming/src/net/workingdev/chat/README.md
```

Figure 5-11. *Recent Changes*

Open Target Type

There are times when you're working with types that you're not very familiar with. A quick peek at the documentation (or the actual code implementation) could be very useful during these times. IntelliJ lets you do exactly this. Place the cursor on the type that you'd like to investigate — as shown in Figure 5-12, where I've got the cursor on the Employee type. Then, use **cmd + B** (macOS) or **CTRL + B** (Linux and Windows) to open the source file where the type is defined.

```
C  MainProgram.java  ×    C  Programmer.java  ×    C  TestDeveloper.java  ×
1       package net.workingdev.intellijbook.ch5;
2
3       public class Programmer implements Employee{
4           @Override
5           public void work() {
6
7           }
8       }
9
```

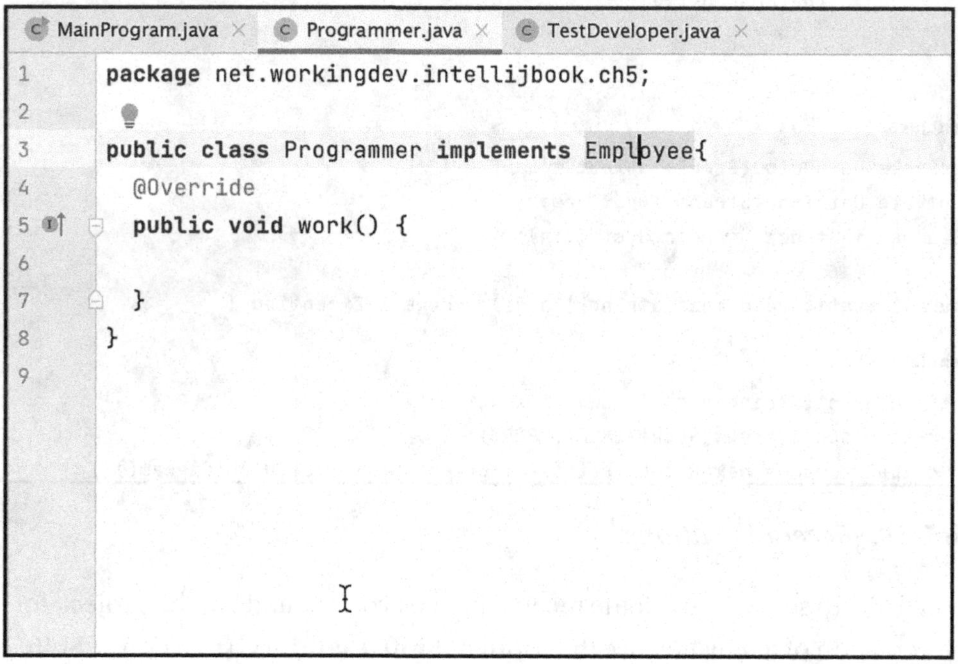

Figure 5-12. *Programmer source file*

IntelliJ launches the source file where the type is defined (shown in Figure 5-13).

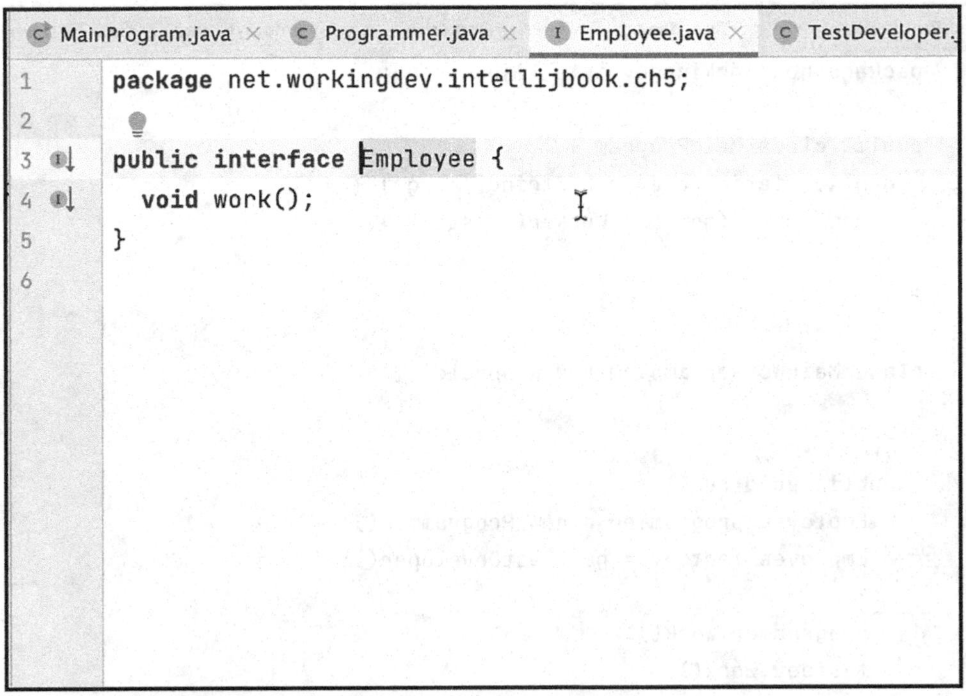

```
  MainProgram.java ×     Programmer.java ×     Employee.java ×     TestDeveloper.
1        package net.workingdev.intellijbook.ch5;
2
3        public interface Employee {
4          void work();                              I
5        }
6
```

Figure 5-13. *Employee source file*

You're not limited to files within your solution; you can peek at files that are in the standard Java libraries as well. Figure 5-14 shows my cursor positioned at the *Thread* type; pressing **cmd + B** quickly takes me to the definition of the Thread class (shown in Figure 5-15).

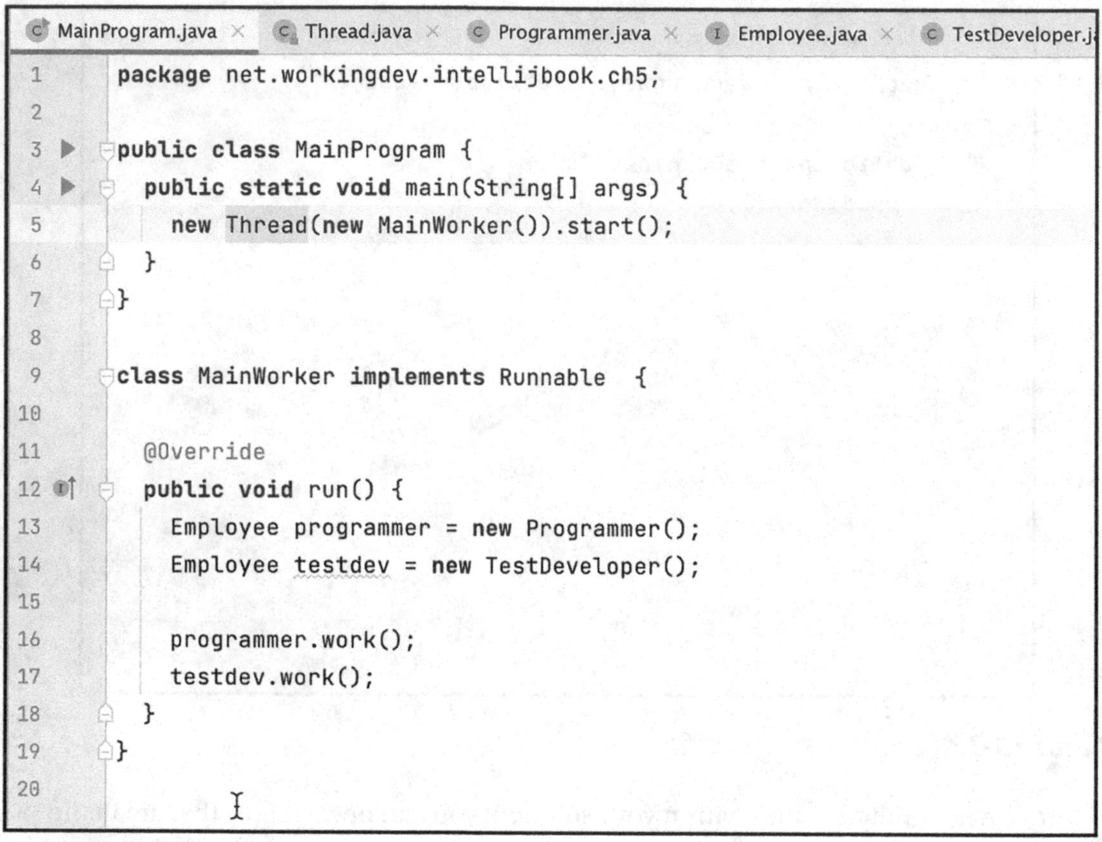

MainProgram.java
Thread.java
Programmer.java
Employee.java
TestDeveloper.j
package net.workingdev.intellijbook.ch5;
public class MainProgram {
public static void main(String[] args) {
new Thread(new MainWorker()).start();
}
}
class MainWorker implements Runnable {
@Override
public void run() {
Employee programmer = new Programmer();
Employee testdev = new TestDeveloper();
programmer.work();
testdev.work();
}
}

Figure 5-14. *MainProgram source file*

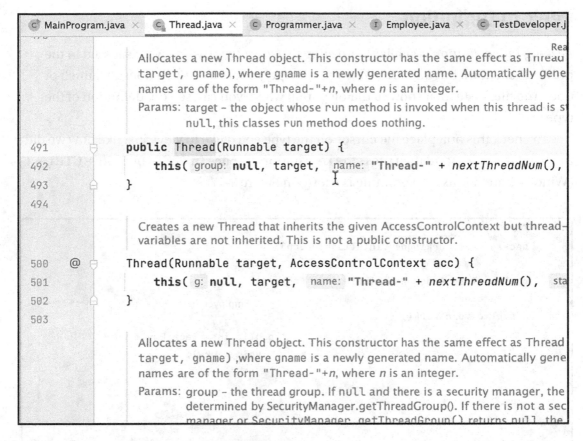

Figure 5-15. *Thread class definition*

The **cmd + B** shortcut isn't limited to types alone – it also works on methods. When you use this shortcut on methods, the IDE will show you all the usages of the method within the solution (shown in Figure 5-16).

```java
package net.workingdev.intellijbook.ch5;

public class TestDeveloper implements Employee{
    @Override
    public void work() {

    }
}
```

							Usages of work() — Results in 'Project Files'
MainProgram.java	16	programmer.work();
MainProgram.java	17	testdev.work();

Figure 5-16. *The usages of the methods within the solution*

Peek to Definition

Peeking into definition is similar to *opening the target type* (which we discussed in the previous section), but unlike the *open target type*, *peek to definition* doesn't launch or open the file. Instead, it shows a dialog popup where you can see the definition of the type.

To check this out, place the cursor on the type you'd like to view, just like how we did in *open target type*, and then press the keys **option** + **space** (macOS) or **Shift** + **CTRL** + **I** (Windows and Linux). An example is shown in Figure 5-17.

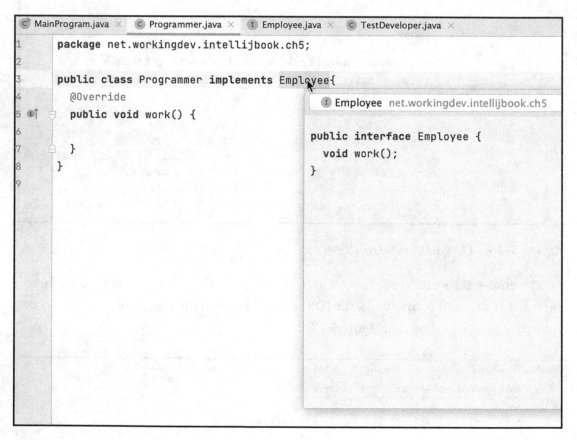

Figure 5-17. *Peeking at the definition of the Employee type*

Show Members

Where do you put your member variables? Do you define them all in one go at the beginning of the class, before all the methods, or do you define them close to the point of use? Flame wars have been waged in the name of the one true coding convention, but it shouldn't matter anymore since IDEs like IntelliJ can show you all the class members in one neat window.

There are at least two ways to see all the members of the class. The first one is by using **cmd + F12** (macOS) or **CTRL + F12** (Windows and Linux); a sample is shown in Figure 5-18.

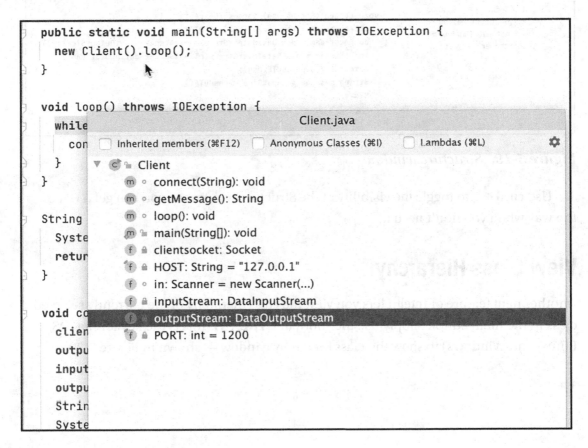

Figure 5-18. *Show members*

Another way to view the members is by revealing the structure window (Figure 5-19); use **cmd + 7** (macOS) or **Alt + 7** (Windows and Linux).

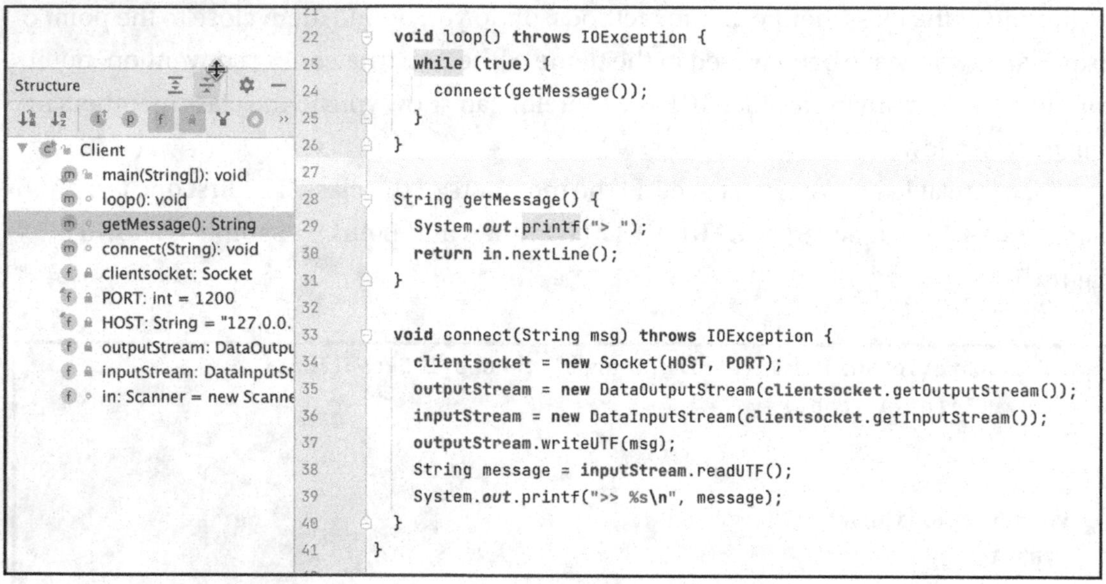

Figure 5-19. *Structure window*

Use **cmd + 7** to toggle the visibility of the Structure window so you can get it out of the way when you don't need it.

View Class Hierarchy

Another neat feature of IntelliJ lets you view the class hierarchy of the currently selected class in the main editor. Simply use the shortcut **CTRL + H** (this is the key for macOS, Linux, and Windows) to show the class hierarchy window — shown in Figure 5-20.

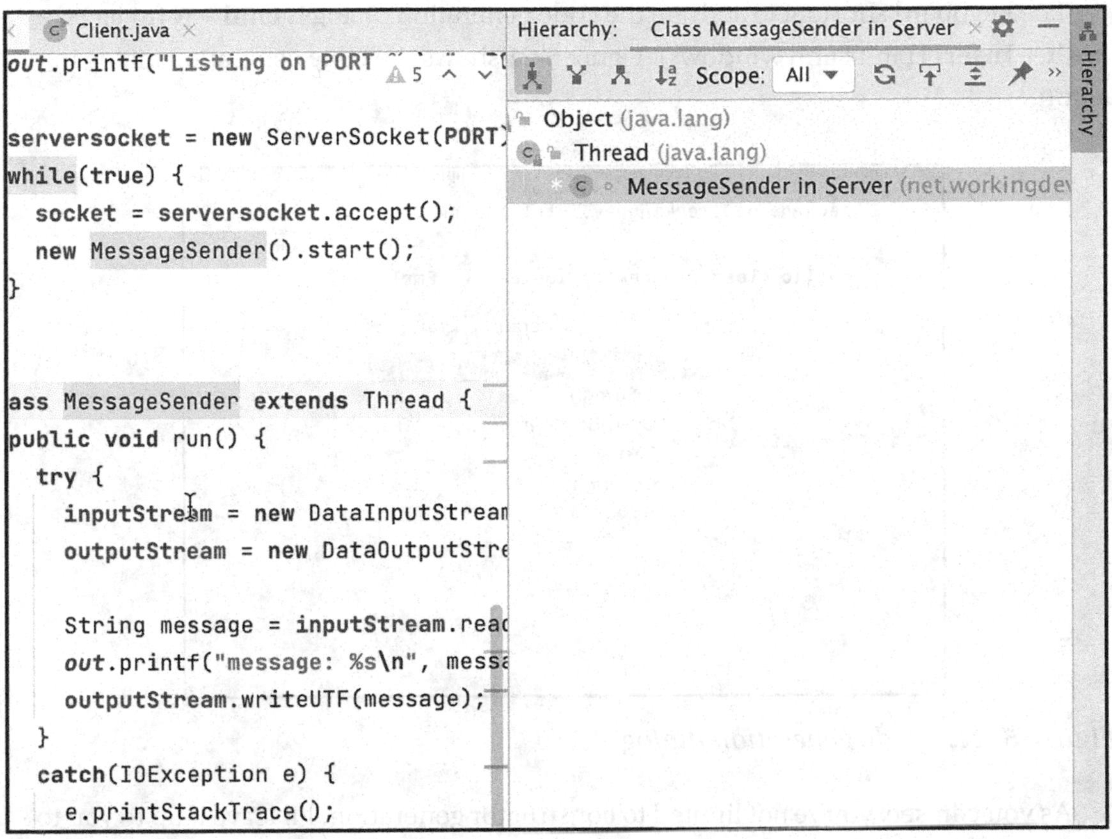

```
  C Client.java ×                          Hierarchy:    Class MessageSender in Server × ⚙ —
out.printf("Listing on PORT ⚠5 ∧ ∨        ↟ ⋎ ↡ ↓ᶻ Scope:  All ▼   ↺ ⬆ ⬇ ✦ »
                                          ⬡ Object (java.lang)
serversocket = new ServerSocket(PORT)     C ⬡ Thread (java.lang)
while(true) {                                  * C ○ MessageSender in Server (net.workingde
  socket = serversocket.accept();
  new MessageSender().start();
}


ass MessageSender extends Thread {
public void run() {
  try {
    inputStream = new DataInputStream
    outputStream = new DataOutputStre

    String message = inputStream.read
    out.printf("message: %s\n", messa
    outputStream.writeUTF(message);
  }
  catch(IOException e) {
    e.printStackTrace();
```

Figure 5-20. *Show class hierarchy*

This is the last tip I want to show you on code navigation. Next stop, code generation.

Code Generation

Another time-saving feature of IntelliJ is the code generator; it's aptly named because it does exactly what you think it does — it generates code.

The keyboard shortcut to activate the code generation dialog is **cmd + N** (macOS) or **Alt + Insert** (Linux and Windows). Figure 5-21 shows the code generation dialog in action.

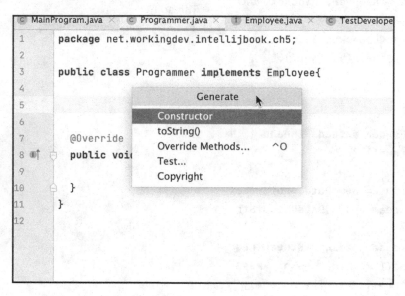

Figure 5-21. *Code generation dialog*

As you can see, you're not limited to constructor generation. I'll leave it up to you to experiment with the other options.

The next example I'd like to show is how to generate code for getters and setters — which is a very common task in Java programming.

Figure 5-21 shows class Programmer with two member variables, *mLastname* and *mFirstname*. Show the code generation dialog, and then choose *Getter and Setter*, as shown in Figure 5-22.

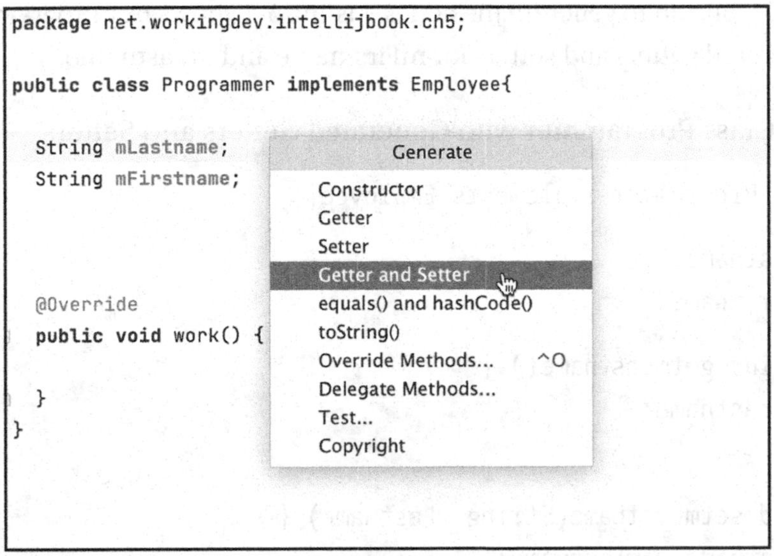

```
package net.workingdev.intellijbook.ch5;

public class Programmer implements Employee{

    String mLastname;                    Generate
    String mFirstname;
                                    Constructor
                                    Getter
                                    Setter
                                    Getter and Setter
    @Override                       equals() and hashCode()
    public void work() {            toString()
                                    Override Methods...      ^O
    }                               Delegate Methods...
}                                   Test...
                                    Copyright
```

Figure 5-22. *Generate getters and setters*

IntelliJ shows all the autodetected member variables (shown in Figure 5-23). You can select all the members for which you'd like to generate getters and setters — you can make multiple selections here.

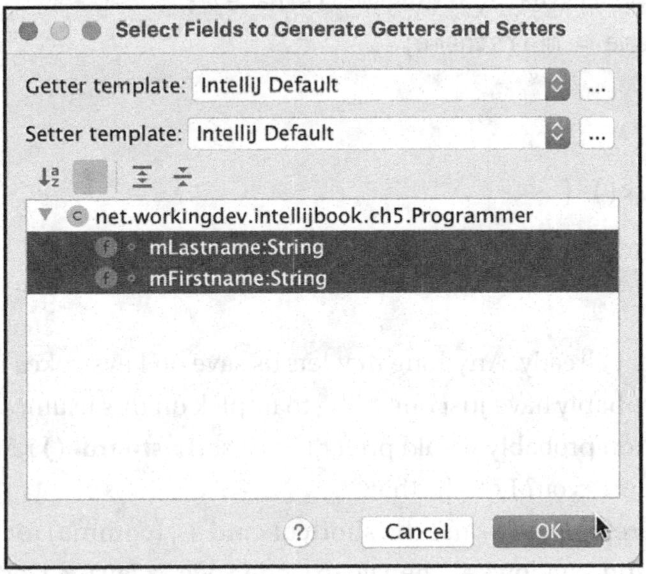

```
●  ●  ●   Select Fields to Generate Getters and Setters

Getter template:  IntelliJ Default                 ⌄   ...

Setter template:  IntelliJ Default                 ⌄   ...

↓ᵃz   ■   ⊼  ⊻

▼ ©  net.workingdev.intellijbook.ch5.Programmer
     🅕 ∘  mLastname:String
     🅕 ∘  mFirstname:String




                         ?      Cancel        OK
```

Figure 5-23. *Select fields to generate getters and setters*

Click the OK button to generate the codes. Listing 5-1 shows our Programmer class with autogenerated getters and setters for mFirstname and mLastname.

Listing 5-1. Class Programmer with Generated Getters and Setters

```java
public class Programmer implements Employee{

  String mLastname;
  String mFirstname;

  public String getmLastname() {
    return mLastname;
  }

  public void setmLastname(String mLastname) {
    this.mLastname = mLastname;
  }

  public String getmFirstname() {
    return mFirstname;
  }

  public void setmFirstname(String mFirstname) {
    this.mFirstname = mFirstname;
  }

  @Override
  public void work() {

  }
}
```

This is pretty neat already. Anything that lets us save on keystrokes is a good thing. I'm guessing you probably have just one thing to nitpick on this example; the method naming isn't right. You probably would prefer to call **setLastname()** rather than **setmLastname(),** don't you? Let's fix that.

Go to IntelliJ's Preferences — use the shortcut **cmd + ,** (comma) for macOS. It's **CTRL + Alt + S** for Linux and Windows — then go to Code Style ➤ Java ➤ Code Generation, as shown in Figure 5-24.

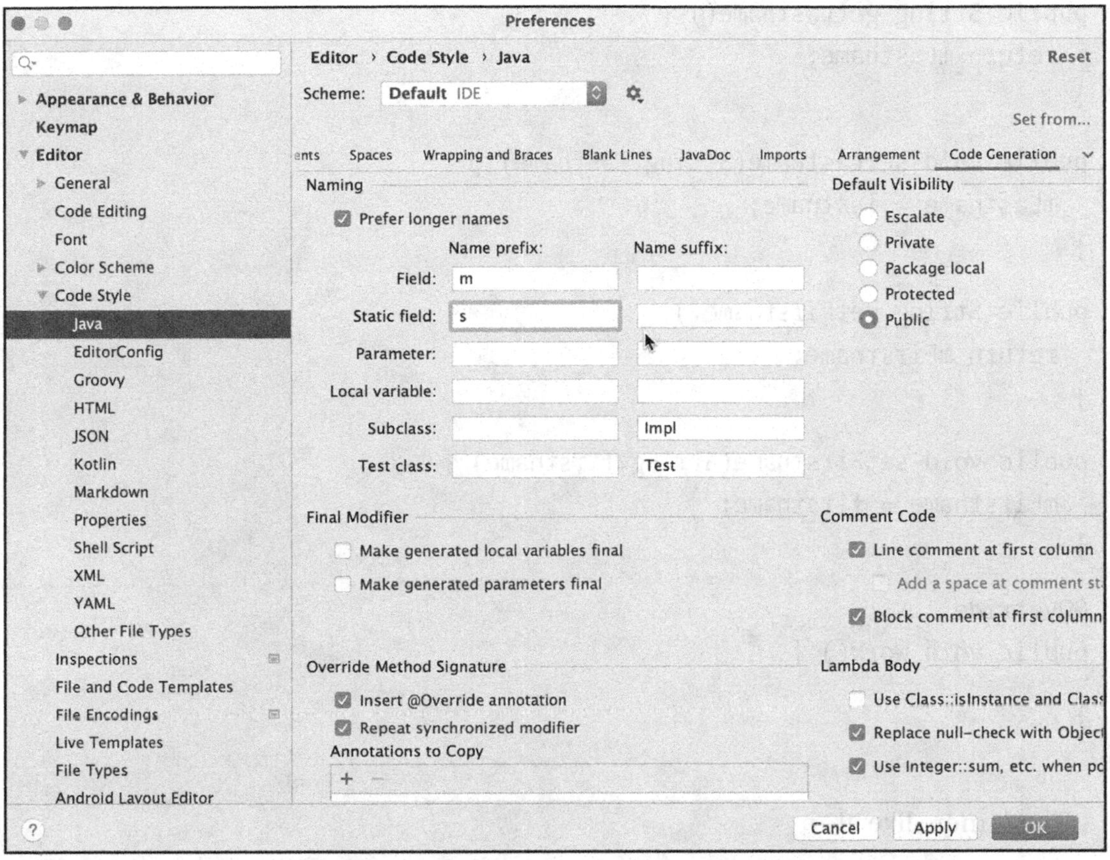

Figure 5-24. *Preferences* ➤ *Code Style* ➤ *Java* ➤ *Code Generation*

In the Field name prefix, tell IntelliJ how you are prefixing your member variables. In my case, I prefix my member variables with the letter *m*, hence, *mLastname* for the lastname variable.

Click Apply or the OK button to save the changes, and then generate the getters and setters for mFirstname and mLastname again.

Listing 5-2 shows the regenerated Programmer class.

Listing 5-2. Programmer Class with Autogenerated Getters and Setters

```
public class Programmer implements Employee{

  String mLastname;
  String mFirstname;
```

```
public String getLastname() {
  return mLastname;
}

public void setLastname(String lastname) {
  mLastname = lastname;
}

public String getFirstname() {
  return mFirstname;
}

public void setFirstname(String firstname) {
  mFirstname = firstname;
}

@Override
public void work() {

}
}
```

That's more like it!

Key Takeaways

- All IDE actions can be performed via the main menu bar, but the fastest way to activate these actions is via a keyboard shortcut.

- The second fastest way to activate an action in IntelliJ is by searching for the action using the **cmd + A** (macOS) or **Shift + CTRL + A** (Windows and Linux).

- You'll save a lot of time if you commit some keyboard shortcuts to memory, but if you can only remember one keyboard shortcut, let it be the double Shift. Just press Shift twice in succession to get the search everywhere dialog.

CHAPTER 6

Inspections and Intentions

In this chapter, we will cover the following:

- Code inspections

- Intentions

You've been using IntelliJ for a while now. I'm pretty sure you've seen the light bulbs (both red and yellow), the yellow triangles with an exclamation mark, and the green check sign with a squiggly line below — these are the icons that IntelliJ uses to tell us that there's something wrong with the code. They're called inspection icons. We'll talk about them in this chapter.

Code Inspections

IntelliJ IDEA is intelligent (pun intended); it knows more about your code than you do. As you type, it's working hard in the background trying to see which parts of the code you botched; and where code is botched, IntelliJ gives you warning signs — mind you, this all happens even before you compile the code. The IDE wouldn't be called IntelliJ if it was dumb. The name is well deserved.

Code inspection is an IDE feature that scans, detects, and corrects anomalous code in the project, even before you compile it. The IDE can find and highlight a wide range of problems. It can locate dead code, find spelling problems (more than you'd like to), and improve overall code structure.

The problems that IntelliJ can find range from benign to critical — like a trailing semicolon (shown in Figure 6-1). A yellow light bulb indicates a warning; they're benign because they won't keep you from compiling, but IntelliJ is warning you because the code is not optimal.

© Ted Hagos 2022
T. Hagos, *Beginning IntelliJ IDEA*, https://doi.org/10.1007/978-1-4842-7446-0_6

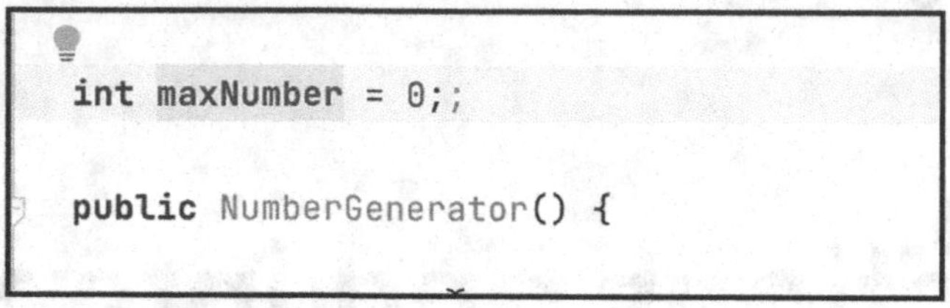

```
int maxNumber = 0;;


public NumberGenerator() {
```

Figure 6-1. *IntelliJ flagging a trailing semicolon*

Other times, you'll see a red light bulb (like the one in Figure 6-2).

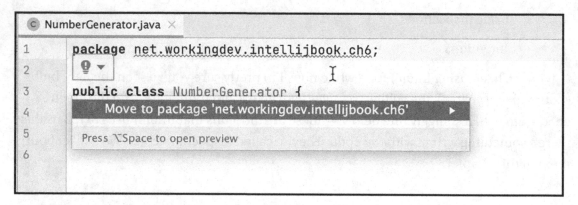

Figure 6-2. *Red light bulb, which indicates an error*

Red light bulbs are error flags. You need to make changes to the offending code, lest your project will not compile.

Addressing Inspections

The easiest inspections to deal with are the ones that are fairly obvious, for example, unreachable statements, like the one shown in Figure 6-3.

```
public int getRandomNumber() {
  Random random = new Random();
  int randomNumber = random.nextInt(maxNumber);


  return randomNumber;

  System.out.println("Random Number generated");
}
```

Figure 6-3. *Unreachable statement*

The red squiggly lines under the last *println()* statement are a dead giveaway that something is wrong with your code. Suppose you press **option + ENTER** (macOS) or **Alt + ENTER** (Windows and Linux), the quick fix of IntelliJ kicks in. The IDE shows you the inspection actions that you might want to take so you can resolve the problem, as shown in Figure 6-4.

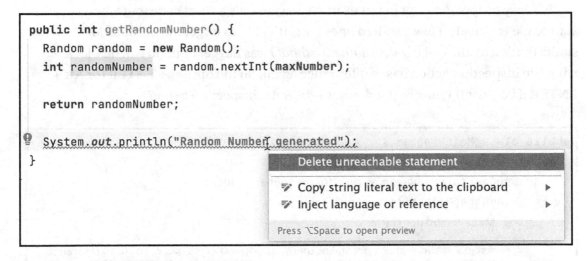

Figure 6-4. *Inspection action*

In our case, the action is straightforward; just *delete the unreachable statement*, which, if you choose, the problem immediately goes away — but this is obvious; of course, you could see that the *println()* was unreachable. You didn't need the inspection for that. Let's try another one.

See if you can spot this one. In Figure 6-5, line 6, I made a call to **this.AnotherMethod()** and IntelliJ raised a flag by underlining the call to *this* with red squiggles. Can you tell why?

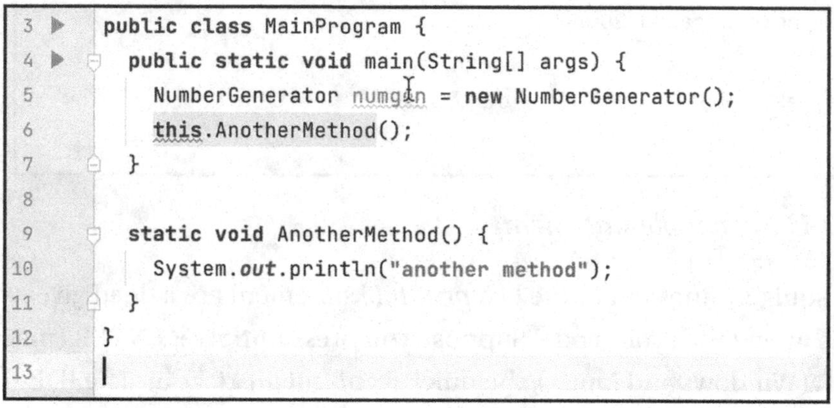

```
3  ▶  public class MainProgram {
4  ▶     public static void main(String[] args) {
5           NumberGenerator numgen = new NumberGenerator();
6           this.AnotherMethod();
7        }
8
9        static void AnotherMethod() {
10          System.out.println("another method");
11       }
12    }
13
```

Figure 6-5. *Inspection action on the non-static call to AnotherMethod()*

It's easy to spot the error in our example because it's a short code, but when your source file is already a few hundred lines long, it's easy to forget that *AnotherMethod()* is static; that's why the call to ***this.****AnotherMethod()* was flagged. But no worries, let's see what the inspection action has to offer. Once again, do the **option + ENTER** (or **Alt + ENTER** if you're on Linux or Windows) to show the inspection action.

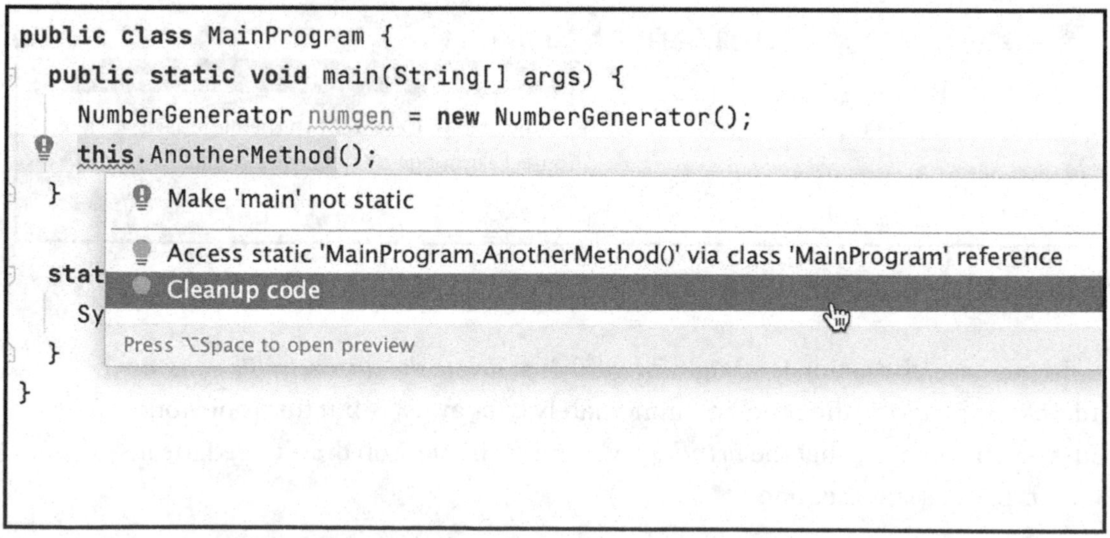

```
public class MainProgram {
  public static void main(String[] args) {
    NumberGenerator numgen = new NumberGenerator();
    this.AnotherMethod();
  }                    Make 'main' not static

                       Access static 'MainProgram.AnotherMethod()' via class 'MainProgram' reference
  stat                 Cleanup code
    Sy
  }       Press ⌥Space to open preview
}
```

Figure 6-6. *Inspection action options*

There's a couple of suggestions from the inspection:

- **Make main, not static** – This is a no-go. The main method has to be static. There are times when the options presented by the inspection action aren't helpful (nor right), and this is one of them.

- **Access static MainProgram.AnotherMethod() via class MainProgram reference** – It is just a fancy way of saying, "remove the *this* keyword in line number 6 and simply call AnotherMethod() without the self-reference." This will solve our problem.

- **Clean up code** – This will do exactly the same thing as the second (preceding) option. It will simply remove call AnotherMethod() without the self-reference. Most of the time, this is the correct option. So, let's choose this, Listing 6-1 shows the resulting code.

Listing 6-1. The resulting code

```java
public class MainProgram {
  public static void main(String[] args) {
    NumberGenerator numgen = new NumberGenerator();
    this.AnotherMethod();
  }

  static void AnotherMethod() {
    System.out.println("another method");
  }
}
```

Most of the time, the inspection actions are just plain handy, like when you use a type in your code without stopping to import it first — why bother? It's just an **Alt + ENTER** away (see Figure 6-7).

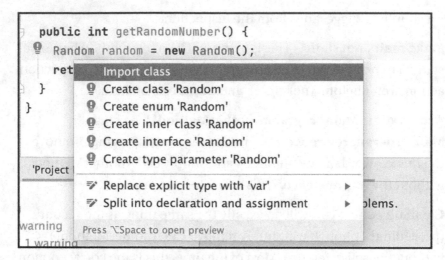

Figure 6-7. *Using the inspection action to import a class*

Inspecting Code

IntelliJ flags our errors as we type; that's quite handy if you'd like to be alerted of suboptimal code as you go. IntelliJ, in the background, actually checks the entire project for errors and warnings.

The IDE makes you aware of errors (or warnings) as you tread through the current line, but if you'd like to know the errors/warnings for the entire file, you can do that by clicking the inspection icons on the right — it's the widget in the top-right corner of the editor which displays the number of problems (and their severities) in the current file. It's shown in Figure 6-8.

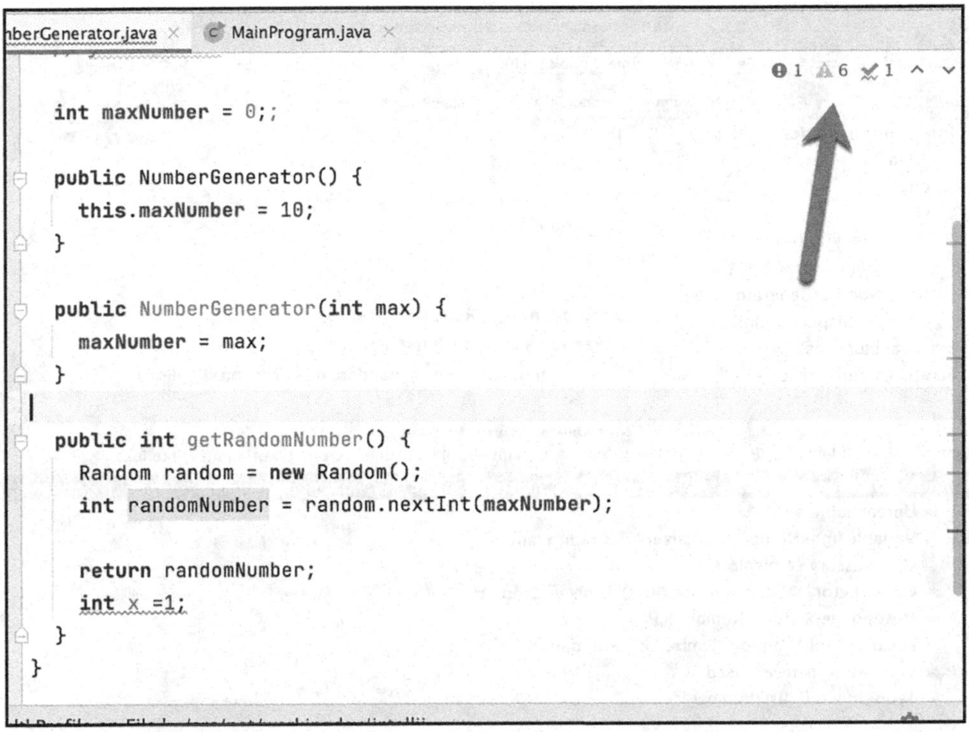

Figure 6-8. *Inspection icons*

If you click the inspection widget, IntelliJ will show the **Problem Tool Window** (shown in Figure 6-9).

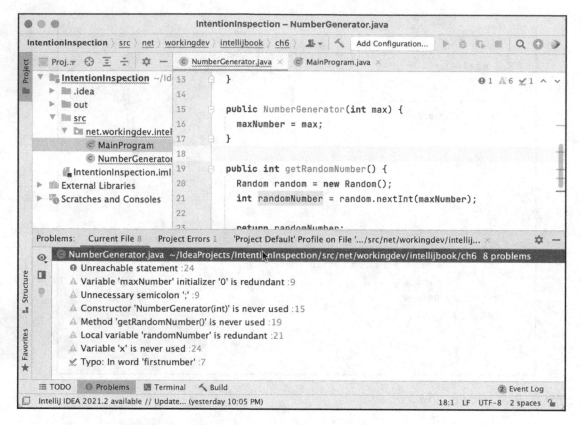

Figure 6-9. *Main editor with the Problem Tool Window shown*

The Problem Tool Window shows a comprehensive list of all the problems in the current file. You can go through them one by one by simply clicking each item on the problem list.

As you click each item, the IDE will take the cursor to the specific line where the problem was found; then, you can use **option + ENTER** (Alt + ENTER for Windows and Linux) to choose a fix (shown in Figure 6-10).

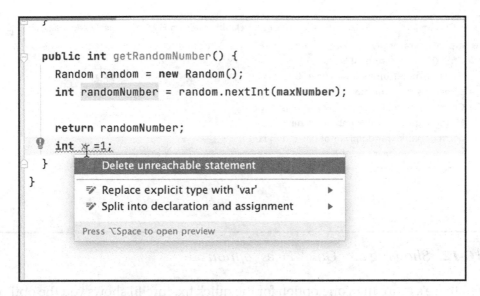

Figure 6-10. *Fixing the unreachable statement*

Alternatively, you can use the context menu for each problem item while you're in the Problem Tool Window (shown in Figure 6-11).

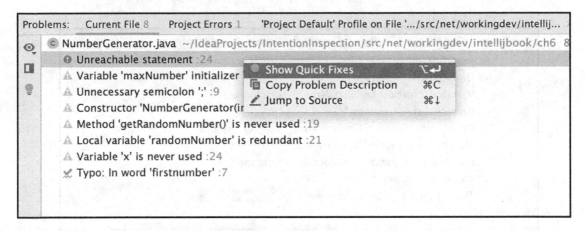

Figure 6-11. *Use the context menu while in the Problem Tool Window*

If you choose "Show Quick Fixes," IntelliJ shows you the options for quick fixes right in the Problem Tool Window (shown in Figure 6-12); that way, you don't have to go back to the source file to perform the fix. This will save you time.

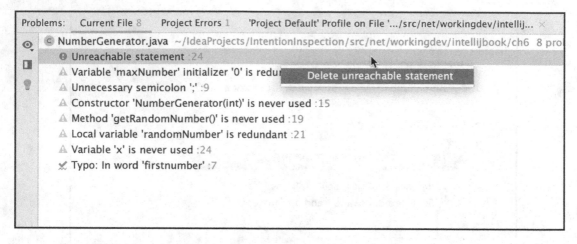

Figure 6-12. *Showing the "Quick Fixes" option*

When there's more than one option for the quick fix, IntelliJ shows you the options so you can scroll and choose the one that's appropriate. In Figure 6-13, IntelliJ tries to be helpful and shows its suggestions to fix what it thinks is a typo error — in my example, I really intended it to be spelled as "firstnumber." IntelliJ doesn't have this entry in its dictionary; that's why it's being flagged as a typo error. I'm just going to ignore it.

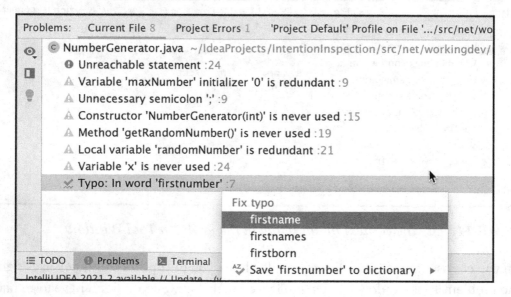

Figure 6-13. *Options for quick fixes*

Another way to navigate the items in the Problem list is to split the pane of the Problem Tool Window. Click the **split pane icon** of the Tool Window (shown in Figure 6-14), so you can see the program source in the Tool Window. You can use the usual quick fix (**option + ENTER** or **Alt + ENTER**) to fix the problem.

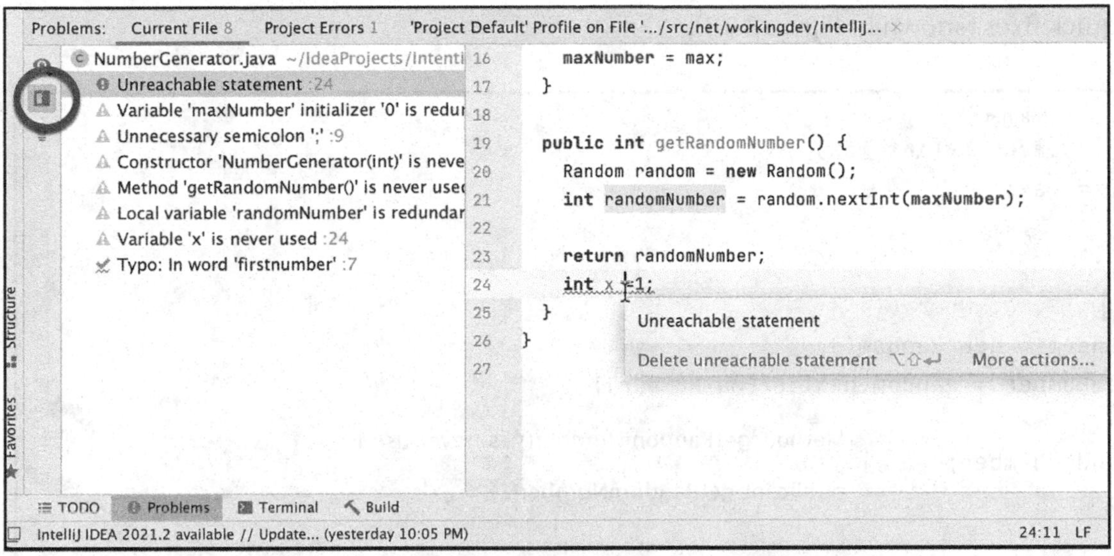

Figure 6-14. *The split pane of the Problem Tool Window*

IntelliJ gives us lots of ways of dealing with inspection problems. Another way to navigate the inspection problems is by hovering on stripes of the scroll bar (shown in Figure 6-15).

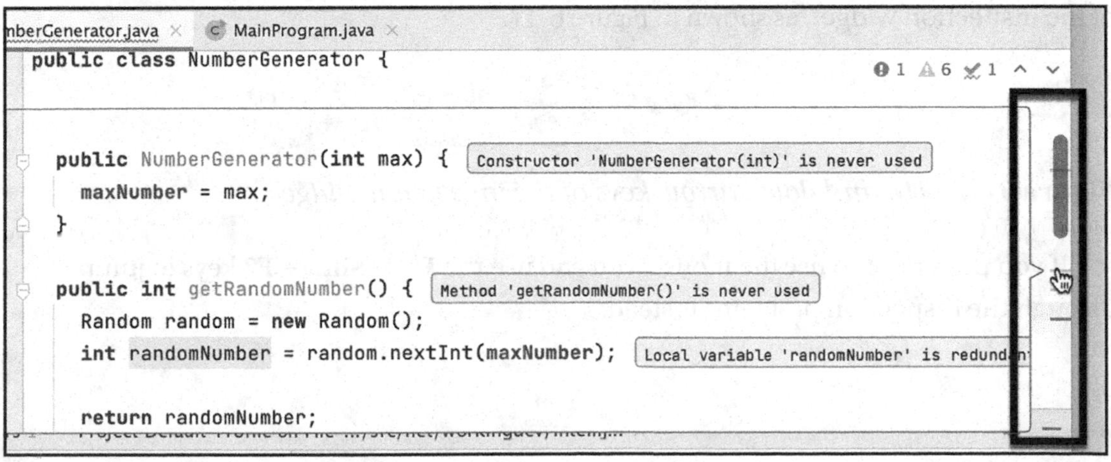

Figure 6-15. *Stripes on the scroll bar*

The yellow stripes show the warnings, and the red stripes show the error. As you hover through the stripes, the warnings and errors are shown in a popup dialog where the inspections are highlighted in callout balloons (so you can easily spot them).

IntelliJ not only makes it easy for you to spot the inspection problems, but it also makes it easy for you to resolve them. From the scroll bar, you also have access to the quick fixes (shown in Figure 6-16).

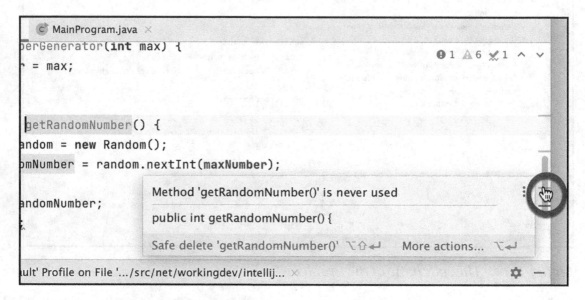

Figure 6-16. *Quick Fix from the scroll bar*

Lastly, you can navigate the inspection problems using the up and down arrow keys of the inspection widget, as shown in Figure 6-17.

Figure 6-17. *Up and down arrow keys of the inspection widget*

If you prefer not to use the mouse, you can use the **F2** or **Shift + F2** keys to jump through the inspection problems instead.

Inspecting the Whole Project

You already know how to handle problems in a single source file; we just click the inspection widget on every source file — job done. But projects typically have multiple source files. If your project has 100 source files, does that mean you need to click the inspection widget 100 times to see the problems for the entire project? Of course not. IntelliJ has a way to run the inspections for the whole project.

To run the inspection on the whole project, go to the main menu bar and then **Analyze ➤ Inspect Code**. Alternatively, use the keyboard shortcut for actions (**Shift + cmd + A** or **Shift + CTRL + A**), then choose *Inspect Code*, as shown in Figure 6-18.

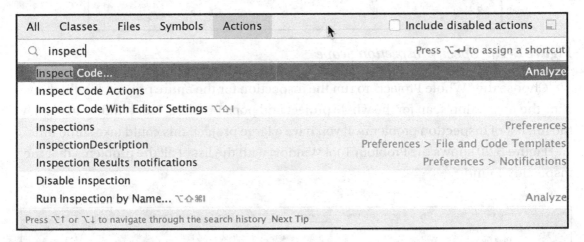

Figure 6-18. *Inspect Code action*

Either way, it'll take you to the *Specify Inspection Scope* dialog (shown in Figure 6-19).

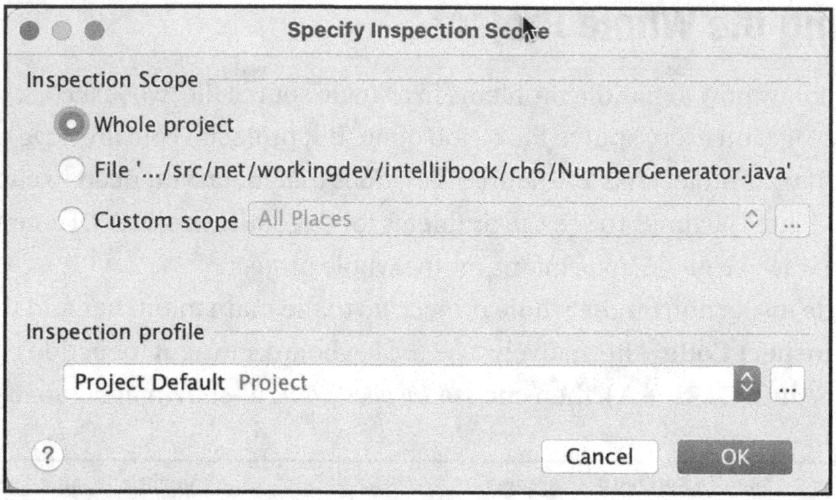

Figure 6-19. *Specify Inspection Scope*

Choose the "Whole Project" to run the inspection for the entire project. IntelliJ then runs the inspection scan for the whole project and pops Problem Tool Window to display the full list of inspection problems. If you have a large project, this could take some time.

Figure 6-20 shows the Problem Tool Window with the list of all the problems that the inspection found.

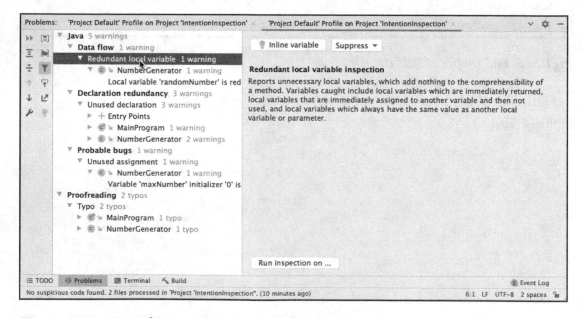

Figure 6-20. *List of inspections for the whole project*

The problems are organized by category, not by location (source file). As you can see in our small sample project, it's listing the problems by categories like Data flow, Declaration redundancy, Probable bugs, and Proofreading.

You can now go through each of the problems and resolve them using various ways of resolution.

Where possible, IntelliJ offers the solution in a nicely laid out array of buttons, as shown in Figure 6-21. It's entirely up to you if you want to use this or if you'd rather use the trusty **option + ENTER** shortcut.

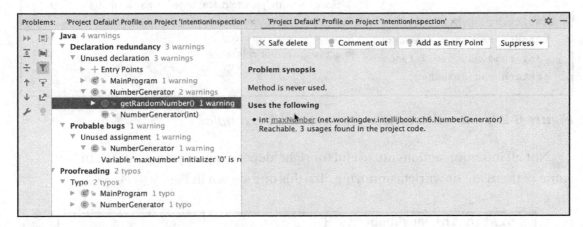

Figure 6-21. *IntelliJ offers possible resolutions.*

Intention Actions

The light bulb doesn't always mean there's something wrong with your code. IntelliJ uses the yellow light bulb to also show you where you can improve the code.

Let's take a quick example of how to use intention actions. Consider the following code shown in Figure 6-22.

```
    System.out.println("Hello" + anyNumber());
    }
```

Figure 6-22. *Intention action on println*

Using our quick fix shortcut (option + ENTER or Alt + ENTER), IntelliJ offers us a couple of ways to improve the code. As you can see in Figure 6-23, we can choose to replace the String expression with either a StringBuilder.append() or the MessageFormat.format() or replace the println with formatted printf() — it's really up to your liking which one to choose. I'm biased on the printf() option, but that's just me.

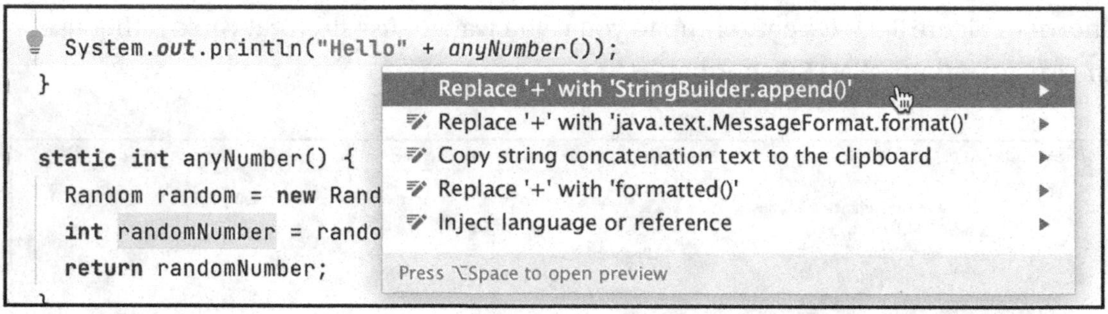

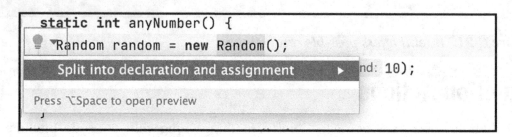

Figure 6-23. *Intention actions for our println example*

Not all intention actions are useful (or right, depending on your context). In fact, some of them are downright annoying, like this one shown in Figure 6-24.

Figure 6-24. *Split declaration intention action*

What it's suggesting is for us to do this.

```
Random random;
random = new Random();
```

Instead of this;

```
Random random = new Random();
```

The suggestion doesn't make sense in this case. The inline declaration and definition make a lot more sense.

Fortunately, you can customize the behavior for any intention. So, let's solve that pesky Split declaration intention now.

Use the quick fix shortcut (option + ENTER or Alt + ENTER), and then click the right arrow (as shown in Figure 6-25).

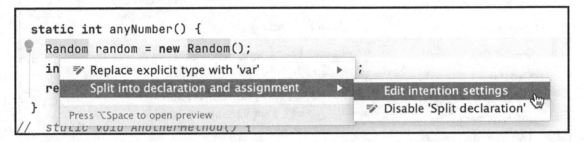

Figure 6-25. *Edit intention settings*

From here, you can either disable the "Split declaration" intention or edit the intention setting; either option will silence the intention action. IntelliJ won't bother you with it again. However, for some reason that you'd like to reinstate the intention action, you may do so in the Preferences or Settings of the IDE. It's under **Editor ➤ Intentions**. Use the search everywhere keyboard shortcut (double Shift), and then type "Intentions" (shown in Figure 6-26).

All	Classes	Files	Symbols	Actions		☐ Include non-project items	▼ ☐
Q intentions						Type / to see commands	
Intentions						Preferences	
Iterate						Preferences > Intentions	
Make open						Preferences > Intentions	
Add braces						Preferences > Intentions	
Add getter						Preferences > Intentions	
Add setter						Preferences > Intentions	
Deannotate						Preferences > Intentions	
Edit range						Preferences > Intentions	
Seal class						Preferences > Intentions	
Create Test						Preferences > Intentions	
Create test						Preferences > Intentions	
Make public						Preferences > Intentions	
Merge 'if's						Preferences > Intentions	
Unroll loop						Preferences > Intentions	

Figure 6-26. *Keyboard shortcut to pop the Intentions dialog*

In the dialog that follows, look for the "Split declaration item" in the Intentions dialog, as shown in Figure 6-27. You can use the search text field in the Intentions dialog to narrow down the options quickly.

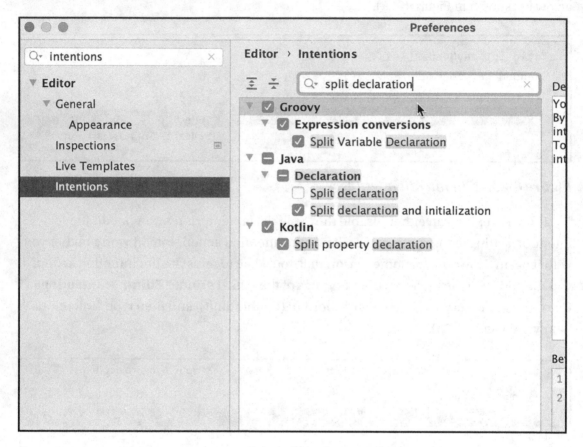

Figure 6-27. *Split declarations entry in the Intentions dialog*

As you can see, the Split declaration is disabled — because we suppressed it a while ago. When you suppress an intention either on the main editor or the Problem Tool Window, that intention action gets disabled on the Preferences (or Settings, if you're on Linux/Windows).

Use the **Preferences ➤ Intentions** to customize IntelliJ's behavior when it comes to suggesting code improvements. If you're annoyed by some intentions, just suppress them.

Key Takeaways

- Pay attention to light bulbs and squiggly lines of the editor. When you see them, it means the IDE found some suboptimal code.

- Wherever you see the light bulbs or squiggly lines, just press option + ENTER (Alt + ENTER for Windows/Linux) to do a quick fix. The quick fix shortcut is your friend.

- IntelliJ isn't always right. Some of the suggestions may not make sense to you. You can turn them off in the **Preferences (or Settings)** ➤ **Editor** ➤ **Intentions**.

CHAPTER 7

Refactoring

In this chapter, we will cover the following:

- Overview of refactoring
- Common (and important) refactoring actions
- How IntelliJ does refactoring

"Technical debt," "DRY principle," "clean code" — ever heard these terms mentioned during code reviews? Dev conferences, maybe? I bet you have. These may be buzzwords now, but they're not empty. These terms were coined (and became popular) for good reasons.

The most exciting parts of building a new app (for me, at least) were the initial coding phase. That was always a blast, but as the project enters the maintenance phase — where your initial technical decisions come to haunt you — it becomes less and less fun. In fact, it begins to feel like a chore. A common reason why the maintenance phase isn't very exciting is that it's a lot more difficult to add new functionality when you're writing it on top of a whole lotta code. The tiniest error can break lots of things, and when you fix one thing, you'll end up breaking two. This is why you should really get into the habit of unit testing your code — but we're getting ahead of ourselves here; that's not what this chapter is about; we'll deal with testing soon enough (Chapter 11). Anyway, the point is, if the code is clean, easy to read, and a bit organized, that makes the job of maintaining the code a little less nightmarish.

Refactoring is basically rewriting and improving source code — making them easily readable — without changing its observable behavior. Organized, neat, and easily readable codes are preferable over disorganized, cluttered, and convoluted codes — it makes codes a lot easier to maintain and extend. In this chapter, we'll talk about refactoring and how IntelliJ makes it easy to do.

© Ted Hagos 2022
T. Hagos, *Beginning IntelliJ IDEA*, https://doi.org/10.1007/978-1-4842-7446-0_7

Refactoring

No one sets out to write convoluted, cluttered, and disorganized code. Code complexity isn't the goal of any programmer when he starts a project. The code starts out simple, if you can believe it; then, as we add more codes, the complexity piles up — one on top of another. If you don't control the complexity, you'll most likely end up with "spaghetti code" that's really hard to untangle. So, how do we manage this situation? Plenty of ways, one of which is through refactoring.

When you refactor, you're simply moving pieces of code around in such a way that it makes more sense organizationally; but it doesn't change the behavior of the code. Let's consider the code in Listing 7-1; the method simply calls a routine to print some banner data, calculates an outstanding balance, prints the invoice, and then, lastly, prints the outstanding balance.

Listing 7-1. printSomething() Method

```java
void printSomething(Invoice invoice) {

  printBanner();
  double outstanding = calculateOutstanding();

  // print details
  System.out.println(customer);
  System.out.println(outstanding);

}
```

At some point, we might have to print the customer invoice and the outstanding balance from somewhere else in the codebase. Wouldn't it make sense to create a method that prints the details so we don't have to write the last two println() statements of the preceding sample code? Listing 7-2 shows us how.

Listing 7-2. Refactored printSomething() Method

```java
void printSomething(Invoice invoice) {
  printBanner();
  double outstanding = calculateOutstanding();

  printDetails(invoice, outstanding);
}
```

```java
private void printDetails(Invoice invoice, double outstanding) {
  System.out.println(invoice);
  System.out.println(outstanding);
}
```

See how simple it is? We just moved some code around. Now, whenever we need to print the details of the customer, we simply need to call printDetails().

The refactoring we just did is called the "extract method" refactor. There's a whole catalog of these refactor actions — which you can find at https://refactoring.com/catalog/. There are over 60 refactor actions that are listed in the catalog. I doubt that you're gonna need all 60. As a matter of experiment, you can go to GitHub and search the names of each of the refactoring actions. For example, search for "rename variable" (as shown in Figure 7-1).

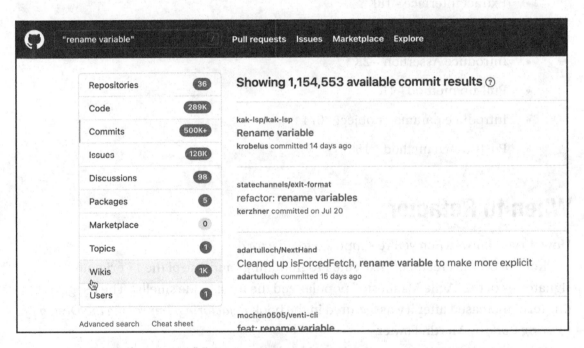

Figure 7-1. *"Rename variable" search on GitHub*

There's over 1M plus commits on GitHub for the "rename variable" operation. Granted, not all refactoring operations are documented on the commit message, but this is not a bad approximation of real-world refactoring activities.

With these crude research methods, here's what I found on GitHub. At the time of writing, the "rename variable" operation tops the list with over 1 million commits.

The following list shows parts of my findings:

- Rename variable – 1M+

- Rename method – 178K

- Rename class – 143K

- Move method – 109K

- Move class – 97K

- Extract method – 95K

- Inline method – 81K

- Extract class – 23K

- Extract interface – 18K

- Extract superclass – 2K

- Introduce Assertion – 2K

- Pull-up method – 1K

- Introduce parameter object - 674

- Push-down method – 168

When to Refactor

How do you know when you're supposed to refactor?

Kent Beck, the creator of "Extreme Programming" and one of the 17 original signatories of the "Agile Manifesto," popularized the term "code smells." The usage of this term increased after it was featured in the book *Refactoring: Improving the Design of Existing Code* by Martin Fowler.

When a code needs refactoring, it's said to have a "smell," not literally – it just means the code isn't appealing or pleasant to read. Here are some examples of code smells:

- **Large class** – It's usually easier to add a new method or behavior to an existing class; that's why a class grows. Over time, too much functionality is crammed into the class. You may need to relocate some of its functionalities to a new class.

- **Long method** – This happens when you cram lots of functionalities into a method. The urge to economize on handoffs and simply keep the behavior within the existing method is too great, and so the method grows. Here's a quick tip: when you feel like you have to write a comment to explain the next lines of code, it's usually a sign you should put the next lines of code into a method of its own.

- **Lots of primitive types being used** – When the number of primitive member variables grows over time, it's probably time to review your abstraction of the problem domain.

- **Too many parameters** – This usually happens in tandem with the "long method" mentioned earlier. There are too many parameters because, probably, the method is doing too much. It's implementing too many algorithms. Either that or it may be time to review your abstractions again. Instead of passing many parameters, it might be better to pass an object instead.

There's plenty of code smells; we won't be able to get to them all in this chapter because we're supposed to talk about how to do refactorings in IntelliJ.

Note   As you gain more experience, your powers to detect "code smells" manually will grow – until then, you may want to use some tools to help you find malodorous code. SonarLink isn't a bad place to start. It's available as a plugin for IntelliJ. You can get SonarLink from the website `www.sonarlink.org`.

Refactoring in IntelliJ

Now that we know a fair bit about refactoring, it's time to see it in action.

To start refactoring, you need to select the code fragment you want to refactor (the target). It can be a symbol or just a piece of code. You can select the symbol either in the editor or in the Structure Tool Window — I usually just select the code in the editor; it just feels more natural that way. It's usually sufficient to have the caret on the symbol. IntelliJ expands the selection automatically, as shown in Figure 7-2, where I placed the caret somewhere in the *lastName* symbol.

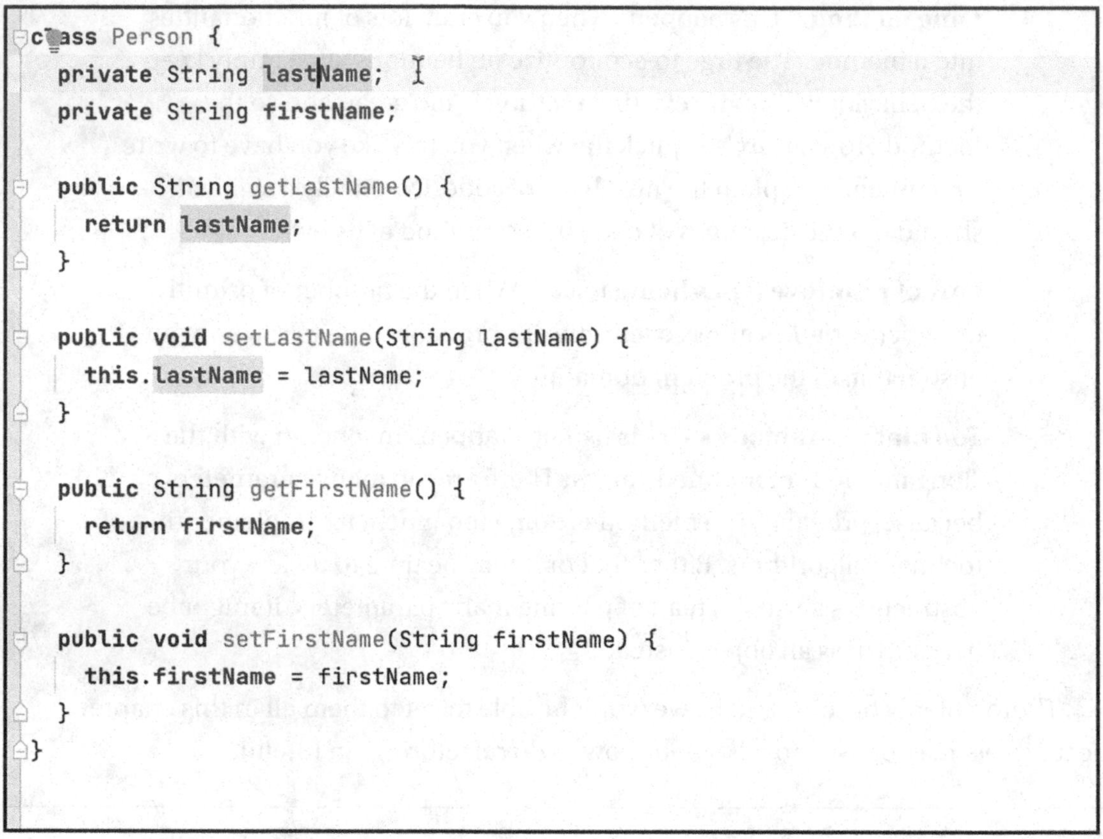

```
class Person {
  private String lastName;   I
  private String firstName;

  public String getLastName() {
    return lastName;
  }

  public void setLastName(String lastName) {
    this.lastName = lastName;
  }

  public String getFirstName() {
    return firstName;
  }

  public void setFirstName(String firstName) {
    this.firstName = firstName;
  }
}
```

Figure 7-2. *IntelliJ expands the selection automatically*

As you can see, IntelliJ already highlighted the usages of the lastName symbol, even if I haven't asked it to do anything just yet. The IDE anticipates your moves.

Once you selected the target, you can now choose the refactoring action. You can do that in a couple of ways:

- Via the main menu bar, choose Refactor, and then choose the refactoring action.

- Use the context menu. Right-click the symbol, and then choose Refactor and then the refactoring action.

- Use the keyboard shortcut **CTRL + T** (macOS) or **CTRL + Shift + Alt + T** (Linux/Windows), and then choose the refactoring action.

To continue our example, let's rename the *lastName* variable to *lname*. Once I have the caret on the *lastName* symbol, I'll use the keyboard to show the "Refactor This" dialog (shown in Figure 7-3). By the way, as you display the "Refactor This" dialog, the keyboard shortcuts for the various refactoring operations are shown: Shift + F6 for rename, F6 for Move members, F5 for Copy class, etc. You can choose to memorize these individual shortcuts (which is the fastest way to access to them), or if you're a bit lazy (like me), I either just use the right-click or the CTRL + T — it gets me to the "Refactor This" dialog anyway.

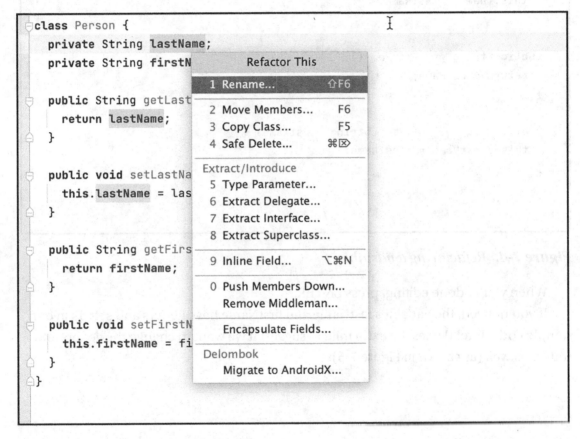

Figure 7-3. *"Refactor This" dialog*

Let's choose "Rename"; after all, we want to rename a variable. Once you choose "Rename," IntelliJ highlights the symbol as it's being edited and instantaneously changes the occurrences of the symbol accordingly as shown in Figure 7-4.

```
class Person {
    private String lname // ☐ ;
    private String firstName;

    public String getLastName() {
        return lname;
    }

    public void setLastName(String lastName) {
        this.lname = lastName;
    }

    public String getFirstName() {
        return firstName;
    }

    public void setFirstName(String firstName) {
        this.firstName = firstName;
    }
}
```

Figure 7-4. *Refactoring a variable*

When you're done editing, press ENTER.

If you noticed, the variables lastName and firstName have getters and setters in our sample code. IntelliJ goes the extra mile to suggest if we want to change the getters and setters as well (as shown in Figure 7-5).

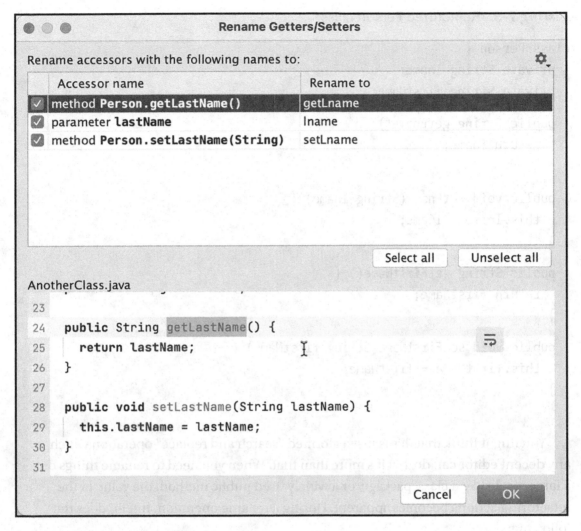

Figure 7-5. *Rename Getters and Setters*

A preview of the code changes is shown in the bottom panel of the dialog (Figure 7-5). Click OK to complete the action.

Listing 7-3 shows the refactored Person class.

Listing 7-3. Refactored Person class

```
class Person {
  private String lname;
  private String firstName;

  public String getLname() {
    return lname;
  }

  public void setLname(String lname) {
    this.lname = lname;
  }

  public String getFirstName() {
    return firstName;
  }

  public void setFirstName(String firstName) {
    this.firstName = firstName;
  }
}
```

You might think that this is just a glorified "search and replace" operation which any decent editor can do, but it's more than that. When you need to rename things on a larger scale like a class, package, or a widely used public method, the value of the refactoring actions becomes apparent. During a rename operation, IntelliJ does the following:

- It checks for name collisions in the current scope.

- It verifies that the new name is syntactically legal.

- In case you're renaming a class or a package, it creates new files and directories and deletes the old ones.

- It updates the version control system of any files that were added or removed from the source tree as a result of the name change.

- It corrects all direct code references to the symbol you renamed to make sure they are using the new name.

- It even updates JavaDoc annotations.

- It updates any import statements that were affected.

Some More Refactorings in IntelliJ

I'm sure you're already getting the hang of it, and I can probably leave it up to you to experiment on how to do the other refactoring actions — but let's just do a couple more, shall we?

Extract Method

You might want to use the "extract method" refactoring action when you "smell" that the code is growing long. You'll extract the method because you want to abstract the operation and encapsulate some behaviors on a separate method; that way, it can be reused from other parts of the code.

Figure 7-6 shows the printSomething() method — you've seen this code earlier. I used this as an example earlier in the chapter. You already know how this will get refactored.

```
8      void printSomething(Invoice invoice) {
9          printBanner();
10         double outstanding = calculateOutstanding();
11
12         // print details
13         System.out.println(invoice);
14         System.out.println(outstanding);
15     }
16
17
```

Figure 7-6. *printSomething() method*

We want to extract lines 13 and 14 and put them in a separate method. To do that, I'll highlight lines 13 and 14 (as shown in Figure 7-7) and then pop the "Refactor This" dialog.

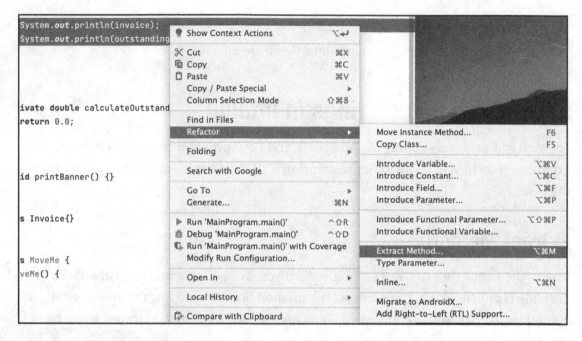

Figure 7-7. *Extract Method*

Choose the "Extract Method" action; once I choose the action, IntelliJ shows a live preview of the change. The extracted method — aptly named "extracted()" — is shown and lit in the background (shown in Figure 7-8).

```
 8   void printSomething(Invoice invoice) {
 9       printBanner();
10       double outstanding = calculateOutstanding();
11
12       // print details
13       extracted ✿ (invoice, outstanding);
14   }
15
16   private void extracted(Invoice invoice, double outstanding) {
17       System.out.println(invoice);
18       System.out.println(outstanding);
19   }
20
```

Figure 7-8. *extracted() method is shown in the preview*

At this point, IntelliJ isn't done with the refactoring action yet. As you can see, the "extracted()" method signature is selected because IntelliJ is waiting for me to type the name of the new method. So, I'll type the name of my newly extracted method. I change the name to "printDetails()," as you can see in Figure 7-9.

Like before, IntelliJ shows you a live preview of your changes as you type.

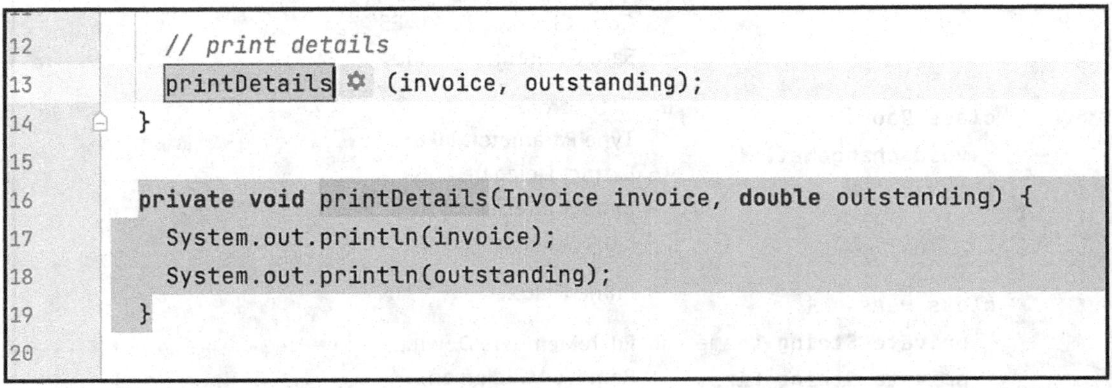

```
12        // print details
13        printDetails ⚙ (invoice, outstanding);
14     }
15
16     private void printDetails(Invoice invoice, double outstanding) {
17         System.out.println(invoice);
18         System.out.println(outstanding);
19     }
20
```

Figure 7-9. *printDetails() method*

When you're happy with your changes on the method name, press ENTER to complete the refactoring action. After refactoring, you may need to do a bit of cleanup — not much, but sometimes little modifications may be necessary.

Move Members

You can move member variables or methods from one class to another, but note that you can only move static members — IntelliJ won't let you move instance members.

To move a class member, position the caret on the symbol you want to move, and then pop the "Refactor This" dialog, as shown in Figure 7-10.

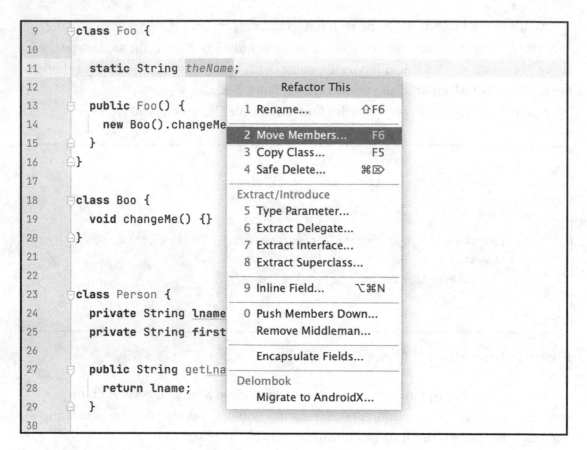

Figure 7-10. *Move Members*

Choose "Move Members." In the screen that follows (Figure 7-11), you get to choose the destination. You need to tell IntelliJ where you'd like to move the member.

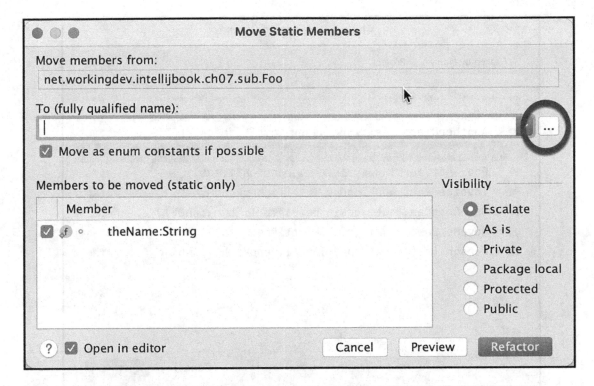

Figure 7-11. *Move Static Members*

Click the ellipsis button (to the right of the "fully qualified name" field). You can choose the destination class in the dialog that follows (shown in Figure 7-12).

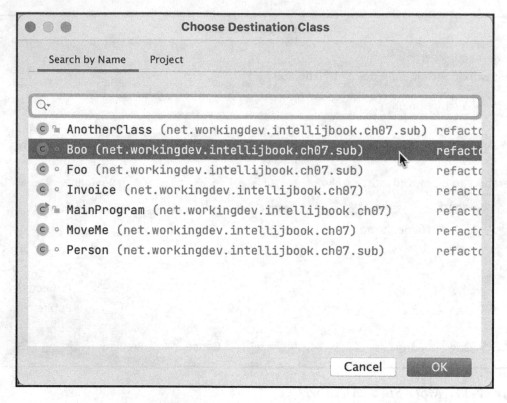

Figure 7-12. *Choose Destination Class*

Click OK to complete the selection, after which you'll go back to the previous dialog, but this time, the destination field contains the fully qualified name of the destination class (shown in Figure 7-13).

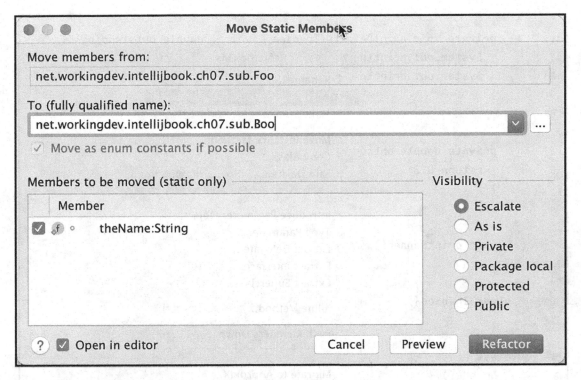

Figure 7-13. *Move Static Members (filled up)*

Click **Refactor** to complete the action.

Change Signature

If you need to change the signature of your methods, think twice before doing it manually. IntelliJ can really save you tons of time in dealing with the aftermath of the change. If you do it manually, you might not get all of the references for the method — the IDE won't miss a beat.

Let's change the signature of our earlier example, "printDetails()" method. Place the caret on the name of the method and pop the "Refactor This" dialog, as shown in Figure 7-14.

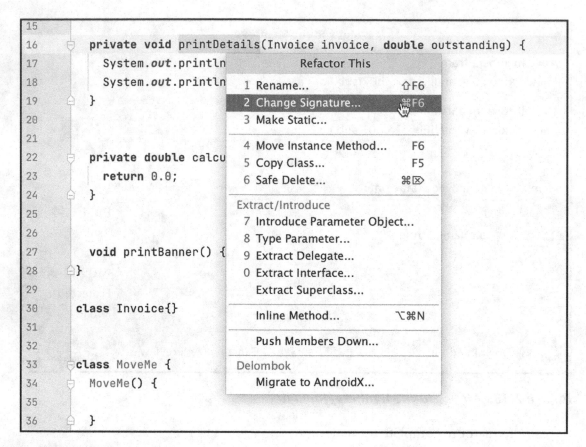

Figure 7-14. *Change Signature of printDetails()*

Choose the "Change Signature" action. The Change Signature dialog pops up (shown in Figure 7-15).

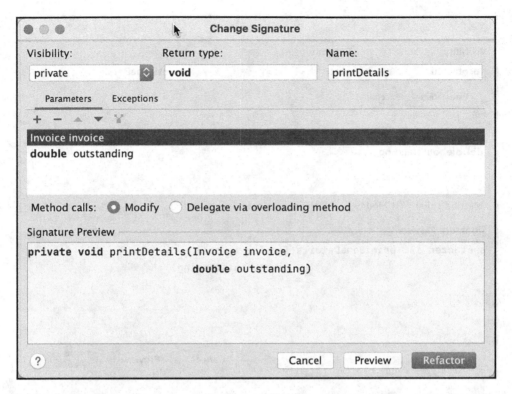

Figure 7-15. *Change Signature dialog*

In this dialog, you can change the visibility of the member, the return type, the name, and even the ordering of the parameters.

Figure 7-16 shows the Change Signature dialog with some of my changes.

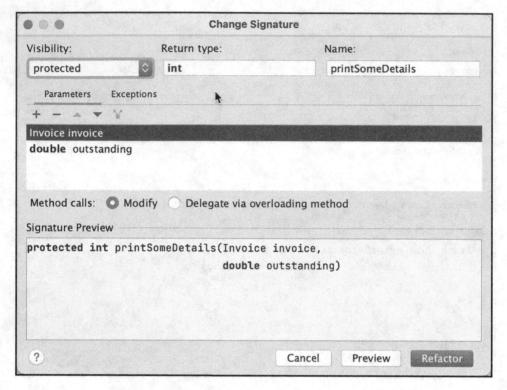

Figure 7-16. *Change Signature (with my changes)*

As you can see, I changed the name of the method to "printSomeDetails()," changed the return type to int, and I also changed its visibility to "protected."

The bottom panel of the dialog shows a preview of the method signature (with your changes). At this point, if you're already happy with your changes, you can click "Refactor" to complete the action. Alternatively, you can click the "Preview" button to see the refactoring preview before you commit to the action. The refactoring preview is shown in Figure 7-17.

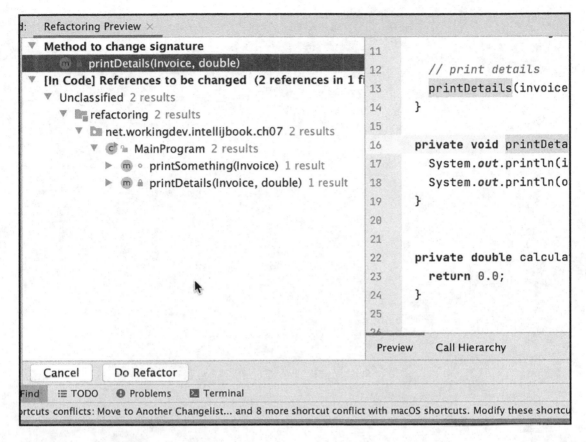

Figure 7-17. *Refactoring Preview*

You can inspect the details of the proposed refactoring in the preview. When you're happy with your changes, click the "Do Refactor" button to complete the action. Otherwise, click the "Cancel" button to abort the action.

Key Takeaways

- Refactoring keeps our codebase sane not only for other people but also for us. Three months from now, you won't remember what your thoughts were while writing that nifty piece of code.

- IntelliJ's refactoring tools are way better than "Find and Replace." Whenever possible, try to use the refactoring facilities before doing it manually.

- If you can remember only one shortcut for refactoring, let that be **CTRL + T** (for macOS folks) or **CTRL + Shift + Alt + T** (for PC folks).

Live Templates

In this chapter, we will cover the following:

- Live templates
- Using live templates
- Creating your own live templates

Java has a love-and-hate relationship with developers for various reasons. If I were a betting person, I'd say one of the reasons why Java is hated is because of verbosity. To get anything done, you have to endure its boiler-plate codes. You have a couple of options:

- **Switch to Python** – you'll need to switch careers and possibly get out of your current employment (drastic).

- **Switch to Kotlin** – It's possible. A lot of Java shops are now adopting Kotlin. You may not need to jump to another employer after all, but do you really want to? Java is your first love, isn't it?

- **Grit your teeth, power through, and type the codes** – Ouch! Hello, carpal tunnel syndrome.

- **Use IntelliJ's live templates** – Yay! Your fingers (and your keyboard) will thank you for it. That's what this chapter is all about.

So What Are Live Templates?

Have you used text expanders before – the ones where you type some letter patterns like *datetoday* and it expands to the current date or *tgif*, and it expands to "thank goodness it's Friday"? Live templates are a lot like that. It's a feature of IntelliJ where you get to type a mnemonic (or something like that), and it expands to an expression or structure.

123

© Ted Hagos 2022
T. Hagos, *Beginning IntelliJ IDEA*, https://doi.org/10.1007/978-1-4842-7446-0_8

You wanna see it in action? The next time you define a class and you need to write the main() method, type the word "main" (as shown in Figure 8-1), and then press either ENTER or TAB to expand the template.

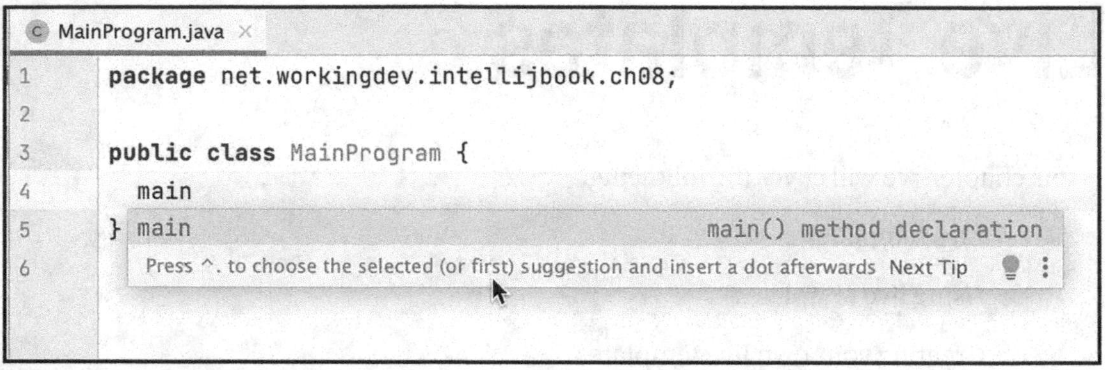

Figure 8-1. *Using the "main" live template to insert public static void main*

When the template expands, you'll have an empty main() method (as shown in Figure 8-2). The IDE will also put the caret on the first blank line of the method. It's very thoughtful. That way, you can start typing the first line inside the method without repositioning the cursor.

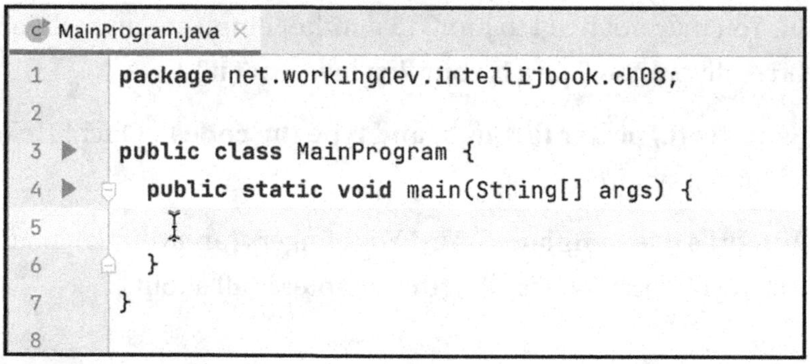

Figure 8-2. *Expanded the "main" live template*

There's another template for the main method. Try typing "psvm," as shown in Figure 8-3.

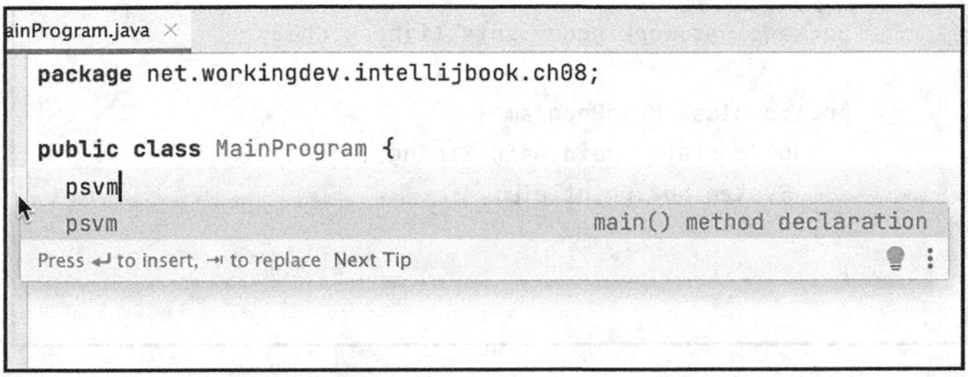

CHAPTER 8   LIVE TEMPLATES

Figure 8-3. *Using the "psvm" template*

Pressing ENTER or TAB also expands "psvm" to `public static void main()` method. Now, after landing on the first blank line of main, try typing "so," as shown in Figure 8-4.

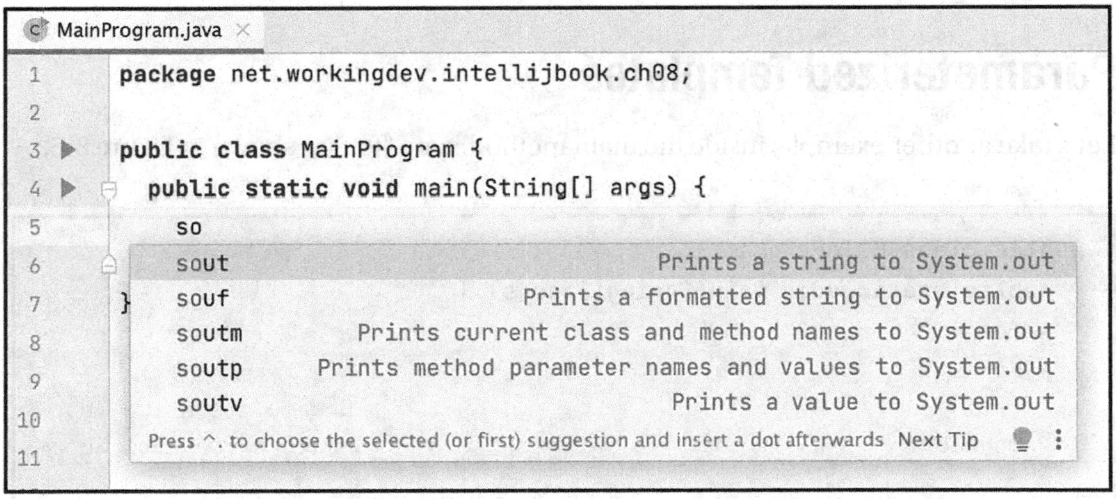

Figure 8-4. *IntelliJ showing some live templates starting with "so"*

We'd like to write *System.out.println(),* so choose "sout." Pressing ENTER or TAB while "sout" is selected expands the template to *System.out.println();* as shown in Figure 8-5.

125

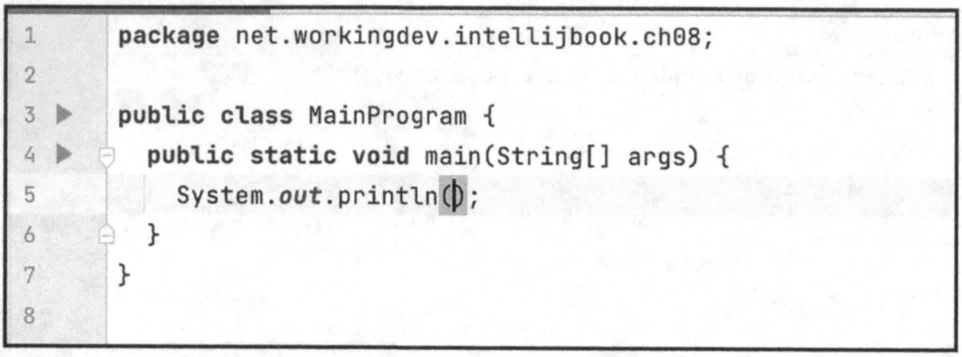

```
1      package net.workingdev.intellijbook.ch08;
2
3  ▶   public class MainProgram {
4  ▶  ⊝  public static void main(String[] args) {
5           System.out.println();
6        }
7      }
8
```

Figure 8-5. *"sout" expands to System.out.println();*

So far, you've typed eight keys ("main" and "so," including the tabs), and it expanded to 58 characters. That's 50 characters you don't have to type anymore — quite neat, right? Imagine if you can actually use all 38 live templates of Java. The savings in keystrokes can be huge.

Parameterized Templates

Let's take another example; inside the main method, type "for," as shown in Figure 8-6.

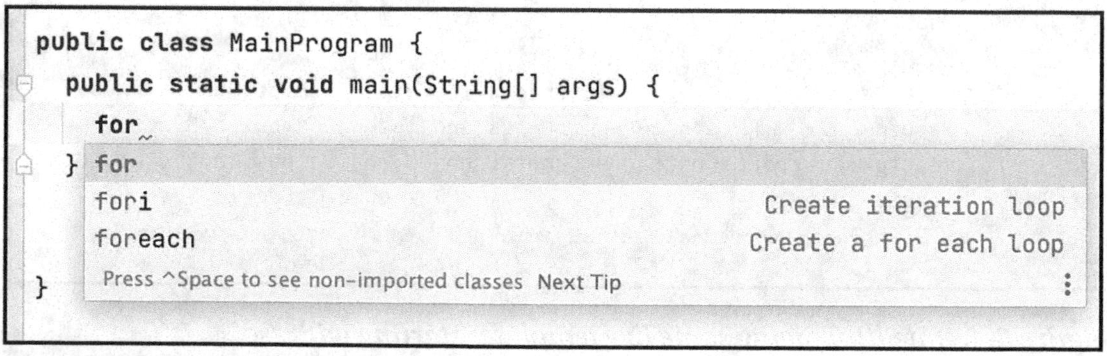

```
public class MainProgram {
⊝   public static void main(String[] args) {
      for⌇
⊝  } for
   fori                                    Create iteration loop
   foreach                                 Create a for each loop
}     Press ^Space to see non-imported classes  Next Tip        ⋮
```

Figure 8-6. *Using the "fori" template*

As you can see, IntelliJ presents us with three options: (1) ***for***, which expands to the for loop structure; (2) ***fori***, which expands into a more comprehensive for loop structure; and (3) ***foreach***, which is what you might use when working with collections. Let's use the "fori"; press TAB or ENTER while "fori" is selected. IntelliJ expands it to a nearly complete for loop structure (as shown in Figure 8-7).

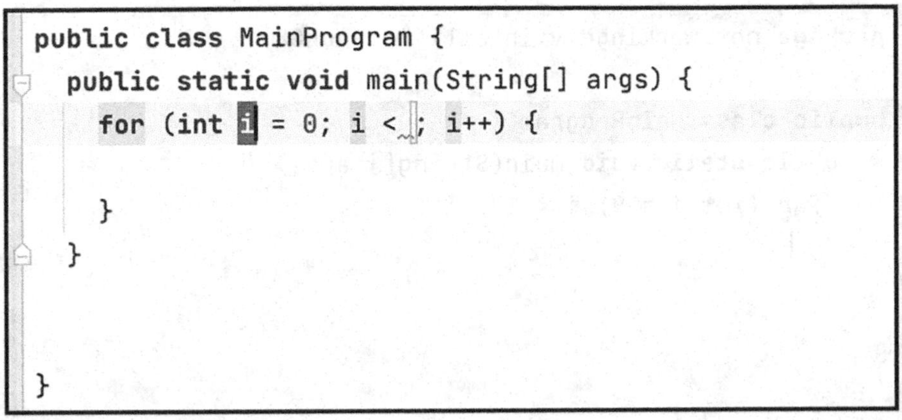

```
public class MainProgram {
  public static void main(String[] args) {
    for (int i = 0; i < ; i++) {


    }
  }



}
```

Figure 8-7. *"fori" expanded*

It has a starting counter value, the limiting expression, and the counter increment expression. As the template expands, the caret lands on "i" in case you'd like to change the counter variable (I usually leave it alone). If you press TAB again, the caret lands on where you should type the value for the limiting expression (shown in Figure 8-8).

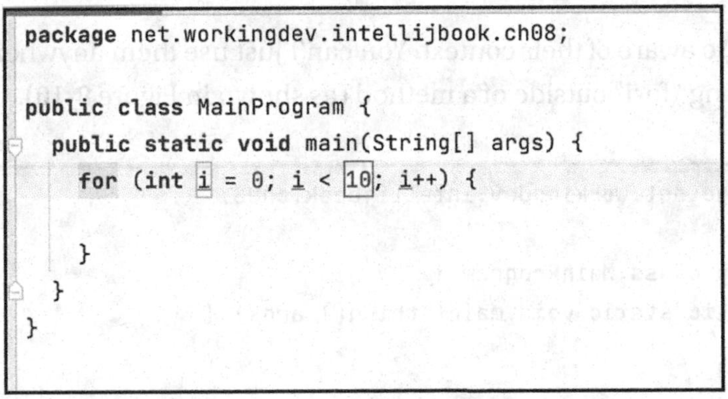

```
package net.workingdev.intellijbook.ch08;

public class MainProgram {
  public static void main(String[] args) {
    for (int i = 0; i < 10; i++) {


    }
  }
}
```

Figure 8-8. *Pressing TAB takes you to the limiting expression*

Notice that each press of the TAB lands the caret to a placeholder where you're supposed to input values in order to complete the statement.

Press TAB one more time, and it should land the caret on the first blank line of the "for" statement (shown in Figure 8-9).

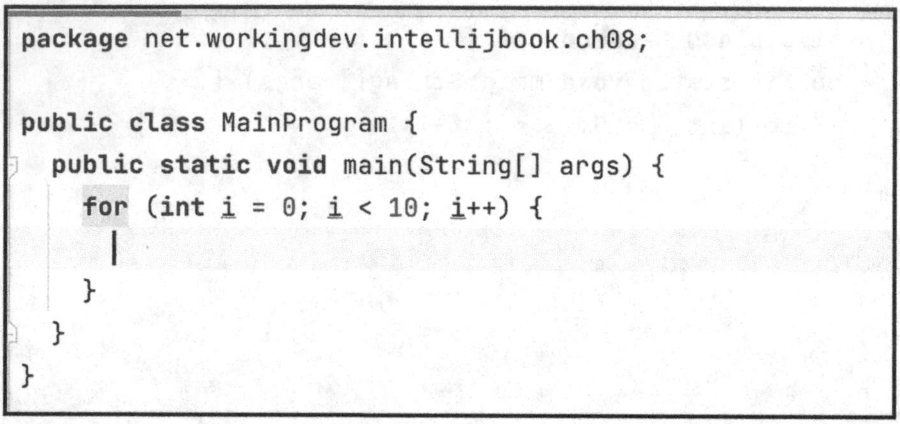

```
package net.workingdev.intellijbook.ch08;

public class MainProgram {
  public static void main(String[] args) {
    for (int i = 0; i < 10; i++) {
      |
    }
  }
}
```

Figure 8-9. *Pressing TAB for the final time*

You should be getting the hang of this already. It's pretty easy to use live templates. You should use them whenever and wherever you can. They're time-savers.

Showing All Available Templates

Live templates are aware of their context. You can't just use them anywhere. For example, try typing "fori" outside of a method (as shown in Figure 8-10).

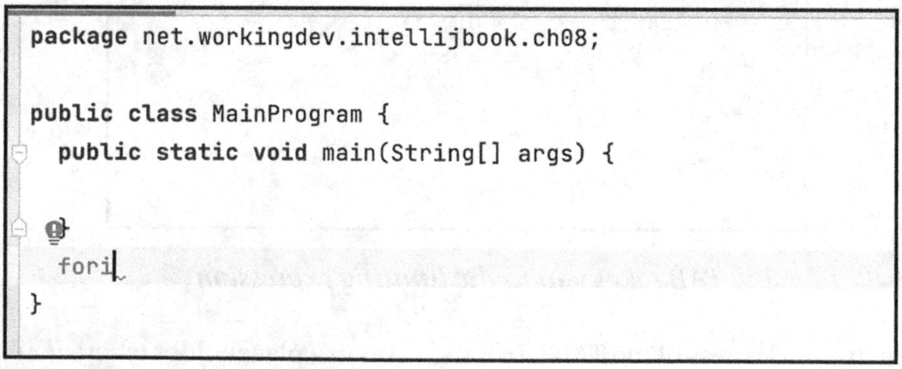

```
package net.workingdev.intellijbook.ch08;

public class MainProgram {
  public static void main(String[] args) {

    fori
}
```

Figure 8-10. *Typing "fori" outside of a method*

See how IntelliJ flags it as an error? The "fori" template doesn't make sense outside of a method. The templates are aware of context. They know where they're supposed to be.

IntelliJ is always trying to be helpful. As you type a bunch of characters in the editor, it works hard to anticipate what you're trying to do. In Figure 8-11, as I type "p," it tries to suggest a bunch of options, and it's hard to tell which ones are live templates and which ones are not. As a rule of thumb, if it (1) doesn't have parentheses or curly braces and (2) doesn't have a helpful description, then it isn't a live template.

Can you spot which are live templates in Figure 8-11?

```
package net.workingdev.intellijbook.ch08;                              1

public class MainProgram {
    public static void main(String[] args) {

    }

    p|
      public
      private
      protected
      prsf                                     private static final
      psf                                       public static final
    m protected Object clone() {...}                        Object
    m public boolean equals(Object obj) {...}               Object
    m public int hashCode() {...}                           Object
    m public String toString() {...}                        Object
    m protected void finalize() {...}                       Object
      psfi                                 public static final int
      psfs                               public static final String
    Press ↵ to insert, ↦ to replace  Next Tip                    ⋮
```

Figure 8-11. *Showing possible templates starting with "p"*

If you guessed prsf, psf, and psfi, then you got it right.

If you want to show the list of all live templates (where the caret is), just use **cmd + J** (macOS) or **CTRL + J** (Windows and Linux) and scroll. Figure 8-12 shows the dropdown for all live templates.

```
package net.workingdev.intellijbook.ch08;

public class MainProgram {
  public static void main(String[] args) {


  }
```

const	Define android style int constant
fixme	adds // FIXME
geti	Inserts singleton method getInstance
key	Key for a bundle
logt	A static logtag with your current classname
main	main() method declaration
newInstance	create a new Fragment instance with arguments
noInstance	private empty constructor to prohibit instance c…
noop	indicate that a method does not have any operations
Parcelable	Create a parcelable block for your current class
ParcelableEnum	Create a parcelable block for your current e…
ParcelableEnumTest	Creates basic parcelable enum test metho…

Figure 8-12.   *List of live templates*

Surround Live Templates

Consider the code in Listing 8-1; it's a typical constellation of Java classes that demonstrates how to do a Singleton — it's not a proper Singleton, so don't use this in production, but it's enough to demonstrate the basic flow on how to control the number of object instances.

Listing 8-1.   TreeFactory, Tree, and MainProgram Classes

```
public class MainProgram {
  public static void main(String[] args) {

    Tree objTree = null;
```

```
    objTree = TreeFactory.getTree();
  }
}

class TreeFactory {
  private static Tree tree;
  private TreeFactory() {
    tree = new Tree();
  }
  public static Tree getTree() throws Exception {
    return tree;
  }
}

class Tree { }
```

Suppose we'd like to surround the getTree() call with try-catch; you can use live templates to save some keystrokes.

To surround a statement with any control flow structure, place the caret on the line you'd like to surround, and then use the keyboard shortcut **cmd + option + T** (macOS) or **CTRL + Alt + T** (Linux and Windows).

The *Surround With* dialog pops up and lets you choose the control structure to use, as shown in Figure 8-13.

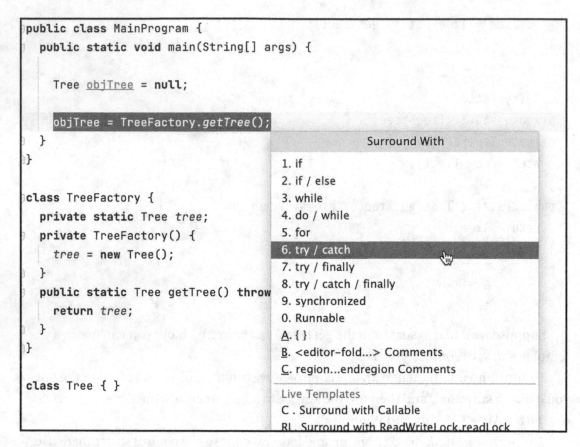

Figure 8-13. *Using the "Surround With" templates*

Choose the try-catch, and then press ENTER.

Figure 8-14 shows the completed action of the live template.

```java
public class MainProgram {
  public static void main(String[] args) {

    Tree objTree = null;

    try {
      objTree = TreeFactory.getTree();
    } catch (Exception e) {
      e.printStackTrace();
    }
  }
}

class TreeFactory {
  private static Tree tree;
  private TreeFactory() {
    tree = new Tree();
  }
  public static Tree getTree() throws Exception {
    return tree;
  }
}
```

Figure 8-14. *Expanded try-catch live template*

As you can see, the try-catch template pre-filled the control structure with the appropriate catch expression and even a printStackTrace() statement.

Let's take our example further. Now, place the caret outside the try-catch structure. We will check if the call to getTree() returns null. Figure 8-15 shows us how to use the live template to do this.

Type "if" and wait for the live template to show the options.

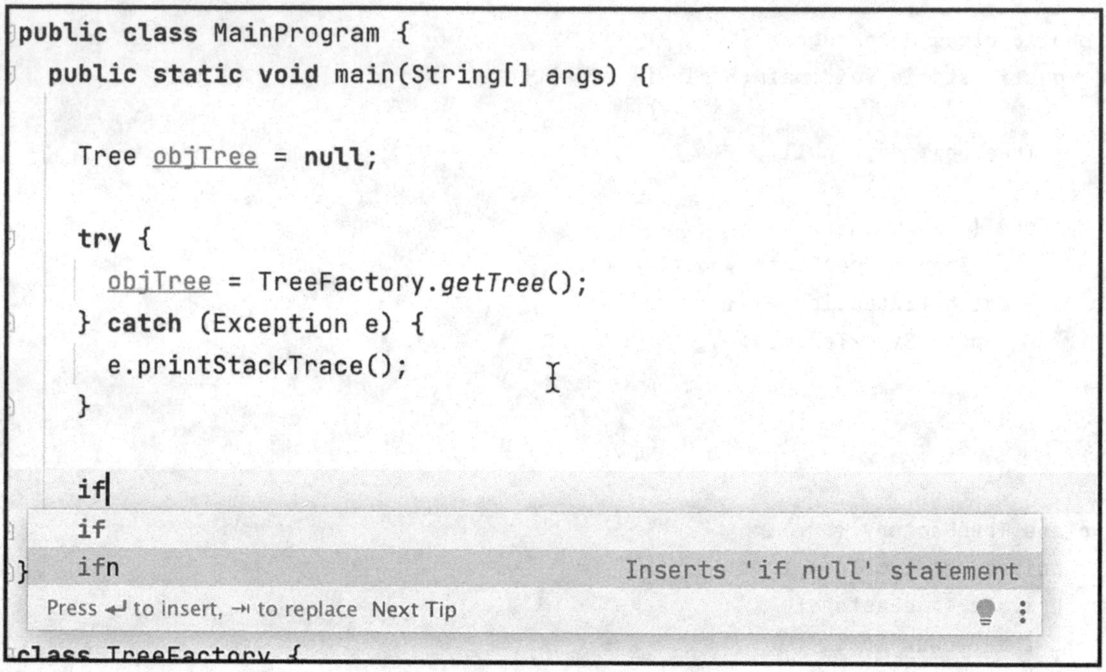

```
public class MainProgram {
  public static void main(String[] args) {

    Tree objTree = null;

    try {
      objTree = TreeFactory.getTree();
    } catch (Exception e) {
      e.printStackTrace();
    }

    if|
    if
    ifn                        Inserts 'if null' statement
    Press ↵ to insert, →| to replace  Next Tip              💡 ⋮
class TreeFactory {
```

Figure 8-15.   *Using the if null (ifn) template*

Choose "ifn" and press ENTER.

Figure 8-16 shows that the live template is aware of which variables are in scope.

```
if (objTree == null) {
  v objTree              Tree
} p args               String[]
}   Press ↵ or →| to replace        ⋮
```

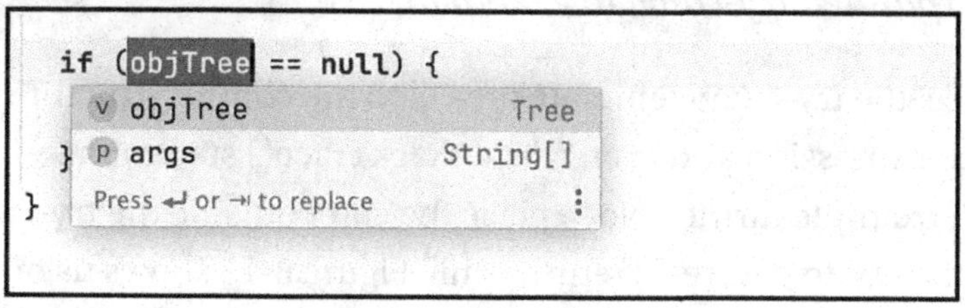

Figure 8-16.   *Live template showing which variables are in scope*

Of course, it's the objTree variable we'd like to test, so choose that. Listing 8-2 shows our completed MainProgram.

Listing 8-2. MainProgram

```java
public class MainProgram {
  public static void main(String[] args) {

    Tree objTree = null;

    try {
      objTree = TreeFactory.getTree();
    } catch (Exception e) {
      e.printStackTrace();
    }

    if (objTree == null) {

    }
  }
}
```

Once you get the hang of this, you'll wonder how you ever coded without these. They really will save you countless hours of typing.

Creating Your Own Templates

You can poke around live templates a bit more on the IDE's Preferences or Settings. To get to it, use **cmd + ,** (comma) on macOS or **CTRL + Alt + S** on Windows/Linux; then go to **Editor ➤ Live Templates**.

You'll see the templates are grouped by language (as shown in Figure 8-17).

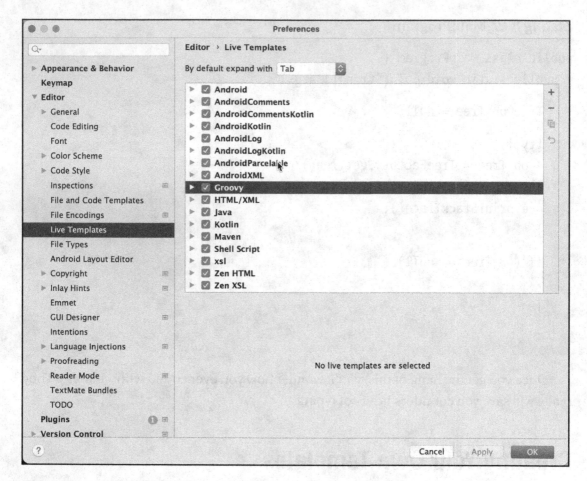

Figure 8-17. *Live Templates on the Preferences dialog*

Click Java language to expand the selection; that reveals all 38 live templates for Java (shown in Figure 8-18).

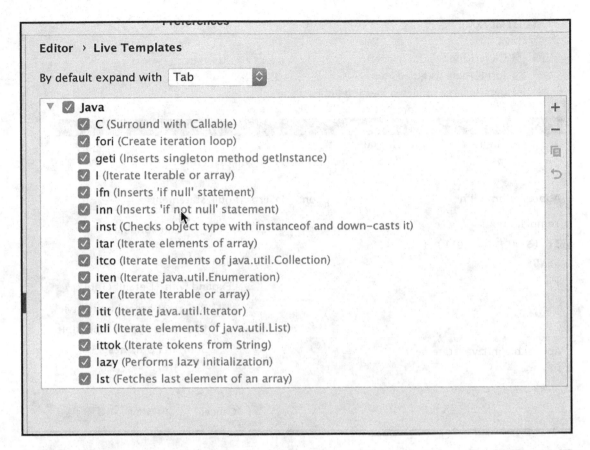

Figure 8-18. *Java Live Templates*

As you click each item, IntelliJ shows the details of each live template. You can see the template text and a couple of other options that affect the behavior of the template, as shown in Figure 8-19.

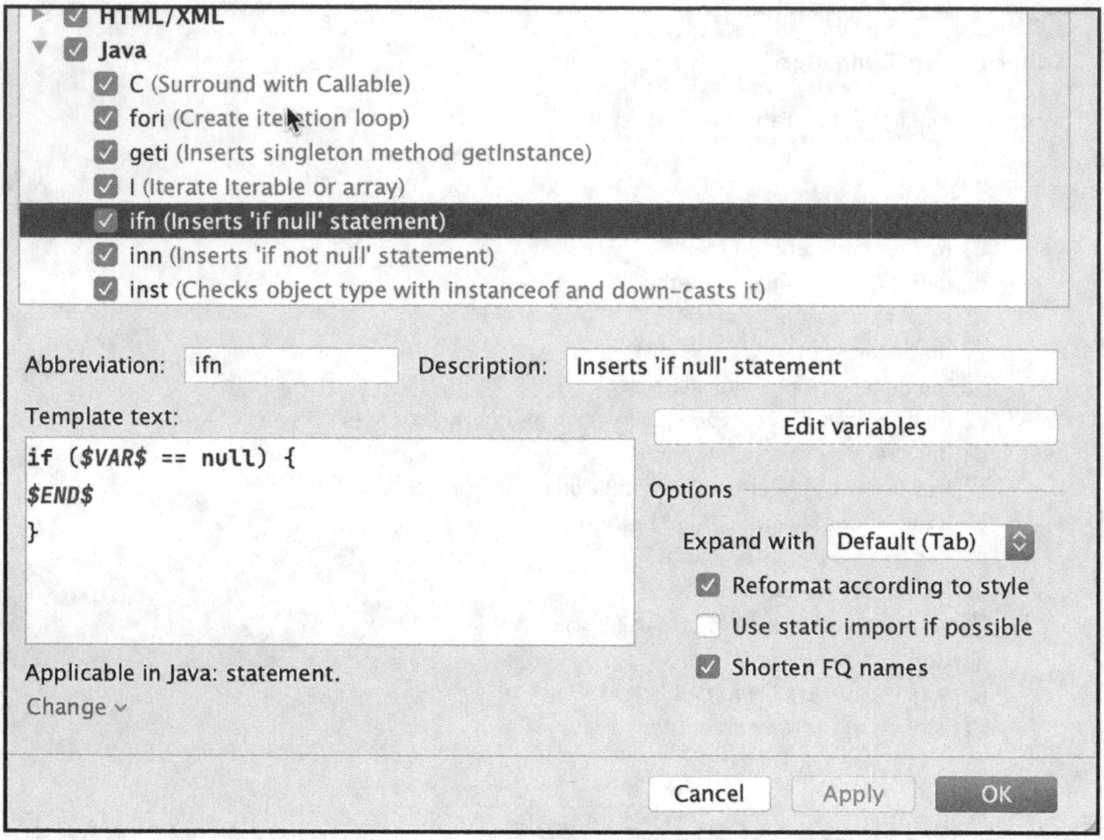

Figure 8-19. *Template text*

To dig deeper into live templates, why don't we create one of our own. We can create a live template and add it to an existing template group, but I wouldn't want to mess around with the existing set of live templates. So, let's create a new template group.

Click the plus sign on the Live Template dialog (shown in Figure 8-20) and click "Template Group."

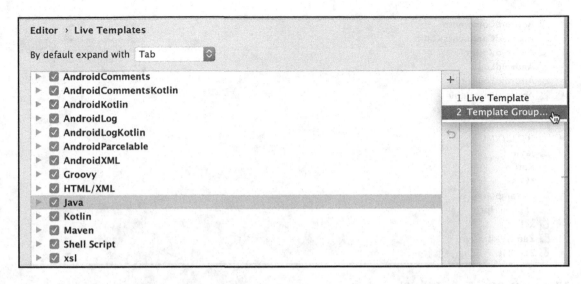

Figure 8-20. *Add a template group*

In the screen that follows, enter the name of the template group; I'll call it "mytemplates," as shown in Figure 8-21.

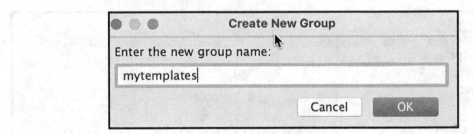

Figure 8-21. *Create New Group*

While the "mytemplates" group is selected, click the plus sign again; this time, click "Live Template," as shown in Figure 8-22.

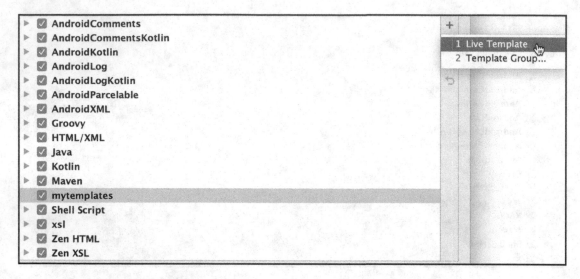

Figure 8-22. *New Live Template*

In the screen that follows, you get to fill out the Template details as shown in Figure 8-23.

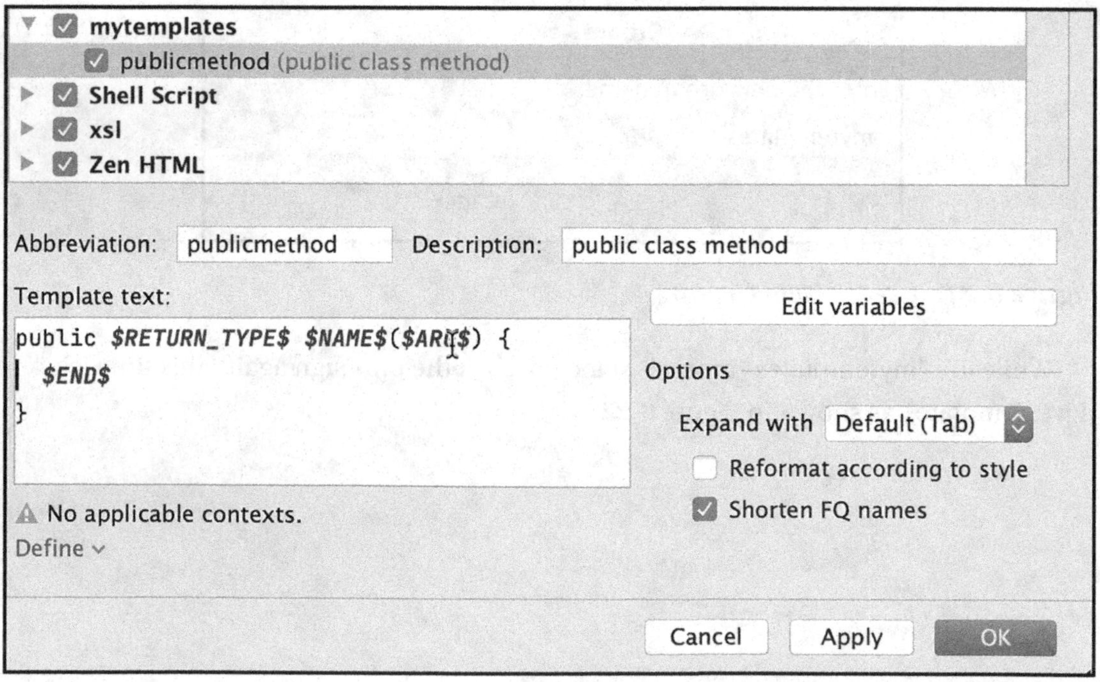

Figure 8-23. *New Template details*

- **Abbreviation** – This will be the keyboard shortcut for the live template. This can't be the same as any existing live template. Also, take the time to think this through; it needs to be easy to memorize as well. As for our example, I'm going with publicmethod.

- **Description** – This is the description that you will see to the right of the live template, as it's shown on the dropdown.

- **Template Text** – This is the body of the template when it gets expanded. The variables in the template text (the ones surrounded by dollar signs) are the ones the programmer has to fill up when the template expands. I used four variables in our example — you can use more (or less). All the variables in the template text are arbitrary, meaning I just made them all up, except the **END** variable; that one is a predefined template variable that has a special meaning to IntelliJ. The END variable indicates the end position of the caret or cursor when the code is complete. You can no longer use TAB to navigate to the next stop.

I'd like to refer to Figure 8-23 again. Notice at the bottom left where it says "No applicable context"? It means we have to tell IntelliJ which context our new template can be called from – whether we can call it outside a method, inside a method, etc.

To define the context for our new template, click the "Define" link, as shown in Figure 8-24. Then choose "Declaration."

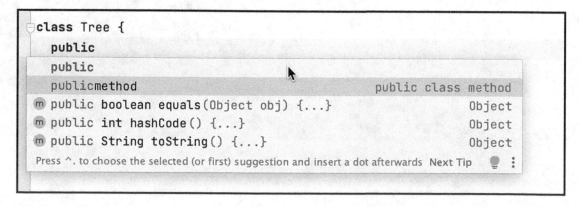

Figure 8-24 dialog content:

- ✓ ▼ ⬜ Everywhere
- ✓ ▶ ⬜ Groovy
- ✓ ▶ ⬜ HTML
- ✓ ▼ ⬜ Java
- ✓   ⬜ Comment
- ✓   ⬜ Consumer function
- ✓   ⬛ Declaration
- ✓   ⬜ Expression
- ✓   ⬜ Statement
- ✓   ⬜ string
- ✓   ⬜ Type-matching completion
- ✓   ⬜ Other
- ▶ ⬜ JSON
- ▶ ⬜ Kotlin
- ⬜ Maven
- ⬜ Shell script
- ▶ ⬜ XML
- ⬜ XML Attribute
- ⬜ Other

Abbreviat...   ate Iterable or array

Template   [Edit variables]

```
for ($E
  $END$
}
```

Options

Expand with [Default (Tab) ⌄]

⬜ Reformat according to style

✓ Shorten FQ names

⚠ No ap...
Define ⌄

[Cancel]   [Apply]   [OK]

Figure 8-24. *Template Context*

When we choose "Declaration," it means we can use our template wherever a declaration is expected.

Now, to test it out (see Figure 8-25).

```
class Tree {
  public
```
```
  public
  publicmethod                                    public class method
ⓜ public boolean equals(Object obj) {...}                    Object
ⓜ public int hashCode() {...}                                Object
ⓜ public String toString() {...}                             Object
Press ^. to choose the selected (or first) suggestion and insert a dot afterwards  Next Tip  💡  ⋮
```

Figure 8-25. *Our new template in action*

Choose "publicmethod," and then press ENTER. Figure 8-26 shows the expanded template — it works!

Figure 8-26. *Expanded publicmethod template*

Share Templates

If you're using other JetBrains' IDE (WebStorm, Rider, PyCharm, etc.), export your IntelliJ templates to those other IDEs — or to other people who also use IntelliJ.

You can share live templates by exporting them; to do that, you need to

1. Go to the main menu bar, then **File ➤ Manage IDE Settings ➤ Export Settings**.

2. In the "Export Settings" dialog (shown in Figure 8-27), make sure the **Live Templates** box is selected, and specify the path and name of the archive where we'll save the exported settings.

3. Click OK to complete the export action.

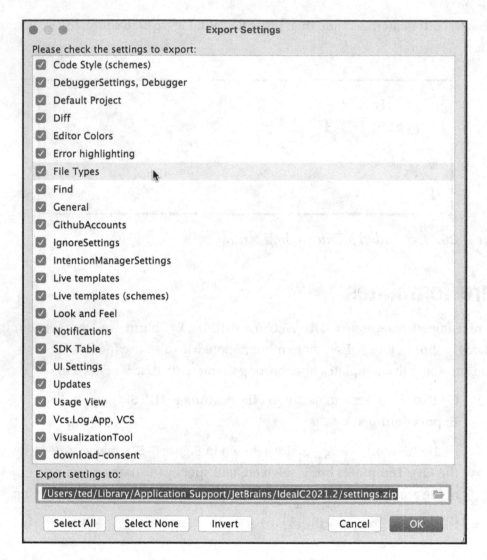

Figure 8-27. *Export Settings*

To import a template, do the following:

1.   On the main menu bar, go to **File ➤ Manage IDE Settings ➤ Import Settings**.

2.   Specify the path to the archive file with the exported template configuration.

3. In the **Import Settings** dialog, select the **Live Templates**
   checkbox, and then click the OK button to complete the import
   action.

4. Restart IntelliJ (or another JetBrains IDE). You should see the
   imported live templates on the **Editor ➤ Live Templates** page of
   the IDE Settings.

Key Takeaways

- Java is quite a verbose language. You can seriously hurt your fingers
  if you don't use text expansion tools. Thankfully, IntelliJ has live
  templates. If you want to find out how many keystrokes you were able
  to save, just go to the main menu bar of IntelliJ, and then go to Help
  ➤ Productivity Guide. It will show you your usage statistics.

- IntelliJ has 38 templates (just for Java alone); learning them well will
  be time well spent. Your fingers (and keyboard) will thank you for it.

- You're not limited to the predefined templates; you can add your own
  templates. It's quite easy to do, as you've seen.

CHAPTER 9

Debugging

In this chapter, we will cover the following:

- Errors that you'll most likely encounter

- Logging debug statements

- Using the debugger

Most (if not all) programs will have errors — I'm talking about the nontrivial programs here, not the "Hello World" kind. Dealing with errors will be a big part of your occupation as a developer. In this chapter, we'll talk about the kinds of errors you will most likely face and how to use IntelliJ to deal with some of these errors.

Types of Errors

Generally, these are the kinds of errors you'll run into:

- Syntax errors

- Runtime errors

- Logic errors

Syntax Errors

Syntax errors are exactly what you think they are – errors in the syntax. It happens because you wrote something in the code that's not allowed in the set of rules of the Java compiler. The compiler doesn't understand it. The error can be as simple as forgetting to close parentheses or a missing pair of curly brace. It can also be complex, like passing the wrong type of argument to a function or a parameterized class when using generics.

You can catch syntax errors with IntelliJ with ease whenever you see red squiggly lines on the main editor, as shown in Figure 9-1.

147

© Ted Hagos 2022

T. Hagos, *Beginning IntelliJ IDEA*, https://doi.org/10.1007/978-1-4842-7446-0_9

```
 1        package net.workingdev.chat;
 2
 3       import java.io.DataInputStream;
 4        import java.io.DataOutputStream;
 5        import java.io.IOException;
 6        import java.net.ServerSocket;
 7        import java.net.Socket;
 8
 9       import static java.lang.System.out;
10
11  ▶    public class Server {
12
13           private ServerSocket serversocket
14           private Socket socket;
15           private final int PORT = 1200;
16           private DataInputStream inputStream;
17           private DataOutputStream outputStream;
18
19  ▶  ⊞    public static void main(String[] args) throws IOException {...}
22
23       ⊟    void startServer() throws IOException {
```

Figure 9-1. *The main editor is showing a syntax error indicator*

When you see a squiggly red line like this, it means you have a syntax error. IntelliJ puts the red squiggly line very near the offending code. If you hover your mouse on the red squiggly line, most of the time, the IDE can tell you, with a high degree of accuracy, what's wrong with the code so you can easily find and fix these codes.

Apart from syntactical errors, you may also encounter compilation errors when you're trying to compile codes that was built using a different JDK (either older or a different JDK altogether).

Runtime Errors

Runtime errors happen when your code hits a situation it doesn't expect. As the name implies, this error happens only when your program is running. It's not something you'll see during compilation.

Java has two types of Exceptions, *checked* and *unchecked*. IntelliJ gives you lots of assistance with checked Exceptions. Figure 9-2 shows what happens in the main editor when you try to call to a method that throws a **checked Exception**.

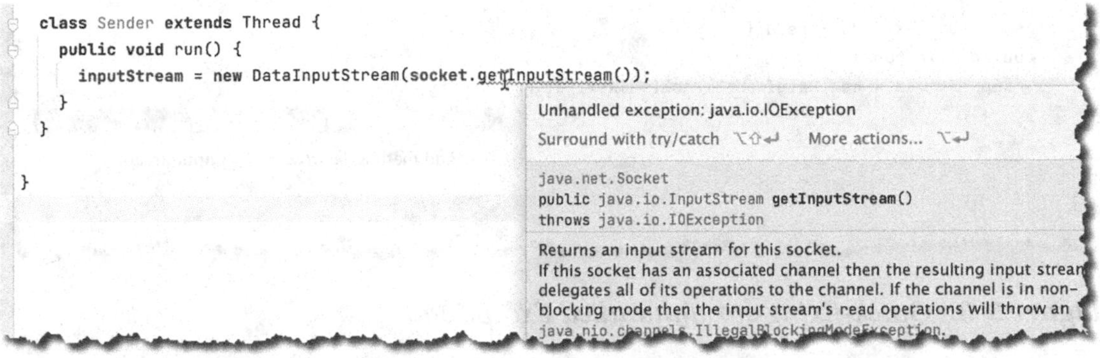

```
class Sender extends Thread {
  public void run() {
    inputStream = new DataInputStream(socket.getInputStream());
  }
}

}
```

Unhandled exception: java.io.IOException
Surround with try/catch ⌥⇧↵   More actions... ⌥↵

java.net.Socket
public java.io.InputStream getInputStream()
throws java.io.IOException

Returns an input stream for this socket.
If this socket has an associated channel then the resulting input stream
delegates all of its operations to the channel. If the channel is in non-
blocking mode then the input stream's read operations will throw an
java.nio.channels.IllegalBlockingModeException.

Figure 9-2. *Main editor showing information about an unhandled Exception*

IntelliJ tries to be helpful by flagging unhandled Exceptions, like the one you see in Figure 9-2. If you hover your mouse long enough on the squiggly red lines, IntelliJ shows the reason why the code is flagged — and even gives you suggestion on how to fix it.

A quick word about checked and unchecked Exceptions: A checked Exception is something that the Java compiler inspects (or checks) during compilation. If a method declares that it throws a checked Exception (e.g., FileNotFoundException, ClassNotFoundException, IOException, SQLException, etc.), then the method must handle the Exception either by enclosing the call within a try-catch or by rethrowing the Exception.

An unchecked Exception, on the other hand, is not checked at compile time, which means you need not bother with try-catches; you can just code like nothing bad can happen to your app. In languages like C++ and Kotlin, all Exceptions are unchecked, so you can dispense with the try-catch blocks — you can still handle the Exceptions if you prefer, but it's optional.

Flagging and hinting at the solution to unhandled Exceptions is already great, but IntelliJ goes the extra mile by offering quick fixes. A quick fix is IntelliJ's repair action for errors that it detects during design time; it's easy to execute – you simply need to press **Alt + ENTER** (for Linux and Windows users) or **cmd + ENTER** (if you're on macOS) at a highlighted code issue, and then choose an appropriate course of action. Figure 9-3 shows this in action.

```
class Sender extends Thread {
  public void run() {
    inputStream = new DataInputStream(socket.getInputStream());
  }
}
```
```
}
```
	Surround with try/catch	
🖋	Add method contract to 'getInputStream'	▶
	Press ⌥Space to open preview	

Figure 9-3. *Quick-fixing our unhandled Exception*

Listing 9-1 shows the Sender class (with the autocorrected code).

Listing 9-1. Class Sender

```
class Sender extends Thread {
  public void run() {
    try {
      inputStream = new DataInputStream(socket.getInputStream());
    } catch (IOException e) {
      e.printStackTrace();
    }
  }
}
```

IntelliJ dutifully adds the proper try-catch structure to your code — it even formats it properly. It doesn't add the *finally* clause, though, that you'll have to write yourself.

Logic Errors

Logic errors are the hardest to find. As its name suggests, it's an error in your logic. When your code is not doing what you thought it should be doing, that's a logic error. There are many ways to cope with it, but the heavy favorites are using **System.out.println()** or the Logger class (from java.util.logging).

As you inspect your codes, you'll recognize certain areas where you're pretty sure about what's going on, but then there are areas where you are less sure; it's in these areas where the println or the Logger are most useful. It's like leaving bread crumbs for you to follow.

Debugger

IntelliJ is a full-featured IDE. It comes with a capable debugger. While you can play sleuth with your code using println and Logger statements, when you're playing code-detective, using the debugger gives better results — it's easier to use too because it doesn't clutter your code.

Let's consider the following code (shown in Listing 9-2) to demonstrate the IDEA debugger.

Listing 9-2. DebugSample Class

```
package net.workingdev.ideabook;

import java.util.ArrayList;
import java.util.List;

public class DebugSample {
  public static void main(String[] args) {
    List sampleNames = createNames();
    printNames(sampleNames);
    addName(sampleNames, "Jane Doe");
    printNames(sampleNames);
  }

  private static List createNames() {
    ArrayList listNames = new ArrayList<String>();
    listNames.add("John Doe");
    listNames.add("Jane Doe");

    return listNames;
  }

  private static void printNames(List<String> names) {
    for (String name : names) {
      System.out.println(name);
    }
  }
}
```

```java
private static void addName(List<String> l, String name) {
  l.add(name);
}

private static void removeNames(List l, String name) {
  int position = l.indexOf(name);
  if (position == -1) {
    // the name is not in the list
  }
  else {
    l.remove(position);
    printNames(l);
  }
}
}
```

The code has five methods (including main). The method **createNames()** creates a List of names and returns it. The method **printNames()** takes in a List of names and print each item on the List. The **addName()** method takes in a List and a String; it then adds the String (second parameter) to the List. Finally, the **removeName()** method takes in a List and a String; it searches the List for an occurrence of the second parameter; if it's found, the String is removed, and the List is printed again.

You can start the Debugger in a number of ways:

1. You can click the Run icon in the gutter area (shown in Figure 9-4), and then select "Debug."

2. You can use the context menu of the class's main method, and then choose "Debug" (shown in Figure 9-5). You can do this either by left-clicking the main method or by using the quick fix key on the main method — the *quick fix* key is **Alt + ENTER** on Windows/ Linux and **cmd + ENTER** on macOS.

3. Alternatively, you can start the Debugger from IntelliJ's main menu bar; go to Run ➤ Debug.

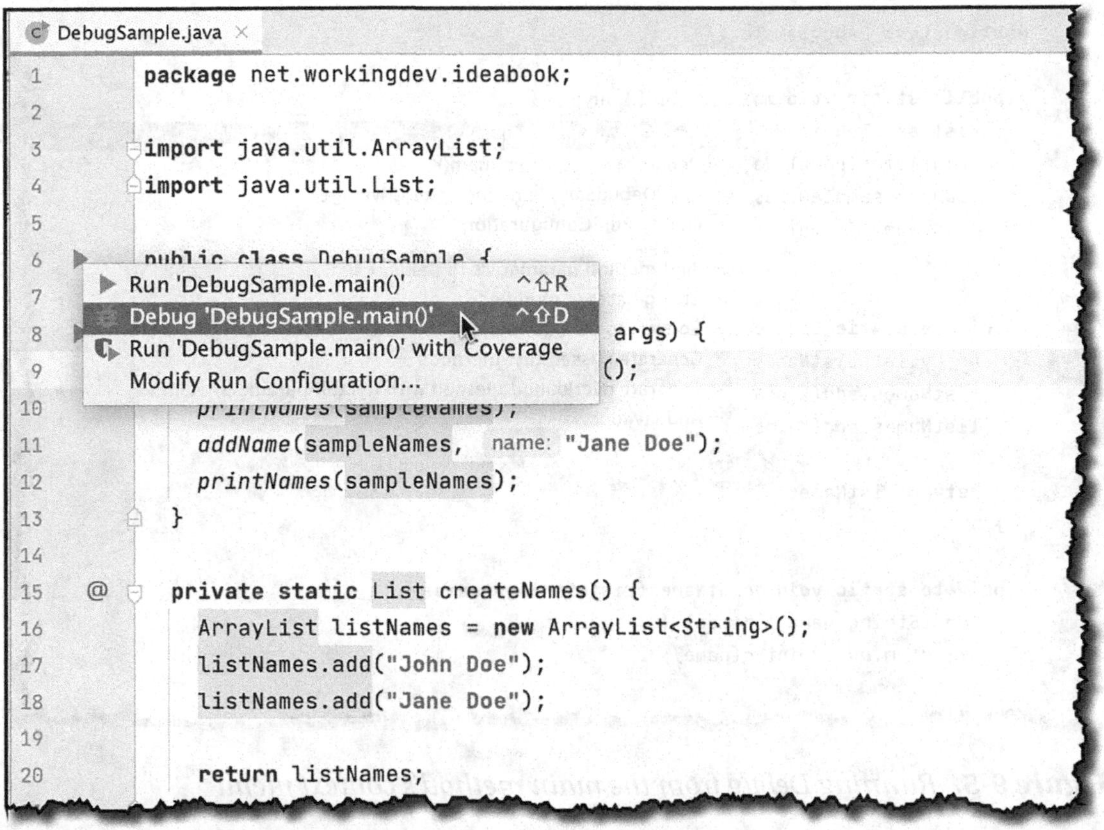

```java
  DebugSample.java ×
1         package net.workingdev.ideabook;
2
3       import java.util.ArrayList;
4       import java.util.List;
5
6       public class DebugSample {
7     ▶  Run 'DebugSample.main()'          ^⇧R
8        Debug 'DebugSample.main()'        ^⇧D        args) {
9     ▶  Run 'DebugSample.main()' with Coverage       ();
          Modify Run Configuration...
10        printNames(sampleNames);
11        addName(sampleNames,  name: "Jane Doe");
12        printNames(sampleNames);
13     }
14
15 @   private static List createNames() {
16        ArrayList listNames = new ArrayList<String>();
17        listNames.add("John Doe");
18        listNames.add("Jane Doe");
19
20        return listNames;
```

Figure 9-4. *Debug from the gutter*

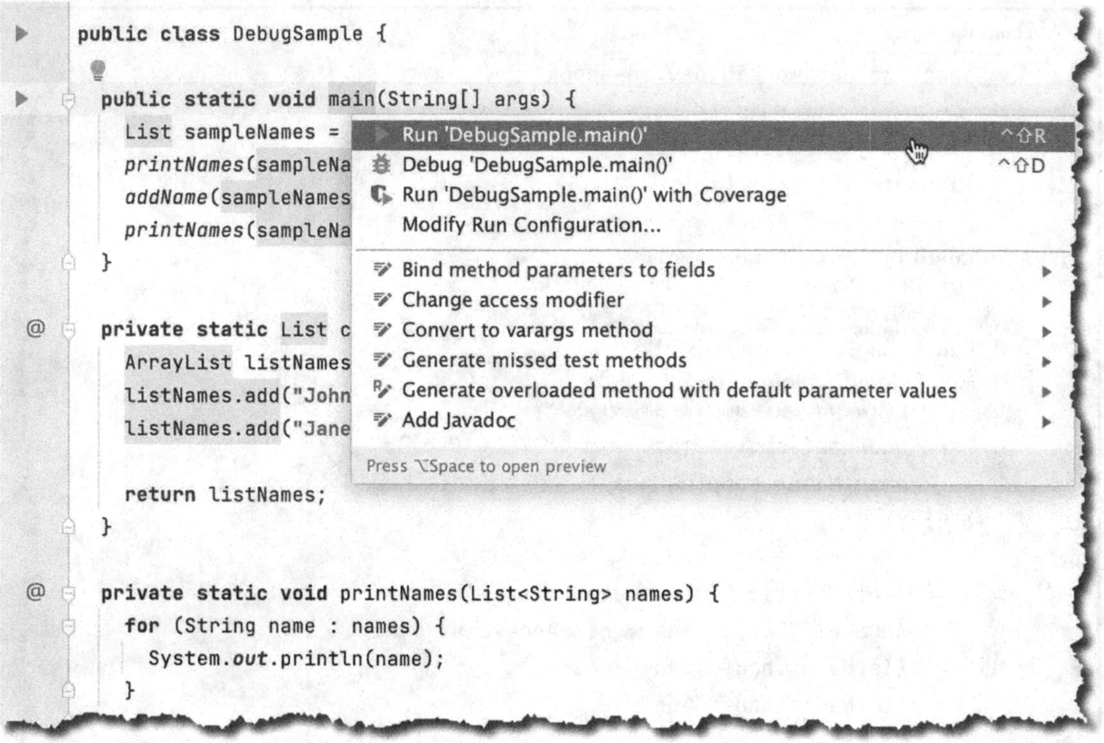

```
   public class DebugSample {
      💡
   public static void main(String[] args) {
      List sampleNames =          ▶  Run 'DebugSample.main()'                          ⌃⇧R
      printNames(sampleNa            🐞 Debug 'DebugSample.main()'                      ⌃⇧D
      addName(sampleNames            🔾 Run 'DebugSample.main()' with Coverage
      printNames(sampleNa              Modify Run Configuration...
   }
                                    ≯  Bind method parameters to fields                ▶
@  private static List c           ≯  Change access modifier                          ▶
   ArrayList listNames              ≯  Convert to varargs method                       ▶
   listNames.add("John             ≯  Generate missed test methods                    ▶
   listNames.add("Jane            ᴾ⁄  Generate overloaded method with default parameter values  ▶
                                   ≯  Add Javadoc                                      ▶
   return listNames;
   }                                Press ⌥Space to open preview

@  private static void printNames(List<String> names) {
   for (String name : names) {
      System.out.println(name);
   }
```

Figure 9-5. *Running Debug from the main method's context menu*

Right now, our code happily cruises through its logic; it creates a list of names, prints the names, adds a name, and prints the names again — you can see that on the output window of IntelliJ (Figure 9-6).

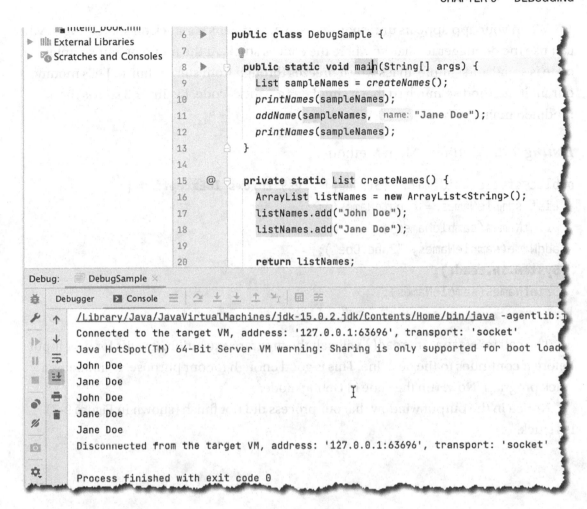

Figure 9-6. *Debug session of our sample code*

The debugger becomes very useful when you want to peek under the (execution) hood — so to speak — and we can do that in a couple of ways. We can pause, resume, restart, or stop the debugger at specified places in the code.

When your app appears unresponsive — which means it's stuck on something — you can use the debugger to analyze where the code is stuck. At the moment, our sample code is small and simple; that's why it breezes through from start to finish. Let's modify our main method so much so that it simulates a "stuck" code. Listing 9-3 shows the modified main method.

Listing 9-3. Modified Main Method

```
public static void main  (String[] args) throws IOException {
  List sampleNames = createNames();
  printNames(sampleNames);
  addName(sampleNames, "Jane Doe");
  System.in.read();
  printNames(sampleNames);
}
```

The call to System.in.read() will halt the program execution; it waits for user input before it continues to the next line. This is good enough for our purpose. It simulates a stuck program. Now, run the code in Debug mode.

Notice in the output window that our process did not finish (shown in Figure 9-7). It's stuck.

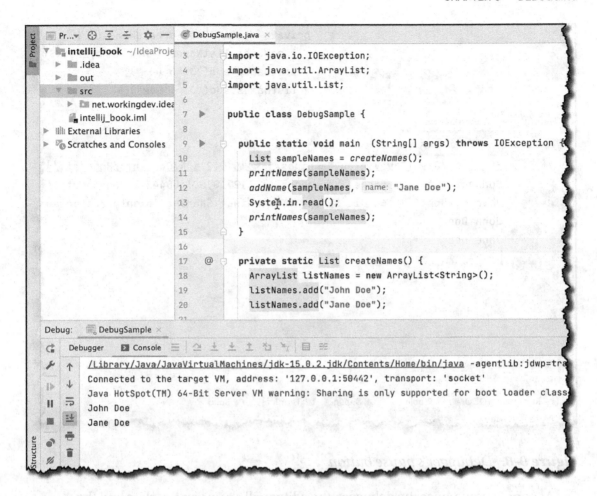

Figure 9-7. *DebugSample is stuck on execution*

Now, click the *Pause* button on the debugger, as shown in Figure 9-8.

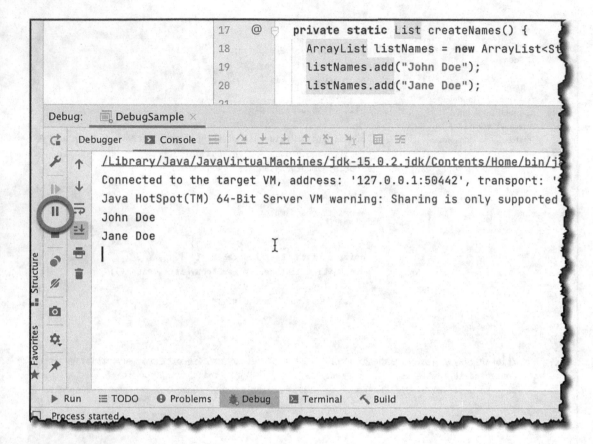

Figure 9-8. *Debugger's pause button*

As soon as you pause the debugger, the editor will show you the class and the method that it's currently running — or stuck on (shown in Figure 9-9). In our example, it's stuck on **System.in.read()**; that's why the editor shows us the **readBytes()** method of the **FileInputStream** class — you can even see the stack trace if you switch to the *Debugger* tab of the *Debug* window (shown in Figure 9-10).

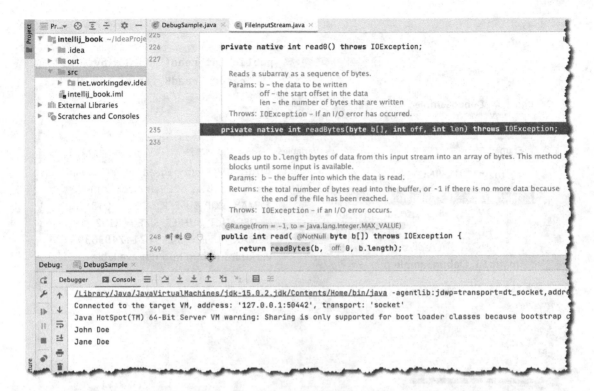

Figure 9-9. Debugger showing what's currently running

Right now, the debug session is waiting for user input. Press any key so that **System. in.read()** can read something from the standard input — that should satisfy the statement.

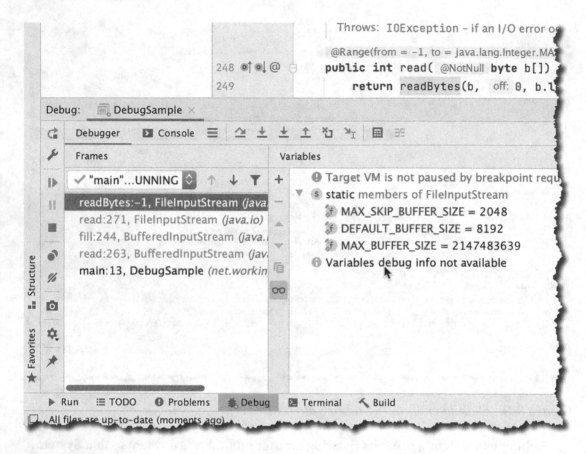

Figure 9-10. *See the stack trace on the "Debugger" tab*

To continue the debug session, you can press the *Resume* button (it's right above the *Pause* button). The other Debugger buttons you will need are the following:

- Restart button – This will restart the Debug session. You can find this button right above the wrench button.

- Stop button – This will stop the Debug session (right below the *Pause* button).

Step Actions

When the Debug session is paused, you can "step through your code" using the various step actions of the Debugger — the step buttons are shown in Figure 9-11.

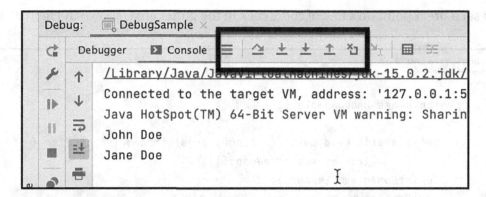

Figure 9-11. *Step actions*

- **Step Into** (F7) – Use this if you want to walk through each line of code. Remember that this walks you through each line of the currently running method inside the currently running class. If the method creates another object and calls another method, you will step into that other method.

- **Step Over** (F8) – This lets you run a line of code and move on to the next line.

- **Force Step Into** – This lets you debug methods defined in the APIs or libraries. If the source code of the API or library is not available, IntelliJ IDEA decompiles and debugs it for you.

- **Step Out** – This lets you skip stepping through the code line by line and return to the calling method. The called method executes but without stepping through each line of code.

- **Drop Frame** – This lets you move back through code execution by dropping a method call.

Breakpoints

Breakpoints are a great way to introduce stopping points to your code. Remember earlier in our debugging example session when I introduced **System.in.read()** to halt our code? We don't really have to do that; we can use breakpoints to halt the program execution at a specific point.

To set a breakpoint on a line of code, click in the gutter area (shown in Figure 9-12).

```java
  6
  7 ▶      public class DebugSample {
  8
  9 ▶ ⊟      public static void main  (String[] args) throws IOException {
 10              List sampleNames = createNames();
 11              printNames(sampleNames);
 12 ●            addName(sampleNames,   name: "Jane Doe");
 13 //             System.in.read();
 14              printNames(sampleNames);
 15 ⊖      }
 16
 17 @ ⊟      private static List createNames() {
 18              ArrayList listNames = new ArrayList<String>();
 19              listNames.add("John Doe");
 20              listNames.add("Jane Doe");
 21
 22              return listNames;
 23 ⊖      }
```

Figure 9-12. Breakpoint set at line 12

I've set the breakpoint at line 12. You'll know that the breakpoint is set when you see a red dot on the gutter next to the line number.

When you start the Debug session, the Debugger will automatically stop execution at the breakpoint (shown in Figure 9-13) — you don't need to press **Pause** anymore.

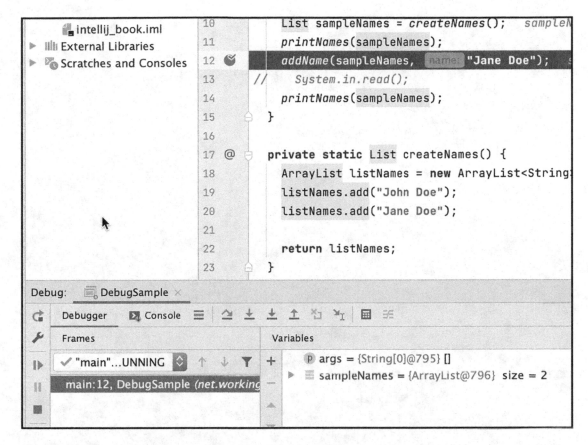

Figure 9-13. Program is halted at a breakpoint

From here, you can use the various stepping tools we've discussed earlier.

Key Takeaways

- The three kinds of errors you may encounter are compile type or syntax errors, runtime errors, and logic errors.

- Syntax errors are the easiest to fix. IntelliJ itself bends over backward for you so you can quickly spot syntax errors. There are various ways to fix syntax errors, but most of the time, the **Quick Fix** should do it.

- You can walk through your code line by line by setting breakpoints and using the various stepping actions.

CHAPTER 10

Source Control

In this chapter, we will cover the following:

- A brief introduction to Git

- Basic operations in Git

- How to set up a local Git repo

- Publishing your project on GitHub

When you're working with other developers, you need a way to share your code with others and share their codes in return. Even if you're working alone, you'll need a way to track the changes you've made to the codebase over time. These are the primary reasons why you need to use source control.

IntelliJ can work with various source control systems, for example, Git, CVS, SVN, Mercurial, and TFS. Git is a widely used version control system, and it's what we'll cover in this chapter.

Git

Git is a free and open source version control system, originally created by Linus Torvalds in 2005 — Linus is responsible for the Linux OS. Git is a distributed system, unlike CVS and SVN, which are centralized. With Git, every developer has the full history of their code repo (short for repository) locally — repo is what you call a folder that's under version control.

The distributed nature of Git makes the initial cloning (copying) of the repo a slow operation — because everything is being copied — but subsequent operations like commit, merge, diff, and log are much faster.

© Ted Hagos 2022
T. Hagos, *Beginning IntelliJ IDEA*, https://doi.org/10.1007/978-1-4842-7446-0_10

We won't go too deep in Git, but here's how it generally works:

1. You'll create a project folder and then place your initial project artifacts, for example, a README file, a couple of source files, etc.

2. Initialize the folder for Git.

3. Add the files in the folder to source control; at this point, you've made your first change in the source control — you've added some files.

4. Commit your changes.

5. At some point, you'll edit some of the files in the project, maybe even add some new files.

6. Add the new files to Git, and then commit the changes again.

There are a lot more operations you can do with Git like a branch, merge, blame, stash, pull, clone, etc., but we'll keep it simple for now.

Before you can use Git with IntelliJ, you need to install it first. To find out if you already have Git, get a terminal window (or cmd in Windows) and run the Git command, as shown in Figure 10-1.

If you run the Git command without any arguments or options, it will print some usage information, like the one you see in Figure 10-1.

```
[ted@macmini ~ % git
usage: git [--version] [--help] [-C <path>] [-c <name>=<value>]
           [--exec-path[=<path>]] [--html-path] [--man-path] [--info-path]
           [-p | --paginate | -P | --no-pager] [--no-replace-objects] [--bare]
           [--git-dir=<path>] [--work-tree=<path>] [--namespace=<name>]
           <command> [<args>]

These are common Git commands used in various situations:

start a working area (see also: git help tutorial)
   clone            Clone a repository into a new directory
   init             Create an empty Git repository or reinitialize an existing

work on the current change (see also: git help everyday)
   add              Add file contents to the index
   mv               Move or rename a file, a directory, or a symlink
   restore          Restore working tree files
   rm               Remove files from the working tree and from the index
   sparse-checkout  Initialize and modify the sparse-checkout

examine the history and state (see also: git help revisions)
   bisect           Use binary search to find the commit that introduced a bug
   diff             Show changes between commits, commit and working tree, etc
   grep             Print lines matching a pattern
   log              Show commit logs
   show             Show various types of objects
   status           Show the working tree status
```

Figure 10-1. *Git*

To find out what version of Git you have, you can pass the version argument when you run the Git command, as shown in Figure 10-2.

```
[ted@macmini ~ % git --version
git version 2.30.1 (Apple Git-130)
ted@macmini ~ %
```

Figure 10-2. *Git version*

If you didn't see the usage information after running Git but instead saw a message like "command not found" or "bad command or file name," it means Git isn't installed yet. You need to install it first before you can use it with IntelliJ.

You can get Git from `https://git-scm.com`; you'll find the version appropriate for your platform. There's also very good documentation and instruction on the git-SCM site on how to install Git, so we won't cover it here.

Figure 10-3 shows the website of **git-scm.com** at the time of writing. The links to download the installer are found on the lower-right portion of the page.

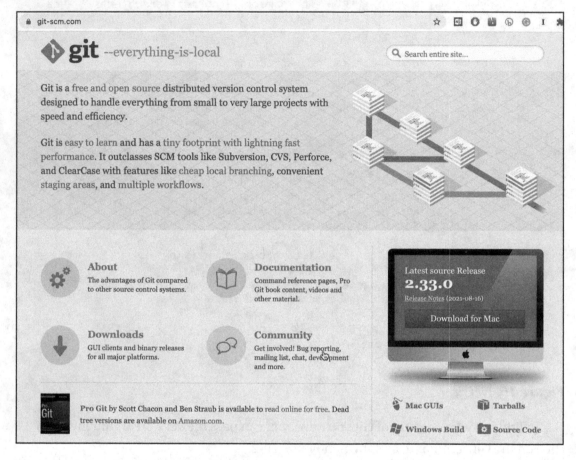

Figure 10-3. *git-scm.com website*

Create Git As a Local Repository

When Git is installed, you can start using it to manage your project.

The first step is to check if the Git plugin is installed and enabled in IntelliJ. If you accepted all the defaults during IntelliJ's setup, then Git, GitHub, and a couple of other plugins would have been installed by default. Anyway, it's easy to check if the plugin is installed — if it isn't, just install it on the Preferences (or Settings) dialog. You can get to Preferences dialog via **cmd + ,** (macOS) or **CTRL + Alt + S** (Linux/Windows).

You can see the Version control plugins in the **Preferences ➤ Plugins** dialog (shown in Figure 10-4).

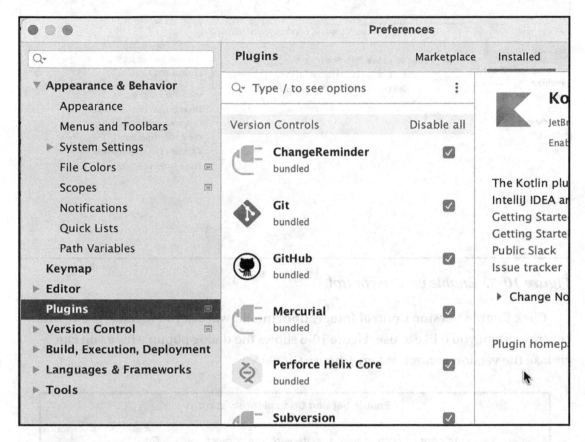

Figure 10-4. *Git plugin*

Open the project that you'd like to put in version control; then, go to the main menu bar and click **VCS**, as shown in Figure 10-5.

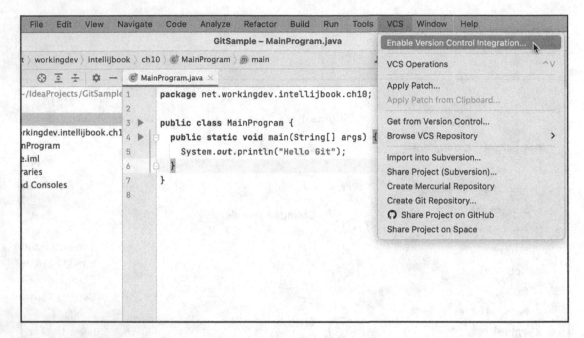

Figure 10-5. *Enable version control*

Click **Enable Version Control Integration**. IntelliJ will ask you to select the version control system you'd like to use. Figure 10-6 shows the dialog popup where you can choose the version control system. Choose Git.

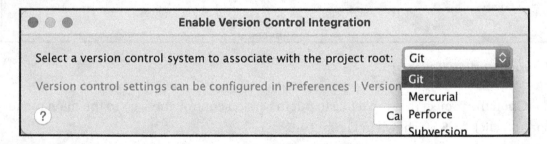

Figure 10-6. *Enable Version Control Integration*

You'll notice a couple of changes in the IDE when you enable Git. First, IntelliJ will ask you if you want to add the **Project Configuration Files** to Git. There's no hard and fast rule on whether you should add Project Configuration Files to source control, but generally, I'd advise you to add them. JetBrains has a pretty good explanation for why we should do this. They articulated in the online help page for IntelliJ IDEA (`www.jetbrains.com/help/idea/2017.1/about-projects.html`). On the section that talks about the directory-based format, JetBrains said

> The .idea directory contains a set of configuration files (.xml). Each file contains only a portion of configuration data pertaining to a certain functional area which is reflected in the name of a file, for example, compiler.xml, encodings.xml, modules.xml.

> Almost all of the files contain information core to the project itself, such as names and locations of its component modules, compiler settings, etc. **Thus, these files may (and should) be kept under version control.**

It's a good thing to keep the Project Configuration Files under source control if you're not using something like Gradle or Maven to manage dependencies. This way, the correct configuration of the project and its dependencies will be available to everyone. But this also means that everybody will have to set their environment exactly the same way you defined it in the config files.

If, on the other hand, you will use Maven or Gradle to manage dependencies, then don't add the Project Configuration Files to source control. All of the information contained inside the config files should be stored in Maven/Gradle files. Then, just let everybody configure their IDE depending on their environment.

So, for now, click "Always Add" — you can override that setting later anyway by adding the whole **.idea** folder in the Git ignore file; we'll get to that later.

Figure 10-7 shows IntelliJ prompting us to include the Project Configuration Files to source control.

```
⚙ —    © MainProgram.java ×
GitSamp  1      package net.workingdev.intellijbook.ch10;
         2
         3  ▶   public class MainProgram {
jbook.ch 4  ▶  ⊟   public static void main(String[] args) {
         5              System.out.println("Hello Git");
         6          ⊝   }
         7      }
         8
```

Project configurations files can be added to Git
View Files   Always Add   Don't Ask Again

⬛ Terminal   ⓘ Event Log
ed to Git // View Files // Always Add // Don't Ask Again (4 minutes ago)   8:1 ▸   UTF–8 2 spaces ⴖ master 🔒

Figure 10-7. *Add Project Configuration Files*

Another change in the IDE you might notice is the addition of a new section in the
left-lower toolbar strip (shown in Figure 10-8).

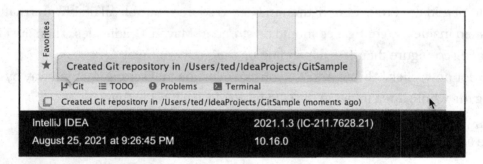

Figure 10-8. *New Git section, added to the toolbar*

A Git button was added to the toolbar.

At this point, we now have the project under version control. We've created a local
repository (repo for short) where our project is stored.

A local repo is a folder under version control, but it doesn't have any upstream
repo yet — upstream repo is just another term for remote repo (like the ones hosted on
GitHub or Bitbucket). We'll get to that later.

You'll also notice that the file name under our **src** folder (in the Project Tool Window) turned to red. File names that are lit in red mean they haven't been added to Git yet. They're still unversioned. The **iml** file is colored in green because I added the Project Configuration Files to Git earlier (when I clicked the prompt to add the configuration files to Git, in Figure 10-7).

Figure 10-9 shows the MainProgram file name lit in red.

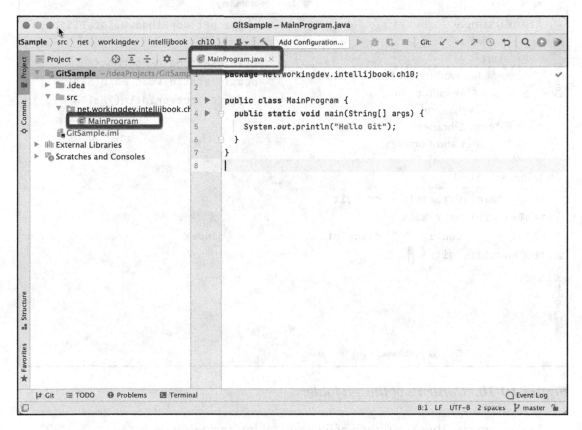

Figure 10-9. *MainProgram lit in red*

There are visual hints that the project is now under source control, but to really know for sure that it is, we can look at the project's directory structure. You won't see any visible change in the project structure because the Git folder is hidden. To look at the Git files, you'll need to go to the Terminal — use the **option + F12** shortcut in macOS or **Alt + F12** (for PCs) to pop the Terminal window in IntelliJ. Alternatively, just click the "Terminal" button on the toolbar strip on the lower-left portion of the IDE.

When the terminal opens, you will automatically be on the project's root folder. Issue a **cd** command to go to **.git** (dot git), and then issue a command to list the contents of the directory (as shown in Figure 10-10).

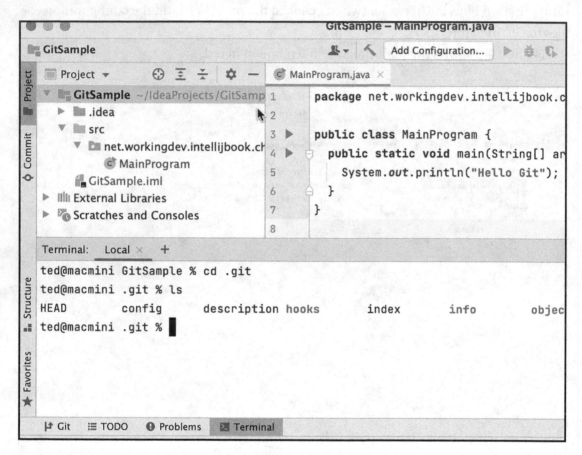

Figure 10-10. *Contents of the .git folder*

As you can see, there's a bunch of files and folders inside .git.

Adding and Committing Changes

So far, the only files I've added to Git are my Project Configuration Files. I haven't added any program files just yet. We can do that in a couple of ways:

- We can go to the main menu bar and choose **Git** — This is a new menu item. It came about when we enabled Git (see Figure 10-11).

- We can right-click *MainProgram.java* (in the Project Tool Window) and then choose **Git ➤ Commit File**.

- Use the keyboard shortcut for "Commit Files," which is **command + K** (macOS) or **CTRL + K** (for PC folks) — This is the fastest way to do it. You should try to "commit" this to memory (pun intended).

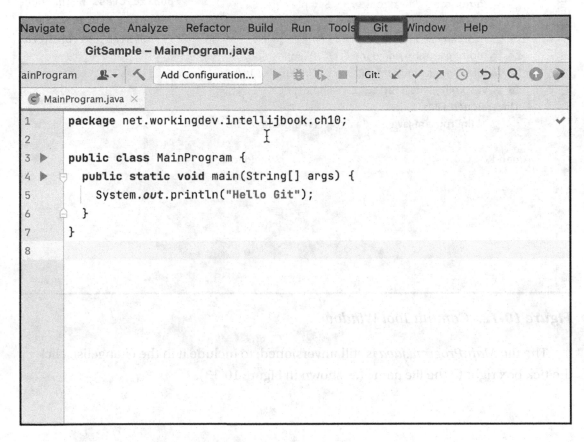

Figure 10-11. *New Git Menu item*

In the screen that follows, you'll see the Commit Tool Window (shown in Figure 10-12).

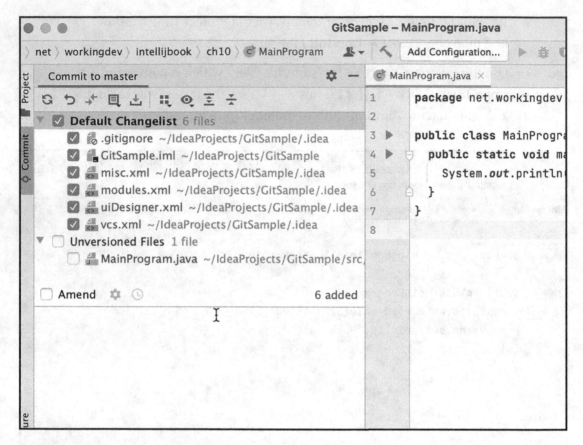

Figure 10-12. *Commit Tool Window*

The file *MainProgram.java* is still unversioned; to include it in the changelist, click the tick box right to the file name (as shown in Figure 10-13).

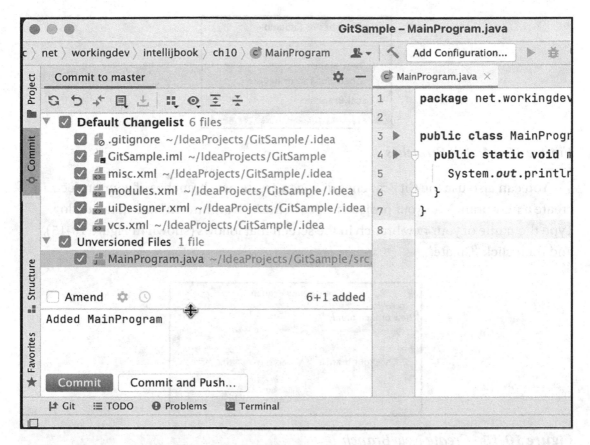

Figure 10-13. *Committing a file to Git*

In the Commit Tool Window, you'll have a chance to include or exclude the files that you'd like to be in the changelist. Tick the box to include that file in the commit; tick it off, and it won't be included. It's that simple.

I put a one-liner comment — "Added MainProgram" — as a commit message, and then I clicked the **Commit** button. Now, all my files are versioned and all changes have been committed to the local repo. You will do this every time you add and/or change something in the project.

Branches

A freshly created Git repo will have one branch named "master." To view the branches of your repo, go to the main menu bar and then **Git ➤ Branches**. The Branches dialog is shown in Figure 10-14.

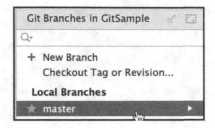

Figure 10-14. *Git Branches*

You can also use the Git Branches dialog to create new branches of your project. To create a new branch for your project, just click the "+ New Branch" link in the dialog. Type the name of your new branch in the screen that follows (shown in Figure 10-15), and then click "Create."

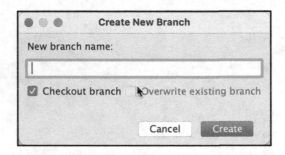

Figure 10-15. *Create New Branch*

By default, the "Checkout branch" setting is on; you'd want to keep it on most of the time. What this means is after creating the branch, you get to check out that branch. Whatever edits or changes you do, it will be on that newly checked-out branch.

Changes in the Changelist

When you're working on a project with many files, knowing which files have changed since the last commit can be useful; the **Commit Tool Window** (shown in Figure 10-16) shows all the files that were changed since the last commit. You can hide or unhide it by clicking its tab on the tool strip. Alternatively, you can also show or hide it from the main menu bar, **View ➤ Tool Windows ➤ Commit** — the quickest way is to just use **cmd + 0** (macOS) or **Alt + 0** (Linux/Windows).

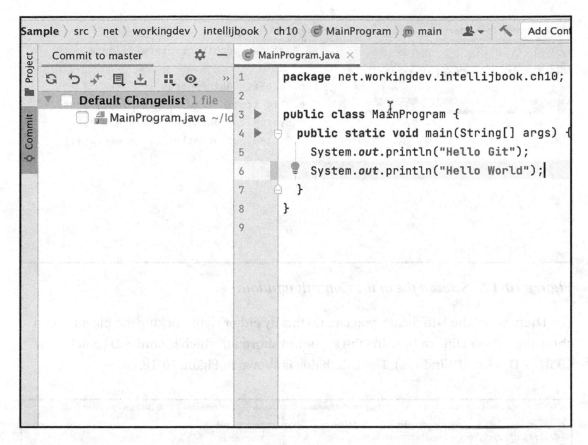

Figure 10-16. *Commit Tool Window*

If you want to view how a file has changed since the last commit, just select the file in the Commit window (as shown in Figure 10-17).

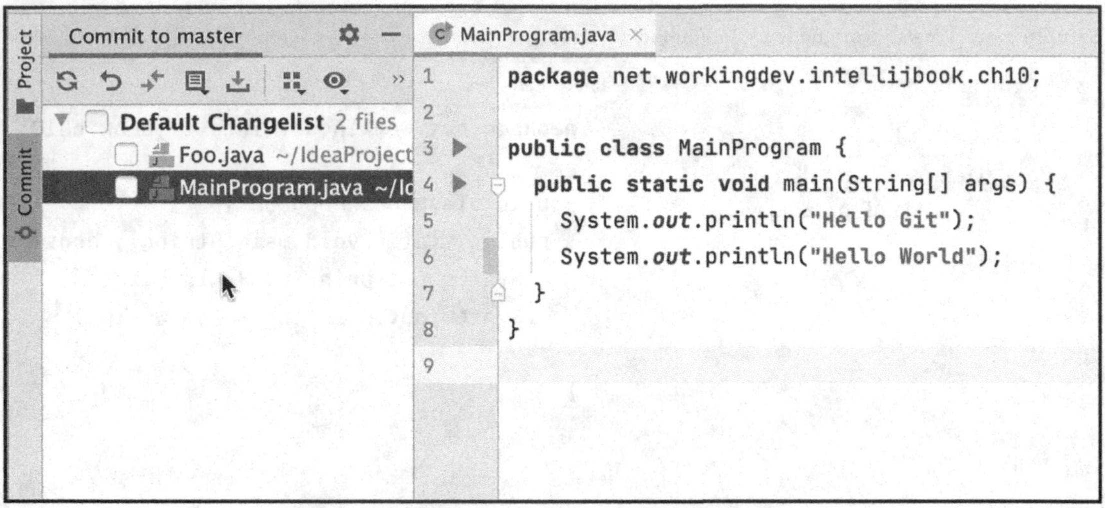

Figure 10-17. *Select a file in the Commit window.*

Then, show the **Diff** dialog; you can do this by either right-clicking the file and then choosing "Show Diff" or by using the keyboard shortcut, which is **cmd + D** (macOS) or **CTRL + D** (Linux/Windows). The Diff dialog is shown in Figure 10-18.

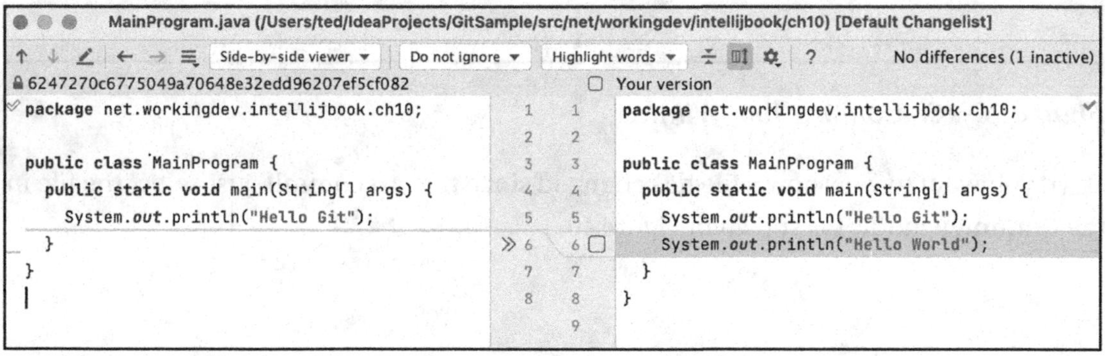

Figure 10-18. *Diff dialog*

The panel on the left shows the file as of your last commit, and the panel on the right shows the file as it stands now (with your changes). The changes or the "diff" between the files are lit in light green on the right panel; this highlight extends to the left panel to point out the location of the differences.

Ignore Files

You'd want to keep most of your project files under version control, but there are some files that you probably don't want under source control. You can filter the files you'd want to keep out of Git during every commit — you just uncheck them in the Commit window — but that would be troublesome, tedious, and prone to error (you might miss something). Fortunately, the solution is simple.

You can create a file named **.gitignore** anywhere in your project folder — but it's usually found on the root folder of the project. An ignore file is a simple text where each line contains a pattern for files or directories to ignore. Any file in the project that matches a pattern in the ignore file will be, well, ignored — they won't be part of the changelist.

You can add an ignore file to the project's root by right-clicking the project as shown in Figure 10-19, and then choose **New ➤ File**.

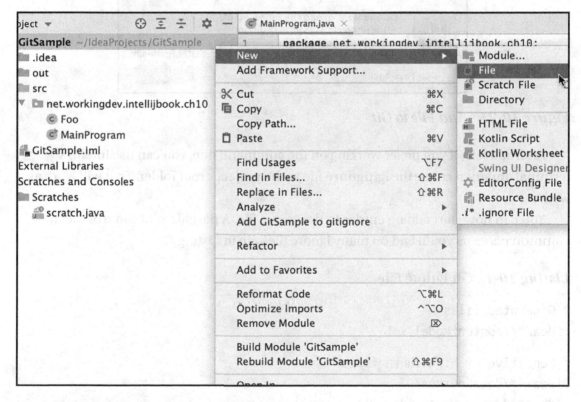

Figure 10-19. *Add a file to the project*

Type the name of the file — .gitignore (as you can see in Figure 10-20) — in the New File dialog.

Figure 10-20. *New File*

Press **ENTER** to complete the action.

IntelliJ adds the **.gitignore** file to the root of the project. Since our project is under version control, the IDE might ask you if you want to add the newly created file to Git (as shown in Figure 10-21). In this case, yes, I'd like to add .gitignore to version control. So, I'll choose "Add."

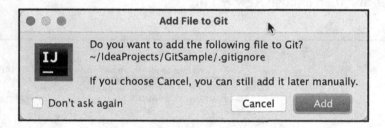

Figure 10-21. *Add File to Git*

Alternatively, if you prefer working on the command line, you can use IntelliJ's terminal and then create the **.gitignore** file in the project's root folder. That will work as well.

You can now start adding entries to the ignore file. A partial list of some of the most common patterns you'll find on many ignore files are in Listing 10-1.

Listing 10-1. Git Ignore File

```
# Generated files
.idea/**/contentModel.xml

# Sensitive or high-churn files
.idea/**/dataSources/
.idea/**/dataSources.ids
```

```
.idea/**/dataSources.local.xml
.idea/**/sqlDataSources.xml
.idea/**/dynamic.xml
.idea/**/uiDesigner.xml
.idea/**/dbnavigator.xml

# IntelliJ
out/

# User-specific stuff
.idea/**/workspace.xml
.idea/**/tasks.xml
.idea/**/usage.statistics.xml
.idea/**/dictionaries
.idea/**/shelf

# macOS
.DS_Store
```

In the generated sample file (Listing 10-1), only selected files in the .idea folder are ignored; but if you want to completely ignore the entire .idea folder, you can simply add the following line to the .gitignore file:

```
.idea/
```

Another way to add files to your ignore list is by using plugins in IntelliJ. Go to Preferences (**cmd + ,** in macOS) or Settings (**CTRL + Alt + S** in Windows/Linux), and then go to Plugins. Go to the Marketplace tab, and then search for "ignore." As you can in Figure 10-22, I installed the **.ignore** plugin (by JetBrains) and the "Add to gitignore" (by euphoricity) — you don't have to install these two. Most devs just install the plugin from JetBrains.

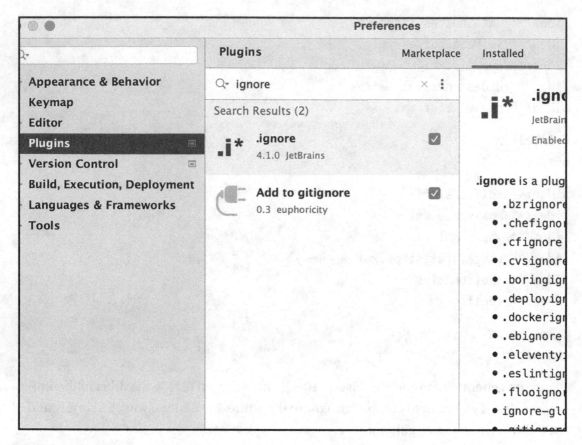

Figure 10-22. *Gitignore plugins*

Once you install the plugin, you can add a Git ignore file to the project by right-clicking the project name (in the Project Tool Window) — as shown in Figure 10-23 — then go to **New ➤ .ignore File ➤ .gitignore**.

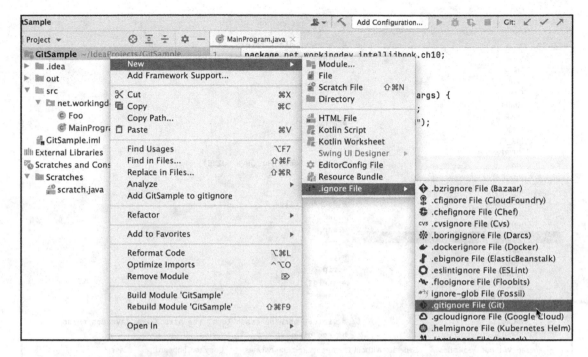

Figure 10-23. *New .gitignore file*

In the screen that follows, you can choose from a wide range of profiles. Since I'm working on a Java project, I selected "Java," as you can see in Figure 10-24.

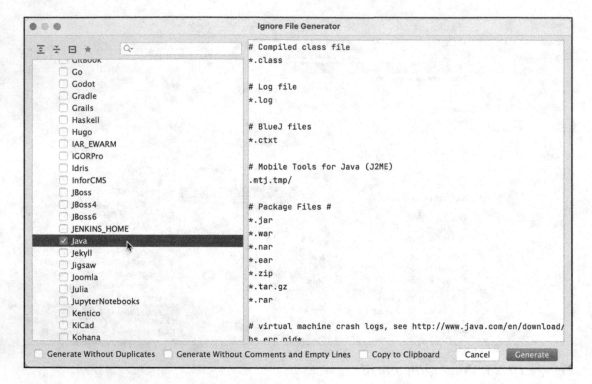

Figure 10-24. *Ignore File Generator*

Click **Generate** to complete the action. The plugin generates an ignore file and preloads it with the most common patterns of files and folders you'd like to ignore in a Java project.

Figure 10-25 shows the generated ignore file.

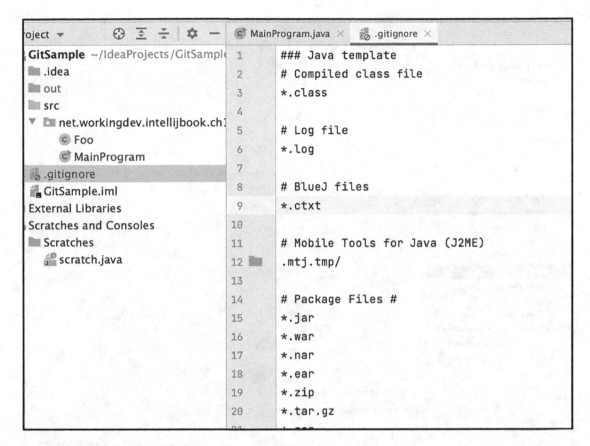

Figure 10-25. Generated .gitignore file

GitHub Integration

GitHub is a first-class citizen in IntelliJ. If you have a GitHub account, integrating it in IntelliJ is simple.

Go to Preferences (**cmd + ,** in macOS) or Settings (**CTRL + Alt + S** in Linux/Windows), and then go to Version Control. Check if GitHub is present. GitHub is available in IntelliJ as a plugin, but it would have been installed during setup. So, in most cases, you should have it — if not, just install GitHub from the Plugin Marketplace.

If you do have the GitHub plugin (like what I have in Figure 10-26), you'll have a chance to add your GitHub account in this dialog.

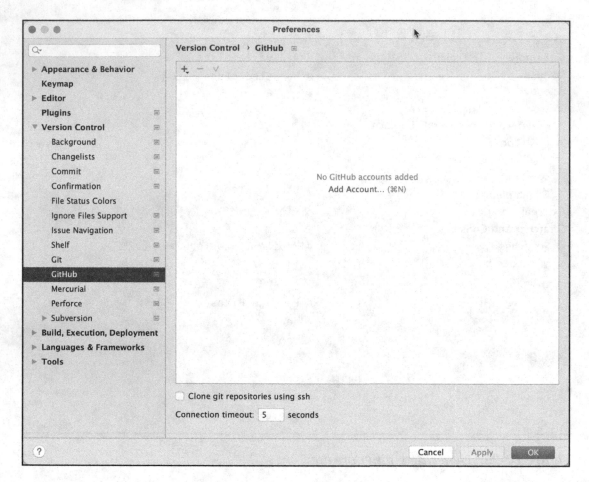

Figure 10-26. *Preferences* ➤ *GitHub*

Click the "Add Account" link. It will launch your default browser and will take you to JetBrains' page where a warning awaits you — "continue only if the page was opened by JetBrains IDE" — as you can see in Figure 10-27.

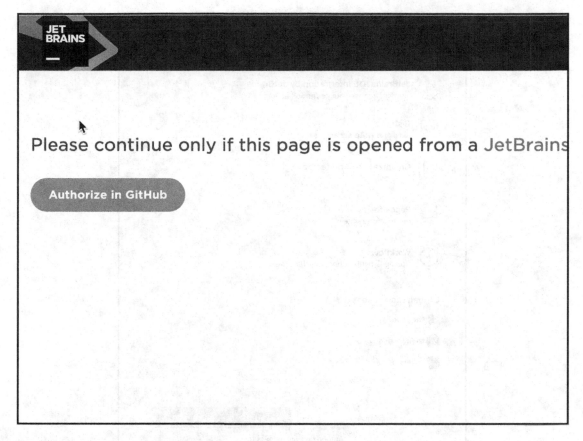

Figure 10-27. *Authorize in GitHub*

Click the "Authorize in GitHub" button to continue the action. Clicking the link takes you to the GitHub page (shown in Figure 10-28). You can now authorize JetBrains to access your GitHub account.

Figure 10-28. *Authorize JetBrains IDE Integration*

Click "Authorize JetBrains" to complete the action. After a short redirect to the
JetBrains site, we'll see the confirmation that we've been authorized in GitHub, as shown
in Figure 10-29.

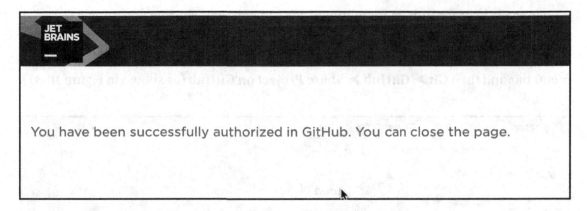

You have been successfully authorized in GitHub. You can close the page.

Figure 10-29. *Confirmation page*

Now we're back to the IDE. You should be able to see your GitHub account in the GitHub section of the Preferences window, as shown in Figure 10-30.

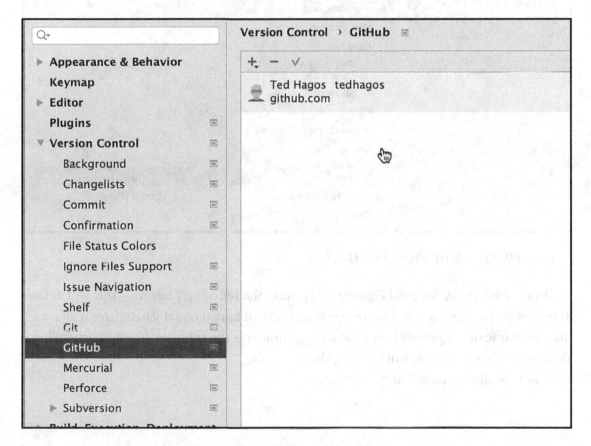

Figure 10-30. *Preferences ➤ Version Control ➤ GitHub*

Once we have GitHub set up in IntelliJ, we can now start sharing any project in GitHub.

To share the currently opened project in GitHub, all you have to do is go to the main menu bar and then **Git ➤ GitHub ➤ Share Project on GitHub** (as shown in Figure 10-31).

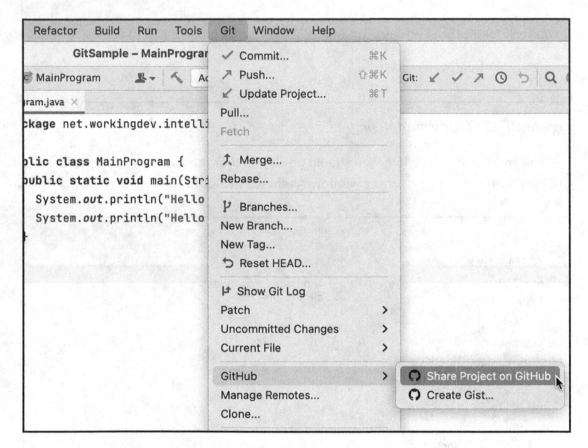

Figure 10-31. *Share Project on GitHub*

In the dialog that follows (Figure 10-32), enter the repository name — this will default to the project's name in IntelliJ, but you can change it here. I usually just leave it alone so that the name of the project in my local environment is the same as its name on GitHub. You can put a description, but that's optional.

Click "Share" to complete the action.

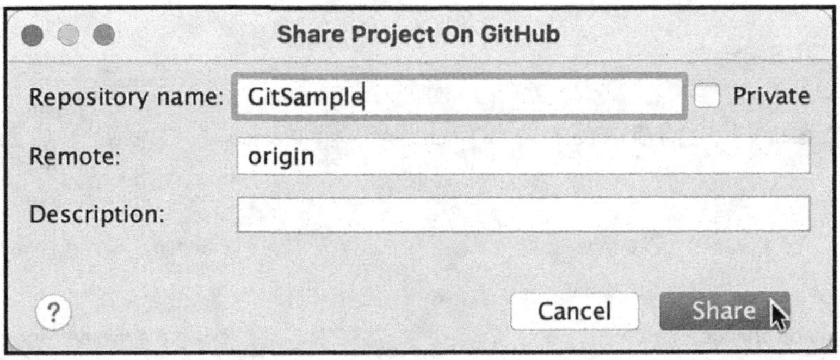

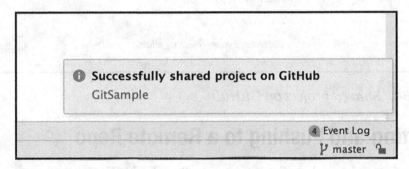

Figure 10-32. *Share Project On GitHub dialog*

Once IntelliJ has completely pushed the local repo to GitHub, you'll get a prompt (shown in Figure 10-33) with a clickable link to the project's page in GitHub.

Figure 10-33. *Successfully shared project on GitHub*

Click the link to go to the project's GitHub page.

Figure 10-34 shows the project on GitHub.

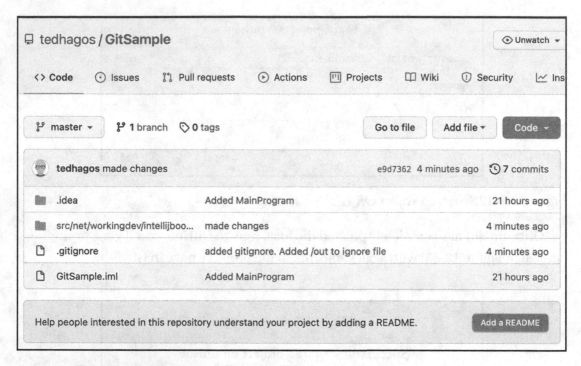

Figure 10-34. Shared project on GitHub

Committing and Pushing to a Remote Repo

When our project exists only in the local repo, all we had to do was to "commit" changes. This was enough since we didn't have a remote repo then, but since our project is now hosted in GitHub, you'd want to reflect the changes in your local repo to your upstream repo as well. To do that, instead of just clicking "Commit," you now need to choose "Commit and Push," as shown in Figure 10-35.

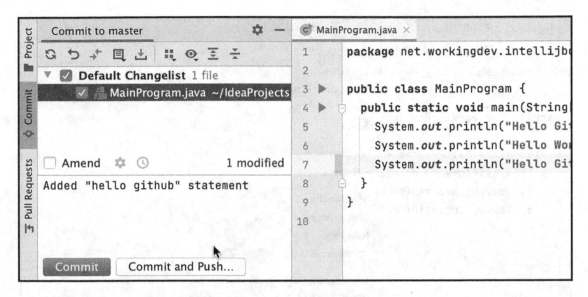

Figure 10-35. *Commit and Push*

Clicking "Commit and Push" commits all the changes and pushes those changes to the upstream repo.

Creating Gist

GitHub has another feature that allows its members to share code snippets, ala pastebin. com. These code snippets are known as gists. GitHub has as a facility on its website to create new gists. With IntelliJ, you can create gists by sharing a source code in the currently opened project.

To start sharing your code as a gist, select a source file in the currently opened project — select the file in the Project Tool Window, and then go to the main menu bar, **Git ➤ GitHub ➤ Create Gist** (as shown in Figure 10-36).

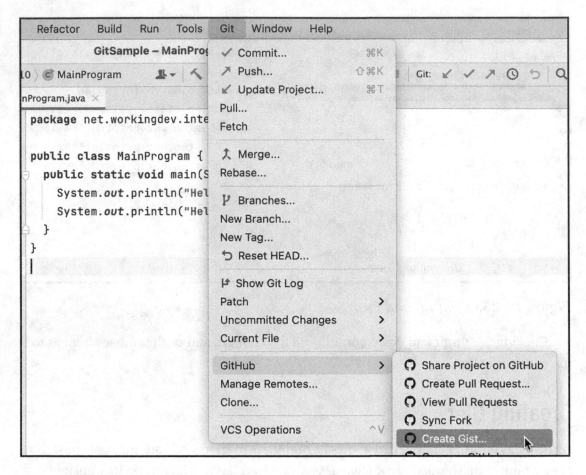

Figure 10-36. *Create Gist*

In the dialog that follows (Figure 10-37), you provide the file name for the gist; it will default to its file name in IntelliJ, but you can change it here. You can provide a description if you prefer.

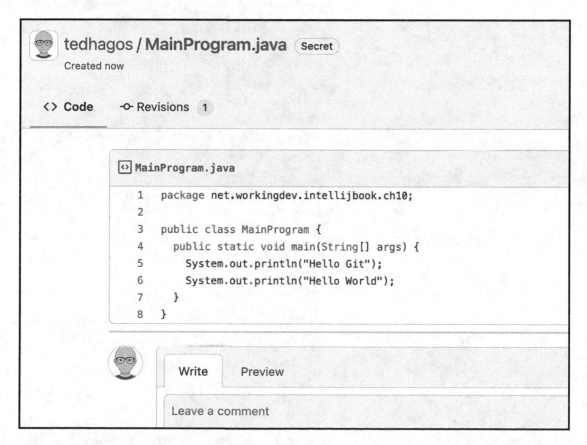

Figure 10-37. *Create Gist*

Click OK to complete the action.

Figure 10-38 shows our gist published in GitHub.

Figure 10-38. *Our newly created gist*

Key Takeaways

- Source control is part of modern software development. You need it to keep track of changes and to share codes with a team.

- Git is one of the most popular source control software. It's widely used and regularly updated. It's easy to use Git within IntelliJ.

- GitHub is a popular hosting site for remote repos. It's also easy to use GitHub within IntelliJ.

- Sharing a project (or just snippets) in GitHub is a cinch in IntelliJ.

CHAPTER 11

Testing

In this chapter, we will cover the following:

- Testing
- Unit testing
- Testing basics
- How to setup in IntelliJ

Testing is an equally important part of the development process. If you ever intend for your app to be used by anyone of consequence (perhaps, a paying customer), then the app can't have rough edges. It can't have any gross or glaring errors. It needs to go through verification and testing.

Types of Testing

There are many kinds of testing; the ones you'll employ depends on what type of app you're building. If you're building a game, you'll most likely include sound testing, soak testing, compliance, or conformance testing in addition to the usual functional, integration, developer, and user acceptance test. Suppose you're building an enterprise e-commerce system. In that case, you'll most likely devote a bit more time to performance or stress testing, in addition to vulnerability testing — there's plenty kind of tests. Here's a short description of some common ones.

Functional Testing. Functional testing is a standard way of testing an app. It's called *functional* because we're testing the app's features (also known as functionalities) as they are specified in the requirement specification — the requirement specification is something you or a business analyst would have written during the planning stages of the app. The requirement specifications would have been written in a document (usually called functional requirements specification). An example of what you might find in a functional specification is "user must log in to the server before entering the app," "user

199

© Ted Hagos 2022
T. Hagos, *Beginning IntelliJ IDEA*, https://doi.org/10.1007/978-1-4842-7446-0_11

must provide a valid email for registration," etc. The testers, usually called QA or QC (short for quality assurance and quality control, respectively), are the ones who carry out these tests. They will create test assets, craft a test strategy, execute them, and eventually report on the results of the executions. Failing tests are usually assigned back to the developer (you) to fix and resubmit. What I'm describing here is a typical practice for a development team that has a separate or dedicated testing team; if you're a one-person team, the QA will most likely be you as well. Testing is an entirely different skill, and I strongly encourage you to enlist the help of other people, preferably those who have experience in testing, to help you out.

Performance Testing. You could probably guess what this type of testing does, just from its name. It pushes the app to its limits and sees how it performs under stress. What you want to see here is how the app responds when subjected to above-normal conditions.

Soak Testing or Endurance Testing. This is a kind of performance testing; usually, you leave the app running for a long time and in various modes of operation, for example, leave the app paused for a long time while it's paused or at the title screen. What you're trying to find here is how the app responds to these conditions and how it utilizes system resources like memory, CPU, network bandwidth, etc.; you will most likely use App Profilers to carry out these measurements.

Volume Testing. This is another form of performance testing; if your app uses a database, you might want to find out how it will respond when data is loaded to the database. What you're checking is how the system responds under various loads of data.

Spike Testing (or Scalability Testing). This is also another kind of performance test. If the app depends on a central server, this test will usually raise the number of users (device endpoints) connected to the central server. You'd want to observe how a spike in the number of users affects the user experience: is the app still responsive, is there an effect on frames per second, lags, etc.

Compatibility Testing. This is where you check how the app behaves on different devices and configurations of hardware/software.

Compliance or Conformance Testing. If you're building a game app for Android, for example, this is where you check the game against Google Play guidelines on apps or games; make sure you read Google Play's Developer Policy Center at `https:// support.google.com/googleplay/android-developer/answer/10959797?hl=en`. Make sure you are also acquainted with PEGI (Pan European Game Information) and ESRB (Entertainment Software Rating Board). If the game app content has objectionable content not aligned with a specific rating, they need to be identified and reported. Violations could be a cause for rejection, which may result in costly rework and resubmission. If you're collecting data from the users, you might want to audit the app to check if it is compliant with applicable data privacy regulations.

Localization Testing. This is essential, especially if the app is intended for global markets. App titles, contents, and texts need to be translated and tested in the supported languages.

Recovery Testing. This is taking edge case testing to another level. Here, the app is forced to fail, and you're observing how the application behaves as it fails and how it comes back after it fails. It should give you insight into whether you've written enough **try-catch-finally** blocks or not. Apps should fail gracefully, not abruptly. Whenever possible, runtime errors should be guarded by try-catch blocks; and when the exception happens, try to write a log and save the state of the game.

Penetration or Security Testing. This is also known as vulnerability testing. This kind of testing tries to discover the weaknesses of the app. It simulates the activities that a would-be attacker will do to circumvent all the security features of the app; for example, if the app uses a database to store data, especially user data, a pen tester (a professional who practices penetration testing) might use the app while Wireshark is running — Wireshark is a tool that inspects packets; it's a network protocol analyzer. If you stored passwords in clear text, it would show up in these tests.

Sound Testing. If your app uses sounds, check if any errors are loading the files; also, listen to the sound files if there are cracking sounds, etc.

Developer Testing. This is the kind of testing you (the programmer) do as you add layers and layers of code to the app. This involves writing test codes (in Java as well) to test your actual program. This is known as unit testing. This is what this chapter is all about.

Unit Testing

Developers test their codes one way or another; some do it by simply running the app, feed it some inputs, and maybe even try to break it by typing special characters in the input fields. They (developers) do this every now and then, typically, after they finish coding a method, which is a natural stopping point, and then they begin some testing activity. We do this because we want to know if the app is behaving consistently with what's expected. More often than not, the kind of test we do is an unstructured one — ad hoc testing, if you want to call it that.

How is unit testing different from ad hoc testing then? And why should we bother with it?

Unit testing and ad hoc testing are both done by the developers. That's where their similarities end. Unit testing is an established testing method where individual units of source code (methods, typically) are tested to determine if the test results are consistent with a set of expected behavior. Unit testing is automated; it's not done manually, like in ad hoc testing. The automated test scripts are written (typically) by the same developer who's building the app.

A unit test is simple; it's a particular thing that a method might do or produce. An application typically has many unit tests because each test is defined as a narrow set of behavior. So, you'll need lots of tests to cover the full functionality. Java developers usually use JUnit to write unit tests.

JUnit (`https://junit.org/`)is a regression testing framework written by Kent Beck and Erich Gamma. You might remember them as the one who created Extreme Programming and the other one from Gang of Four (GoF, Design Patterns), respectively, and among other things.

Why You Should Do Unit Testing

You need to test your code one way or another; why not follow a proven framework for testing?

An automated test is the easiest way to prevent regressions and test those edge cases in the codebase — edge cases are typically overlooked during ad hoc testing.

Another compelling reason to use unit testing is that it gives you the confidence to refactor your code mercilessly. As you introduce changes to the codebase, the unit tests give you a heads-up in case you break something. If you can trust the unit test, recertifying your code is as simple as rerunning the test.

When to Write Tests

This is a hotly debated topic. Advocates of TDD insist that you write the test first before you write the actual code. On the other end of the spectrum, some devs would write the tests after writing a significant amount of code. A lot of devs, I would think, falls in between (yours truly, included) — write a bit of code, and then write a bit of test.

When to Run Tests

You should run your test as frequently as you can. As soon as you make significant changes in the code, run the test.

   If your team has a policy that you should check in all codes at the end of the day, it's a good idea to run all your test before you check the code in. This is to ensure that none of your changes break existing code.

JUnit in IntelliJ

IntelliJ has excellent support for JUnit; it installs the bundled JUnit plugin during setup. You can verify it by looking at IntelliJ's **Preferences (or Settings)** ➤ **Plugin** (as shown in Figure 11-1).

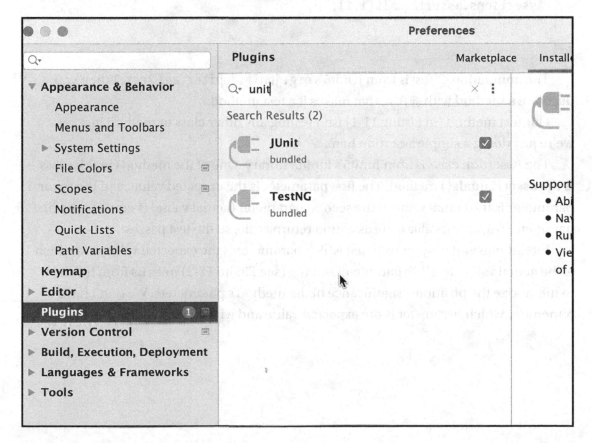

Figure 11-1. JUnit Plugin

Writing a JUnit test is a simple task in IntelliJ. A test is simply a class that uses **@Test** annotations, like the code shown in Listing 11-1.

Note You can use either JUnit 3, 4, or 5 in IntelliJ. For this chapter, as you can see, I used JUnit5.

Listing 11-1. SampleTest.java

```
import static org.junit.junpiter.api.Assertions;

public class SampleTest {
  @Test
  void shouldShowSimpleAssertion() {
    Assertions.assertEquals(1,1);
  }
}
```

The annotation @Test is from JUnit5's `org.junit.jupiter.api.Test`. When you decorate a method with @Test, that makes it a test method.

Our test method (in Listing 11-1) isn't testing any other class or method just yet; we're just doing a simple assertion here.

The Assertion class is from Junit5's jupiter library. One of the methods in this class is the **assertEquals()** method. The first parameter is the expected value, and the second parameter is the actual value. If the second parameter (actual value) is equal to the first parameter (expected value), the assertion returns true, so the test passes.

IntelliJ makes it easy for us to tell which parameter is the expected value and which is the actual value. IntelliJ's parameter hinting (see Figure 11-2) frees us from having to memorize the positional significance of the method's parameters. We don't have to remember which parameter is the expected value and which is the actual value.

```
public class SampleTest {
  @Test
  void shouldShowSimpleAssertion() {                    I
    Assertions.assertEquals( expected: 1, actual: 2);
  }
}
```

Figure 11-2. *Parameter hinting in action on assertEquals() method*

While you can turn off parameter hinting, I advise against it because it's a useful feature. However, if you think you have a valid reason to do so, here's how to do it:

1. Place the caret on one of the parameter hints — in Figure 11-3, I placed the caret in the "expected" hint.

2. Use the **option + ENTER** (macOS) or **Alt + ENTER** (Linux/ Windows) shortcut.

3. A dropdown option will be shown — like the one in Figure 11-3.

4. Choose **Do not show hints for current method**.

That will turn off parameter hints for assertEquals().

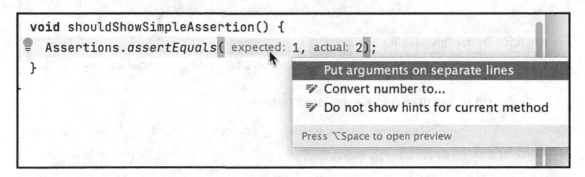

Figure 11-3. *Turn off parameter hints*

IntelliJ will flag the @Test annotation the first time it encounters it. Just use the usual code inspection tools; use **option + ENTER** (macOS) or **Alt + ENTER** (Linux/Windows) to add jUnit5 to the classpath (as shown in Figure 11-4).

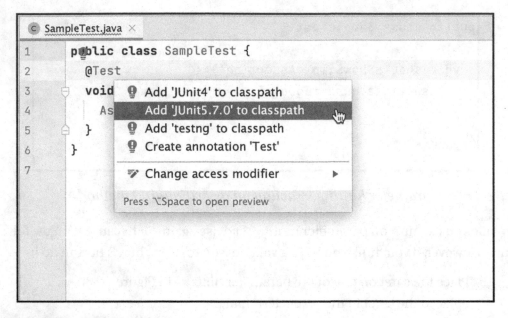

Figure 11-4. *Add JUnit5 to classpath*

While we just added JUnit5 to our classpath, we don't have it yet in our library. In the dialog that follows (Figure 11-5), IntelliJ will offer to download it from the Maven repository. I'd like to download it to my project's library folder; hence, I ticked the box next to **Download to**, as you can see in Figure 11-5.

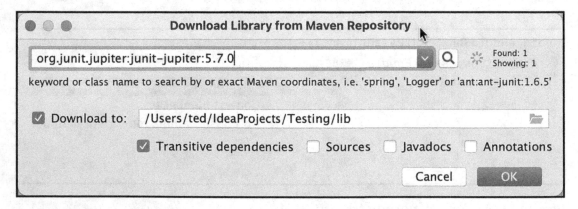

Figure 11-5. *Download Library from Maven Repository*

Click OK to complete the action. When the download finishes, you'll find the JUnit5 libraries in the project's lib folder (as shown in Figure 11-6).

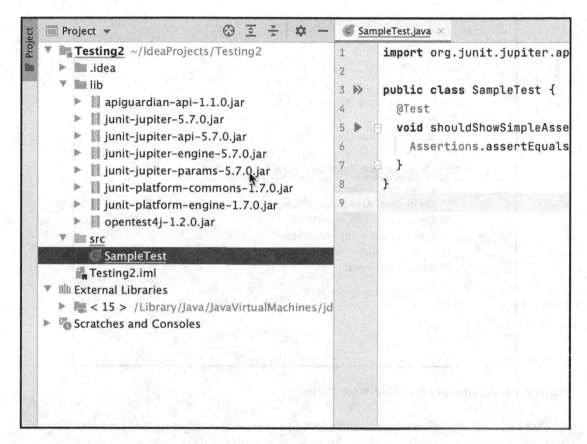

Figure 11-6. *JUnit5 libraries in the lib folder*

We need to add an import statement for the Assertion class. You can quickly take care of that using the code inspection shortcuts (**option + ENTER** or **Alt + ENTER**); choose **Import class** as shown in Figure 11-7.

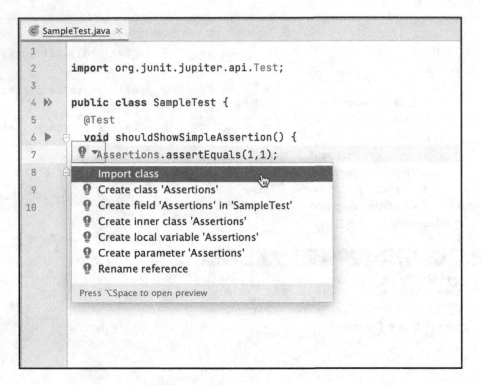

Figure 11-7. *Import the Assertion class*

Now that all is well, we can run the test. Since we have only one test method, I'll just click the green arrow on the gutter next to the test method (shown in Figure 11-8).

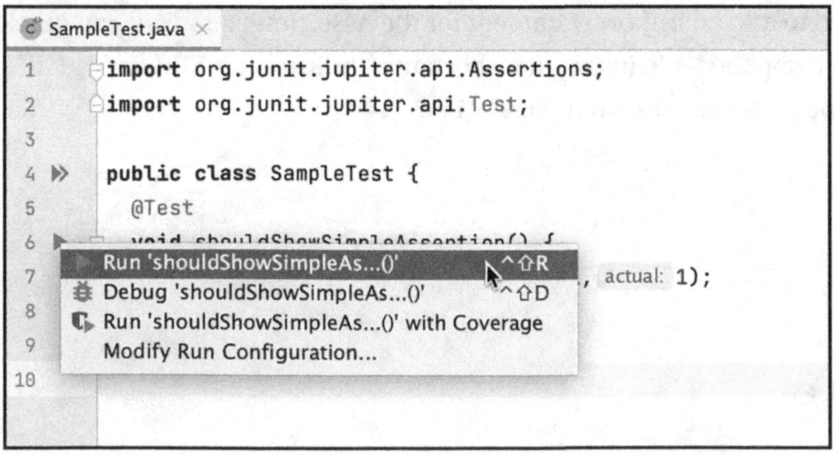

Figure 11-8. *Run shouldShowSimpleAssertion()*

As you might expect, our test passes.

When a test succeeds, you will see green check marks beside the test case method that passes the test and the test class, as shown in Figure 11-9.

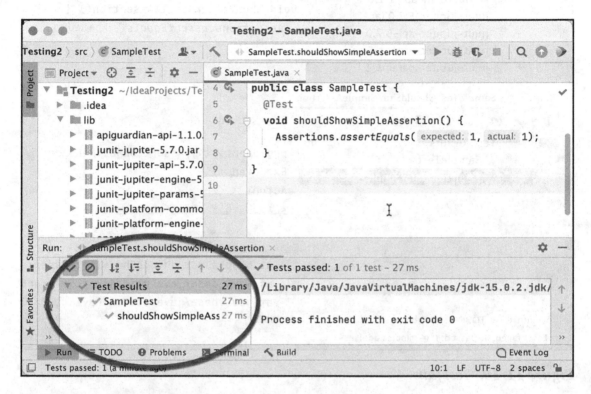

Figure 11-9. *Test is successful*

What happens when a test fails? Well, let's see. Edit the assertEquals() method so it looks like the following code:

```
Assertions.assertEquals(1,2);
```

The test should fail when the expected value (first parameter) is different from the actual value (second parameter).

Rerun the test, and, predictably, it fails. Figure 11-10 shows us the results of a failing test.

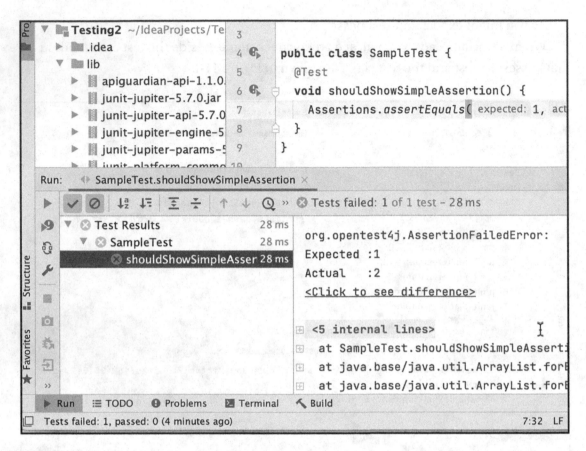

Figure 11-10. *Test fails*

An X mark beside the name of the failing test method and the test class that contains it signifies that the assertion(s) failed.

When you select the failing test (left panel of the **Run** window in Figure 11-10), the test failure details are shown on the right panel. Here, we can see that the expected value is 1 and the actual value is 2 — that's why it failed. The assertEquals() method only returns true if the expected value is the same as the actual value.

Testing an Actual Class

Now that we have enough theory and practical knowledge on setting up the JUnit test, let's use it in an actual class — you might want to set up a new project for this.

Add a new Java class to the new project and edit it to match Listing 11-2.

Listing 11-2. MainProgram

```
public class MainProgram {

  String sayYourName() {
    return getClass().getName();
  }

  int addTwoNumbers(int a, int b) {
    return a + b;
  }
}
```

It's pretty easy to create a test class for an Existing class. Place the caret on the name of the class, and then press **cmd + N** (macOS) or **Alt + Insert** (Linux/Windows), and then choose **Test** (as shown in Figure 11-11).

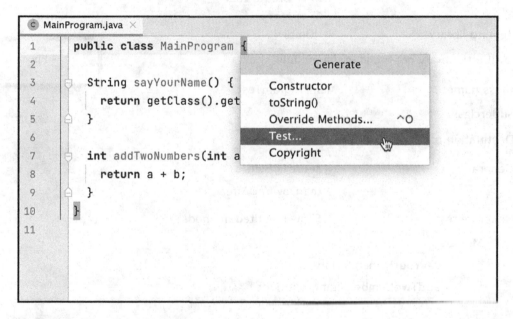

Figure 11-11. *Generate* ➤ *Test*

IntelliJ prompts us that "No Test Roots are found" (Figure 11-12). Ideally, you'd set up a test root folder in your project which will contain all of your test classes. Since we didn't do that, IntelliJ is asking if you'd like the source root to be your test folder as well. I'll click OK for now.

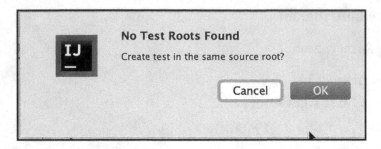

Figure 11-12. *No Test Roots Found*

After clicking OK, the **Create Test** dialog pops up. This is where we can enter some details for the test class that IntelliJ will generate for us (Figure 11-13). There's a bit of a problem. JUnit5 can't be found in the current module — the JUnit5 library has to be imported for each project you use it with.

● ● ●   **Create Test**

Testing library: ◆▶ JUnit5

💡 JUnit5 library not found in the module   Fix

Class name: MainProgramTest
Superclass:
Destination package:

Generate: ☑ setUp/@Before
                       ☐ tearDown/@After

Generate test methods for: ☐ Show inherited methods

	Member
☑ m ○	sayYourName():String
☑ m ○	addTwoNumbers(a:int, b:int):int

?   Cancel   OK

Figure 11-13. *Create Test ➤ JUnit5 not found*

Clicking the "Fix" button will attempt to download the JUnit5 library and create a local copy for our project.

The "Download Library from Maven Repository" pops out next (Figure 11-14) — you've already seen this earlier, so you already know what to do.

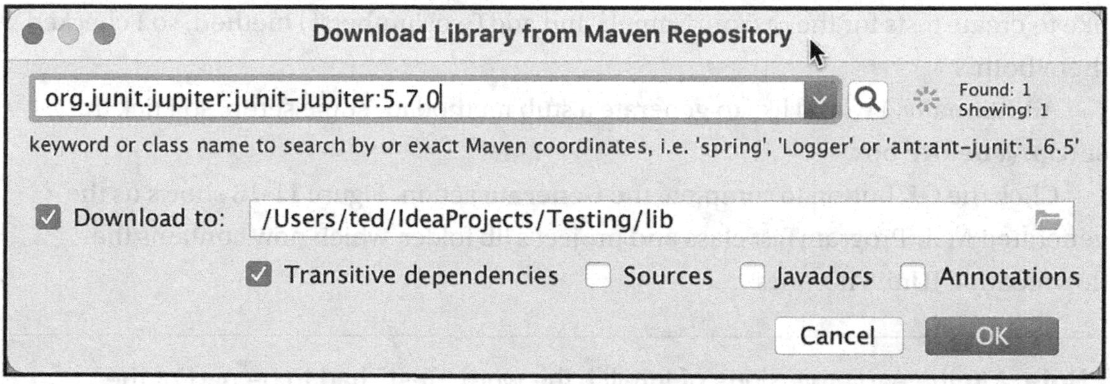

Figure 11-14. *Download Library from Maven Repository*

Click OK to complete the action. When the download finishes, we'll see the "Create Test" dialog again (Figure 11-15).

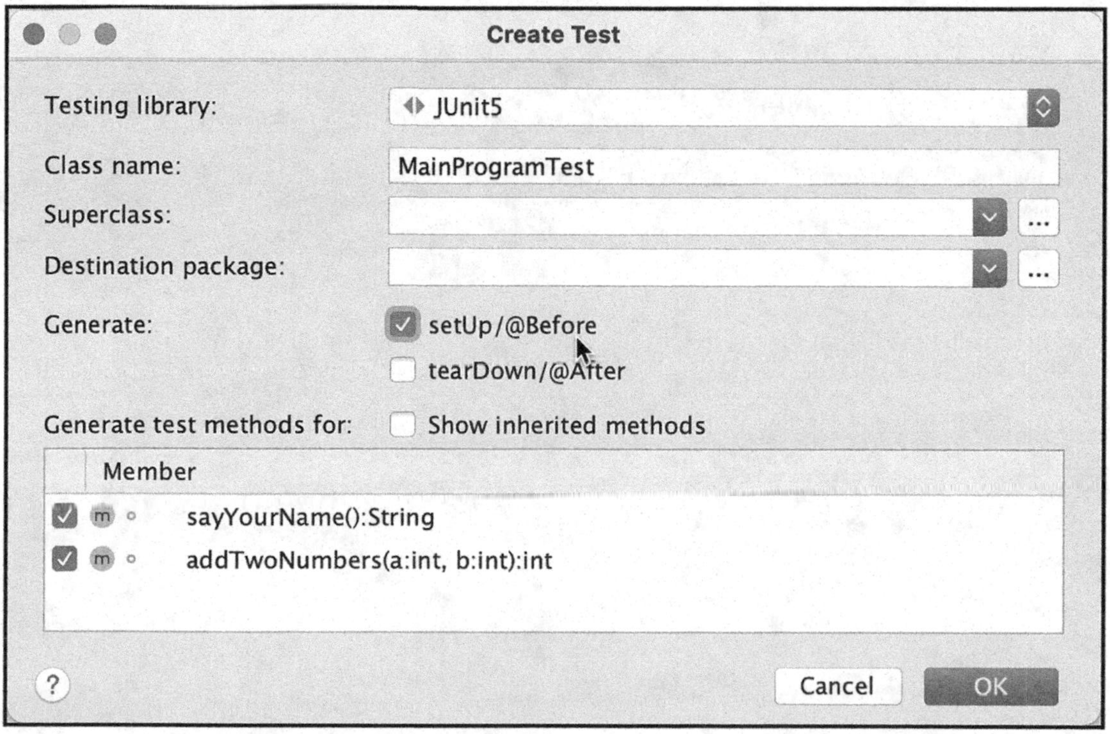

Figure 11-15. *Create Test*

The class name defaults to the name of the class to be tested plus the word "Test." The lower panel of the dialog contains the member methods for MainProgram (the class to be tested). You can check the methods for which you'd like to generate the tests — I'd like to create tests for the sayYourName() and addTwoNumbers() method, so I checked them both.

Additionally, I would like to generate a stub method for some setup, so I tick the **setUp/@Before** box.

Click the OK button to complete the **Generate** action. Figure 11-16 shows us the generated MainProgramTest class and project's lib folder, which now contains the downloaded JUnit5 libraries.

Note   In the earlier versions of IntelliJ, the word "Test" had to be part of the class name. It was a requirement. That's no longer true for the current versions of JUnit — but we still put "Test" as part of the class as a matter of convention.

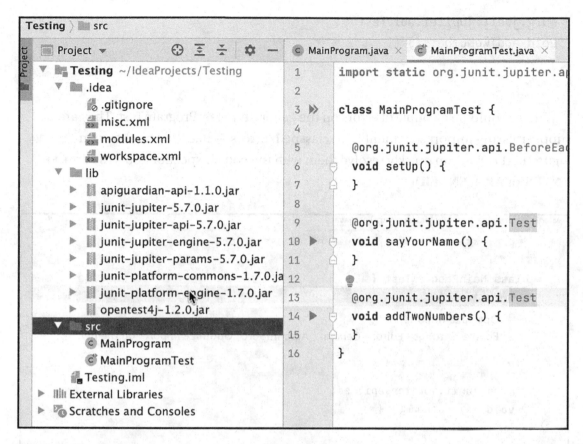

Figure 11-16. *Lib folder in Project Tool Window*

Listing 11-3 shows the generated MainProgramTest class.

Listing 11-3. MainProgramTest

```
import static org.junit.jupiter.api.Assertions.*;

class MainProgramTest {

    @org.junit.jupiter.api.BeforeEach
    void setUp() {
    }

    @org.junit.jupiter.api.Test
    void sayYourName() {
    }
```

```
@org.junit.jupiter.api.Test
void addTwoNumbers() {
}
}
```

There could be a couple of errors on the generated MainProgramTest. They are simply missing import statements and classpath errors — like the one shown in Figure 11-17. You can quickly resolve them with the code inspection tools (**option + ENTER** or **Alt + ENTER**).

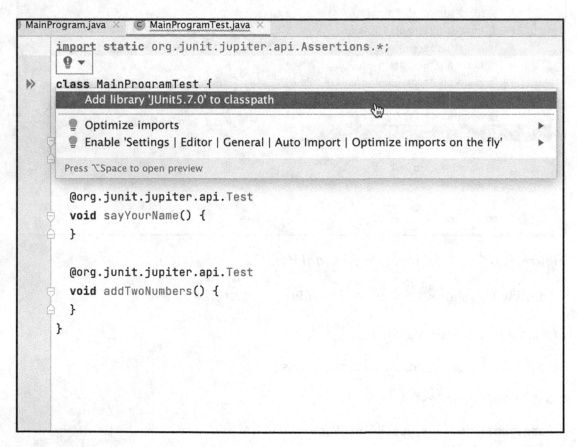

Figure 11-17. *Add JUnit5 to the classpath*

Once you've resolved the missing classpath entries and import statements, we can now start coding the actual test.

Edit the MainProgramTest class and do the following:

1. Add a MainProgram member variable (mp) to the class.

2. Instantiate the **mp** member variable in the setUp() method.

Your code should look like the one in Listing 11-4.

Listing 11-4. Add

```
class MainProgramTest {
  MainProgram mp = null;

  @org.junit.jupiter.api.BeforeEach
  void setUp() {
    mp = new MainProgram();
  }

  @org.junit.jupiter.api.Test
  void sayYourName() {
  }

  @org.junit.jupiter.api.Test
  void addTwoNumbers() {
  }
}
```

You can use the setUp() method to instantiate member variables for the test class. You can also use the setUp() method to connect to databases, open files, initiate a connection to a server, etc.

Next, let's add the actual tests for the sayYourName() and addTwoNumbers() method. Listing 11-5 shows the complete code MainProgramTest class.

Listing 11-5. Complete Code for MainProgramTest

```
import org.junit.jupiter.api.Assertions;

class MainProgramTest {

  MainProgram mp = null;

  @org.junit.jupiter.api.BeforeEach
  void setUp() {
    mp = new MainProgram();
  }

  @org.junit.jupiter.api.Test
  void sayYourName() {
    Assertions.assertEquals("MainProgram", mp.sayYourName());
  }

  @org.junit.jupiter.api.Test
  void addTwoNumbers() {
    Assertions.assertEquals(5, mp.addTwoNumbers(3,2));
  }
}
```

The statements marked as bold in Listing 11-5 are statements you would need to write; the rest of the class was generated for us.

Now it's time to run the test.

The completed MainProgramTest is shown in Figure 11-18.

You can run an individual test — clicking the green arrow on the gutter next to line number 13 will run the sayYourName() test; clicking the arrow on line number 18 runs the addTwoNumbers() test.

I'd like to run all the tests, so I'll click the green arrow next to line number 3 (the MainProgramTest class).

```
1       import org.junit.jupiter.api.Assertions;
2
3       class MainProgramTest {
4
5         MainProgram mp = null;
6
7         @org.junit.jupiter.api.BeforeEach
8         void setUp() {
9           mp = new MainProgram();
10        }
11
12        @org.junit.jupiter.api.Test
13        void sayYourName() {
14          Assertions.assertEquals( expected: "MainProgram", mp.sayYourName());
15        }
16
17        @org.junit.jupiter.api.Test
18        void addTwoNumbers() {
19          Assertions.assertEquals( expected: 5, mp.addTwoNumbers( a: 3, b: 2));
20        }
21      }
```

Figure 11-18. *Run MainProgramTest*

Figure 11-19 shows the result of our test run.

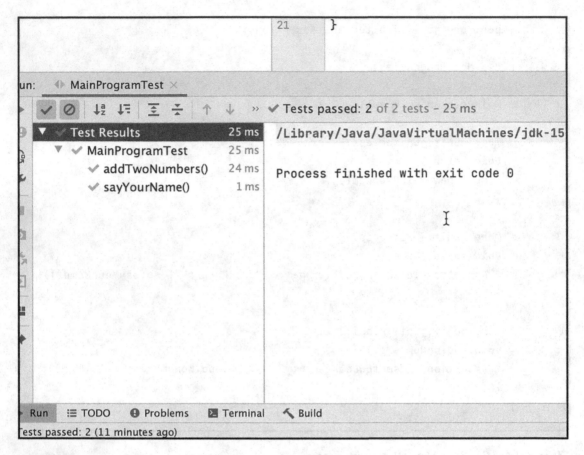

Figure 11-19.   *Test run for MainProgramTest*

All green marks. All of our tests passed.

More Examples

I created a new project for this new example; as you can see in Figure 11-20, it's quite pristine.

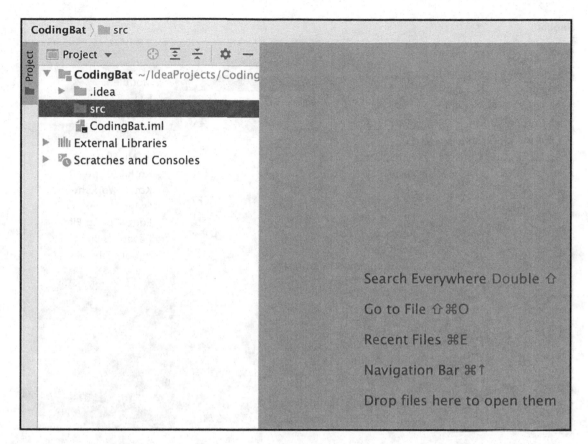

Figure 11-20. *New Project*

I will set up a proper test root folder for this project. The guidance from JetBrains (www.jetbrains.com/help/idea/testing.html) is that we need to set up a test root folder before we create any test classes. In our previous examples, we were able to get away without creating a dedicated test root folder — and for the most part, we were okay. But if you're working on a nontrivial project, it's best to follow proper guidance — that's why we're setting up a test root folder.

Folders in IntelliJ are processed differently. There is a particular treatment for the src folder and quite another for the test root folder. Like I said earlier, it's best to follow proper guidance from the toolmakers themselves.

The src folder is already created by default when you create a project, but the test folder isn't. You'll have to create it yourself — to do that, right-click the project name in the **Project Tool Window**, as shown in Figure 11-21.

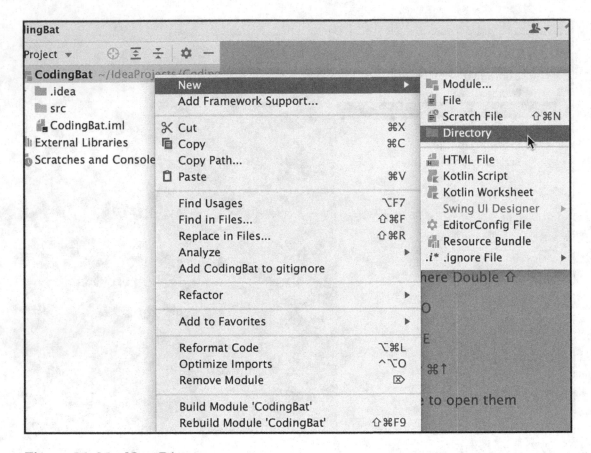

Figure 11-21. *New Directory*

Choose New ➤ Directory, and then provide the new directory name. We'd like to create a test root directory, so we'll call this one "test" — as you can see in Figure 11-22.

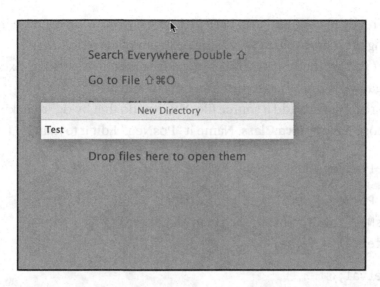

Figure 11-22. *New Directory name*

Pressing ENTER after typing the name of the new directory creates the folder in the **Project Tool Window**.

Next, right-click the newly created **test** directory and choose **Mark Directory as ➤ Test Sources Root**, as shown in Figure 11-23.

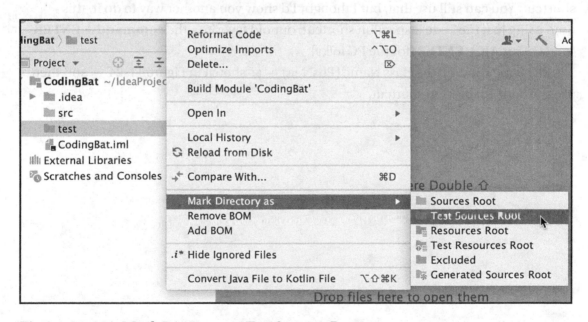

Figure 11-23. *Mark Directory as Test Sources Root*

Now we're ready to code and test. Let's pick an easy warm-up exercise from
https://codingbat.com/prob/p159227; the problem reads as follows:

"Given 2 int values, return true if one is negative and one is positive. Except if the
parameter 'negative' is true, then return true only if both are negative."

So, on the src folder, we add a source file. You can do that by right-clicking the src
folder, and choose **New ➤ Java Class**. Name it "PosNeg." Edit it to match Listing 11-6.

Listing 11-6. PosNeg Class

```
public class PosNeg {
  boolean posNeg(int a, int b, boolean negative) {
    boolean retval = false;

    return retval;
  }
}
```

This should be a good starting point for us.

Let's create the tests.

Earlier, I showed you how to generate test classes using the Generate keyboard
shortcut. You can still use that, but I thought I'd show you another way to do it, this
time using just the code inspection shortcut, our old favorite – the **command + ENTER**
(macOS) or **Alt + ENTER** (for the PC folks).

Place the caret on the class Name (PosNeg) — as shown in Figure 11-24 — and then
use the code inspection shortcut.

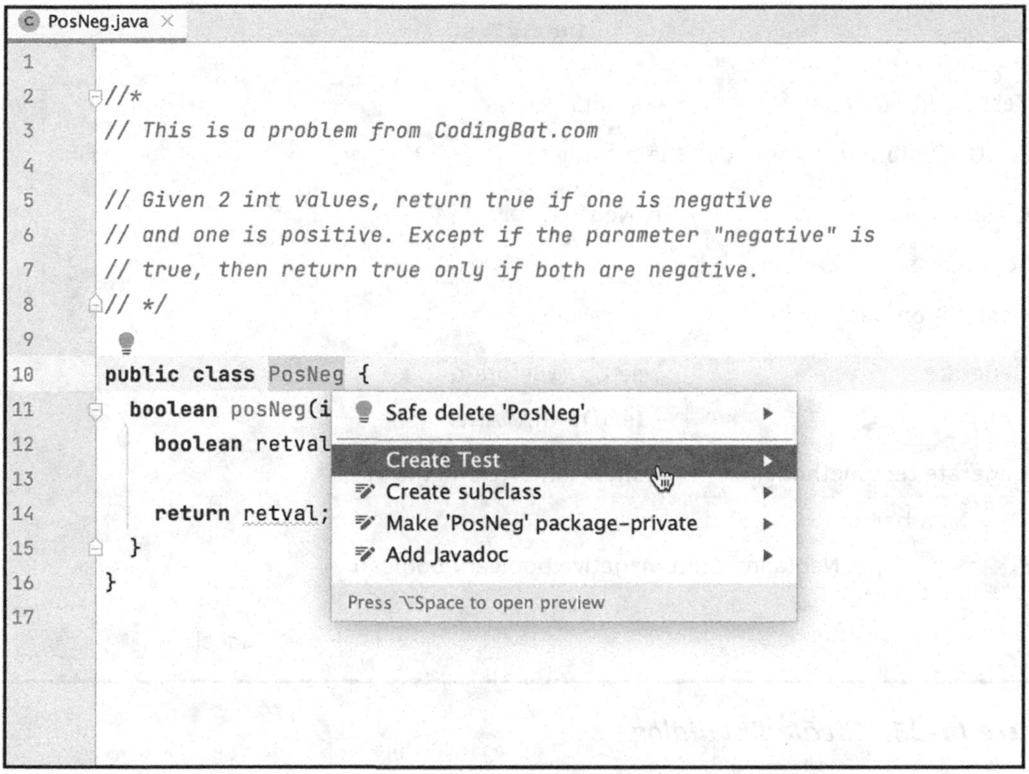

```java
1
2    //*
3    // This is a problem from CodingBat.com
4
5    // Given 2 int values, return true if one is negative
6    // and one is positive. Except if the parameter "negative" is
7    // true, then return true only if both are negative.
8    // */
9
10   public class PosNeg {
11     boolean posNeg(i
12       boolean retval
13
14       return retval;
15     }
16   }
17
```

Safe delete 'PosNeg'   ▶

Create Test   ▶

Create subclass   ▶

Make 'PosNeg' package–private   ▶

Add Javadoc   ▶

Press ⌥Space to open preview

Figure 11-24. *Create Test via quick fix shortcut (command + ENTER)*

Choose "Create Test." In the screen that follows (Figure 11-25), enter the name test class and choose the stub methods to generate — oh, and by the way, you need to fix that "JUnit5 library not found in the module" error. You already know how to do all that.

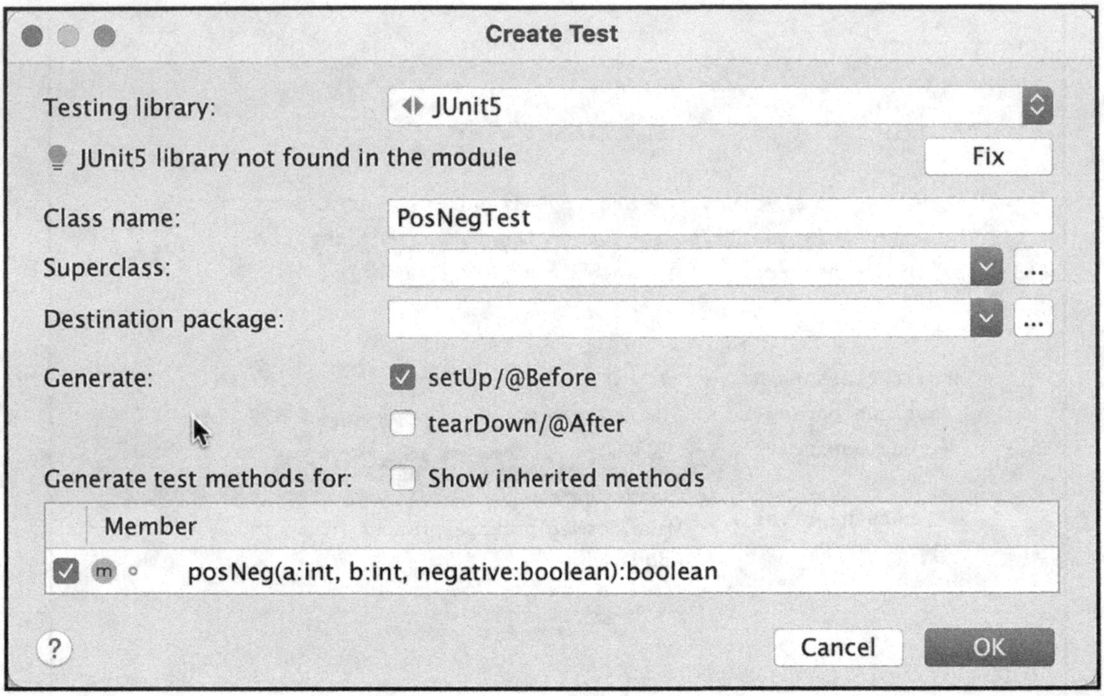

Figure 11-25. *Create Test dialog*

Click OK to complete the action; by the time it finishes, you should have a class in the test folder (as shown in Figure 11-26).

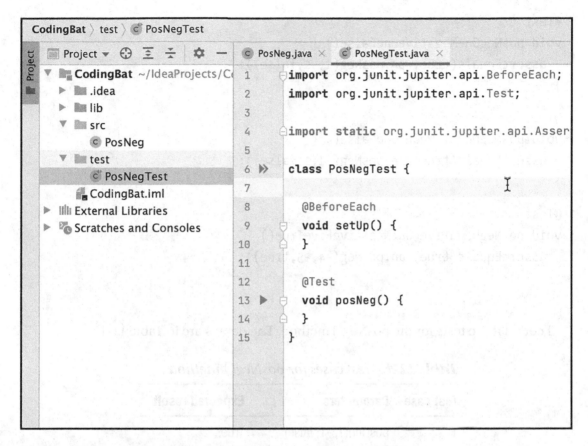

Figure 11-26. *The generated PosNegTest class*

Edit the PosNegTest class to match Listing 11-7.

Listing 11-7. PosNegTest Class

```java
import static org.junit.jupiter.api.Assertions.*;

class PosNegTest {

  PosNeg pn = null;
  @BeforeEach
  void setUp() {
    pn = new PosNeg();
  }
```

```
@Test
void posNegOneNegativeOneFalse() {
  assertEquals(true, pn.posNeg(1,-1,false));
}

@Test
void posNegNegativeOneOneFalse() {
  assertEquals(true, pn.posNeg(-1,1,false));
}

@Test
void posNegNegativeFourNegativeFiveTrue() {
  assertEquals(true, pn.posNeg(-4,-5,true));
}
}
```

I coded three tests for the posNeg() method. The details are in Table 11-1.

Table 11-1. *Test cases for posNeg() method*

Test case	Parameters	Expected result
1	posNeg(1, -1, false)	True
2	posNeg(-1, 1, false)	True
3	posNeg(-4, -5, true)	True

Typically, you'd have more test cases for each method you will test. That's because you'd like to see how your code will behave under a variety of conditions. Ideally, you should cover boundary conditions. In our simple test cases, I have a test for when both inputs are positive and both inputs are negative and another test when one input is negative and the other is positive. It's not exhaustive coverage, but it's a good start.

Let's run the test.

Figure 11-27 shows all three tests failing. Not surprising. We haven't done anything yet on our posNeg() method. It's a good start. This is actually where you're supposed to start — a failing test. Now, take our first stab at a solution.

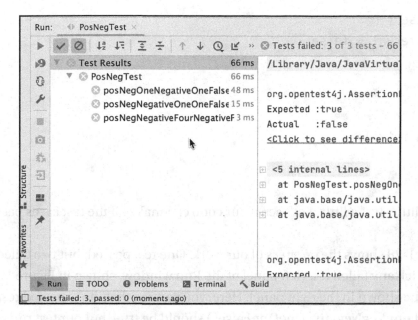

Figure 11-27. *Three tests failed*

Edit the PosNeg class to match Listing 11-8.

Listing 11-8. PosNeg Class

```java
public class PosNeg {
  boolean posNeg(int a, int b, boolean negative) {
    boolean retval = false;

    if (negative) {
      if ((a * b) < 0) {
        // one is positive and the other negative
        retval = false;
      }
      else {
        // either they're both positive or negative
        if (a < 0) {
          // both numbers are negative
          retval = true;
        }
```

```
        else {
          retval = false;
        }
      }
    }

    return retval;
  }
}
```

Code a little, test a little. Let's see if our code can make all the test cases pass. Rerun the test class.

Figure 11-28 shows the progress of our work. One test passed, but two failed.

If you click any failed test (left panel of the Run window, shown in Figure 11-28), the details will be shown in the right panel. Here, you can see that the expected result for the test method **posNegNegativeOneOneFalse()** should be true, but our test run was false.

So, while our current solution is already partially correct, it fails two out of three tests. So, let's code a little more and test a little more.

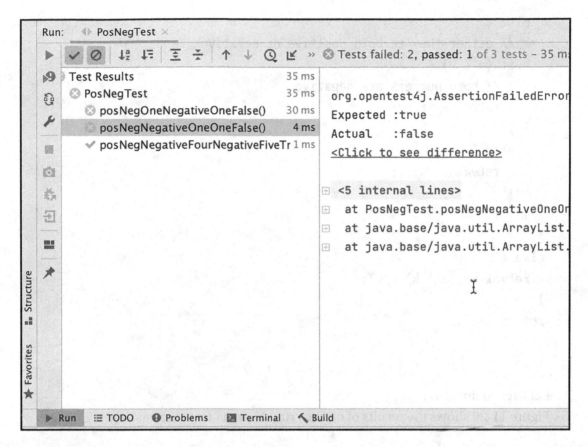

Figure 11-28. *One test passed; two tests failed*

Switch back to PosNeg class, and keep coding until you make all the test pass. Edit it to match Listing 11-9. The statements highlighted in bold are the new additions.

Listing 11-9. Complete Code for PosNeg

```
public class PosNeg {
  boolean posNeg(int a, int b, boolean negative) {
    boolean retval = false;

    if (negative) {
      if ((a * b) < 0) {
        // one is positive and the other negative
        retval = false;
      }
    }
```

```
        else {
          // either they're both positive or negative
          if (a < 0) {
            // both numbers are negative
            retval = true;
          }
          else {
            retval = false;
          }
        }
      }
    else {
      retval = ((a * b) < 0);
    }
    return retval;
  }
}
```

Let's rerun the test.

Figure 11-29 shows the results of our test run. Now, all tests are passing.

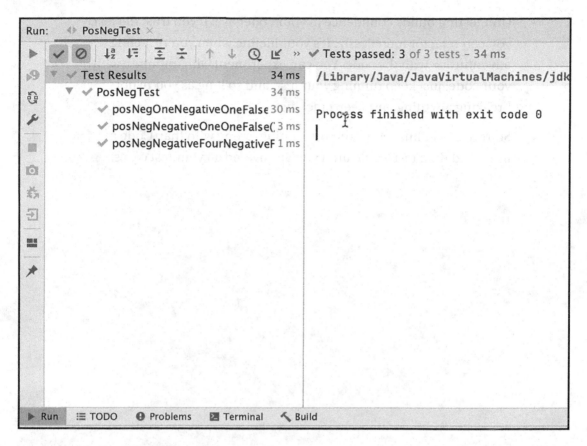

Figure 11-29. *All tests pass*

I hope this gets you started in unit testing. We've only scratched the surface here. I leave it up to you to explore the other assertion methods of the JUnit's Assertion class.

Key Takeaways

- Testing is a vital part of development. Don't skimp.

- Unit testing is pretty easy to set up in IntelliJ. You don't have a reason not to use it.

- Unit testing builds confidence in your codebase. If you trust the test, you can refactor mercilessly. It's your lifeline when you're feeling adventurous with the code. You can experiment with impunity with your code; just keep running your test, and so long as you're not breaking anything, just keep cracking.

- Start with a failing test — there's nothing wrong with that. Code a little, and then test a little until you've covered all your test cases.

## CHAPTER 12

JavaFX

In this chapter, we will cover the following:

- Overview of JavaFX

- How to set up JavaFX and include it in projects

- How to build a basic UI app using JavaFX

- How to set up and use Scene Builder

There are three ways to build user-friendly apps in Java. You can either go the

- **Web App** route, in which case you'll need to know something about JakartaEE apps — Appendix A (an online-only resource for this book) briefly discusses some common JakartaEE apps and how to build them using IntelliJ. You can access this appendix via the **Download Source Code** link located at www.apress.com/9781484274453.

- **Mobile App route**, in which case you'll need to deal with Android.

- **JavaFX route** is the tech stack that will let you build rich desktop applications, which is also our topic for this chapter.

A Brief History

JavaFX isn't the starting point for UI technology on the Java ecosystem. Java's bid for desktop app technology started much earlier. As early as 1995 (Java's debut), developers have used AWT — short for Abstract Window Toolkit — to build Applets (this was a big deal then) and build desktop apps. One of the limitations of AWT was that it used the UI controls of the underlying OS (which was heavy), and it also meant your app would look (and work) differently on each OS.

T. Hagos, *Beginning IntelliJ IDEA*, https://doi.org/10.1007/978-1-4842-7446-0_12

In 1997, Sun Microsystems introduced JFC (Java Foundation Classes), more affectionately known as Swing API. Swing was what you would use if you were building Java desktop apps. Swing was a big hit because, unlike AWT, it did not use the UI controls of the underlying OS, which meant the app would look and behave consistently across platforms.

Sometime in 2008, JavaFX was introduced as the successor of Swing; but JavaFX's history didn't start in 2008 — it started much earlier.

Table 12-1 shows the timeline for JavaFX.

Table 12-1. *History of JavaFX*

Release date	Version	Comments
Early 2000		Chris Oliver at SeeBeyond created F3 (form follows function). F3 was a scripting language for developing GUI applications.
2005		Sun Microsystems acquired SeeBeyond; F3 was renamed JavaFX.
2007		At JavaOne, Sun Microsystems announced JavaFX.
2008	1.0	JavaFX was released.
2009	1.1	Mobile support was included.
2009	1.2	Released sometime in Q2 of 2009.
2010	1.3	Released sometime in Q2 of 2010.
2010	1.3.1	Released sometime in Q3 of 2010.
2011	2.0	JavaFX script was dropped. JavaFX now supports Java API. Support for JavaFX mobile was dropped.
		Lots of changes under the hood took place. Support for lazy binding, binding expressions, bound sequence expressions, and partial bind reevaluation was added. Also, JavaFX is now open source.
2012	2.1	macOS desktops are now supported.
2012	2.2	Released sometime in Q3 of 2012. Now, Linux is supported.

(*continued*)

Table 12-1. (*continued*)

Release date	Version	Comments
2014	8.0	Up until now, you need to download JavaFX separately to use it. Starting with this release, JavaFX was included in the JDK. So, once you installed the JDK, you automatically have JavaFX.
		Also, there was a significant change in the versioning of JavaFX. Starting with this release, JavaFX version will follow the version number of JDK.
		Changes under the hood included support for 3D graphics, sensor support, MathML, printing and rich text support, etc.
2017	9.0	JEP 253 (JDK Enhancement Proposal), now we can style JavaFX with CSS.
2018	11.0	Oracle removed JavaFX from the JDK. Starting with this release, you'll have to download JavaFX separately from the JDK.
2019	12	Released in Q1 2019.
2019	12.0.1	Released in Q2 2019.
2019	13	Released sometime in Q4 2019.
2020	14	Released in Q1 2020.
2020	15	Released in Q4 2020.
2021	16	Released in Q1 2021.

Setup

The best way to learn a new tech is to start building an app using that tech. So, let's build a new project that uses JavaFX.

Download the JavaFX SDK for your OS from GluonHQ `https://gluonhq.com/products/javafx/`. Unzip it in your preferred location, for example, /Users/username/javafx-sdk-16.

Create a JavaFX project. On the New Project dialog (Figure 12-1), choose **JavaFX**.

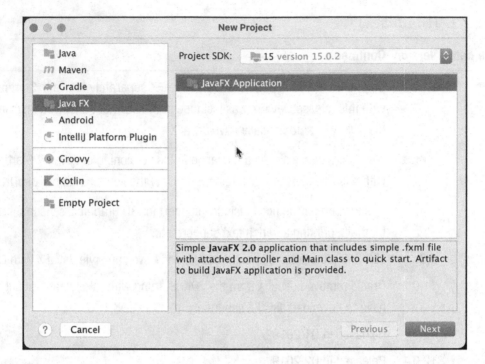

Figure 12-1. *Create a New JavaFX project*

Give the project a name, just like the other projects you've created in the past. Click the Next button to continue the action.

You'll be asked to download the **javafx-fxml** library from the Maven repository (Figure 12-2).

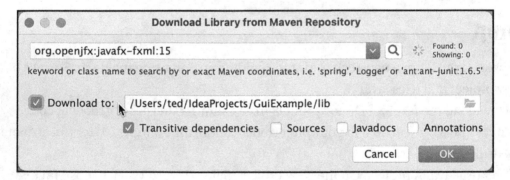

Figure 12-2. *Download JavaFX library from Maven Repository*

Download it so the library becomes part of your project; click the OK button to complete the action.

IntelliJ creates the project. As you can see in Figure 12-3, it created three files.

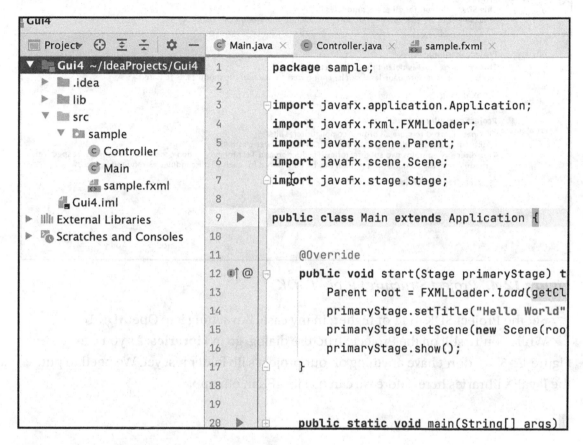

Figure 12-3. *New JavaFX project*

Next, from the main menu bar, go to **File ➤ Project Structure ➤ Project**, as shown in Figure 12-4.

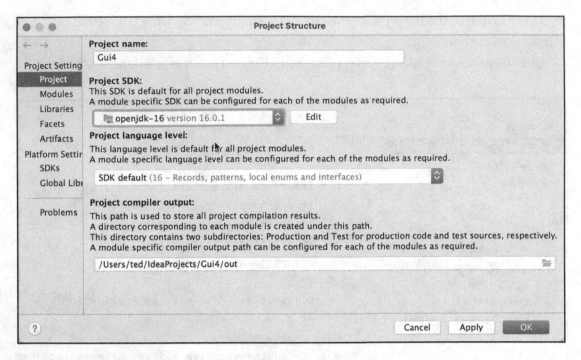

Figure 12-4. *Project Structure | Project SDK*

Set the Project SDK to 11 or higher; in my case, I'm setting it to OpenJDK 16.

While you're still on the Project Structure dialog, go to **Libraries**. As you can see in Figure 12-5, we don't have anything on our project's lib folder just yet. We need to put the JavaFX libraries here before we can use JavaFX in our app.

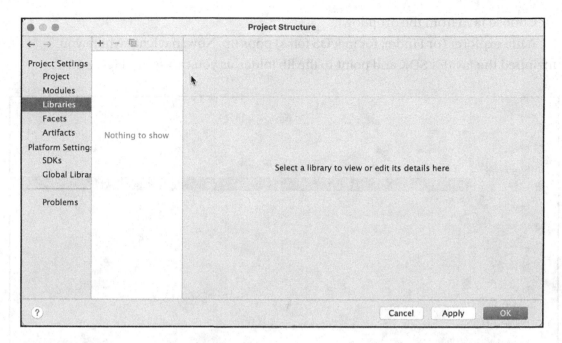

Figure 12-5. *Project Structure | Libraries*

Click the plus sign to add a new library (as shown in Figure 12-6).

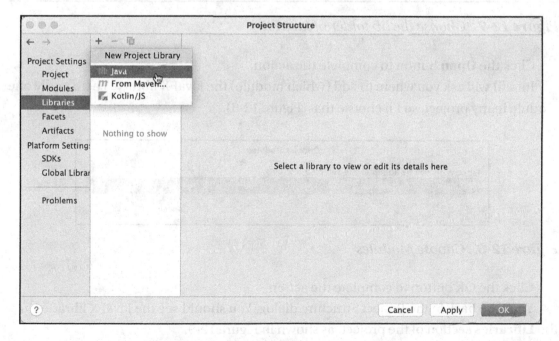

Figure 12-6. *Project Structure | Libraries | New Project Library*

Choose **Java** from the dropdown.

A file explorer (or Finder, for macOS folks) pops up. Now, navigate where you unzipped the JavaFX SDK and point to the lib folder, as you can see in Figure 12-7.

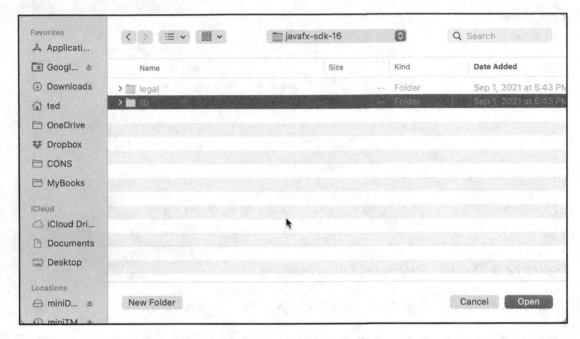

Figure 12-7. Choose the lib folder of JavaFX

Click the **Open** button to complete the action.

IntelliJ will ask you where to add (which module) the JavaFX library. There's only one module in my project, so I'll choose that (Figure 12-8).

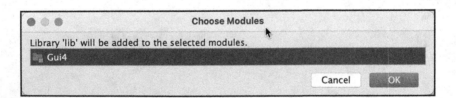

Figure 12-8. Choose Modules

Click the OK button to complete the action.

You'll be back to the Project Structure dialog. You should see the JavaFX libraries in the **Libraries** section of the project, as shown in Figure 12-9.

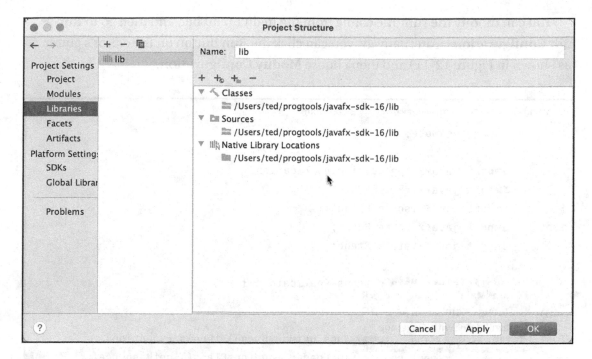

Figure 12-9. *Project Structure | Libraries*

If you try to run the project at this point, you will get a runtime error — "JavaFX runtime components are missing," as shown in Figure 12-10.

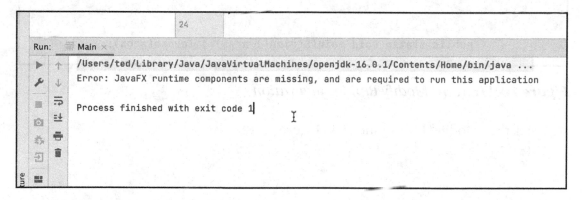

Figure 12-10. *Runtime error*

To solve this, we need to add some options to the VM; to do that, we need to modify the runtime configuration.

You can modify the runtime config from the main menu bar, and then go to **Run ➤ Edit Configurations**. Alternatively, you can click the Run button on the editor's gutter (as shown in Figure 12-11) and then choose **Modify Configuration**.

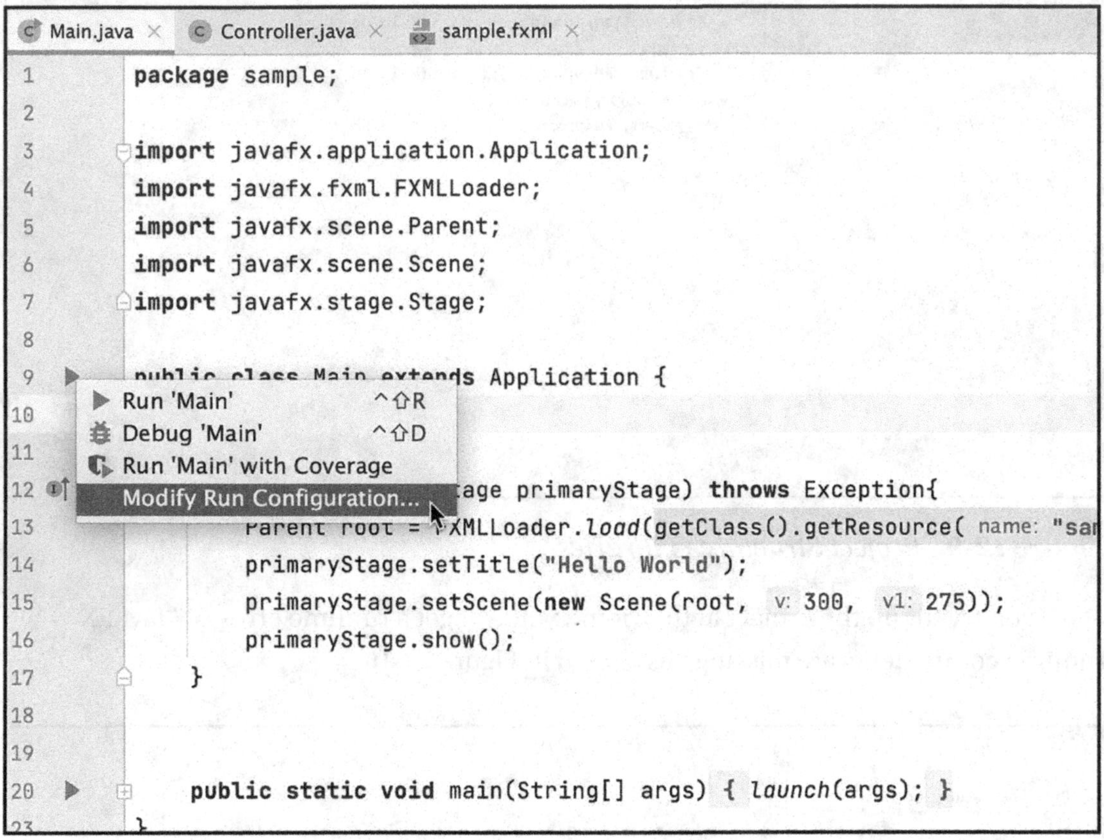

Figure 12-11.   *Run | Modify Run Configuration*

Click the "Modify" link, as shown in Figure 12-12.

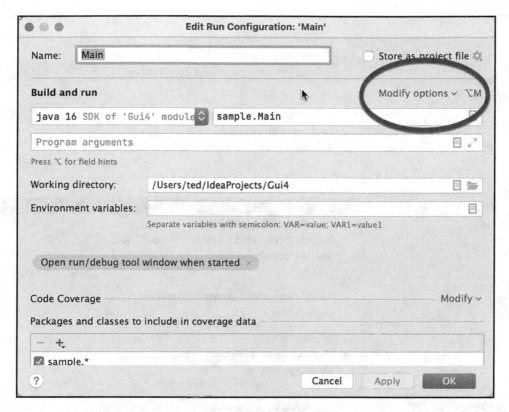

Figure 12-12. Edit Run Configuration | Modify Options

Choose **Add VM options**, as shown in Figure 12-13.

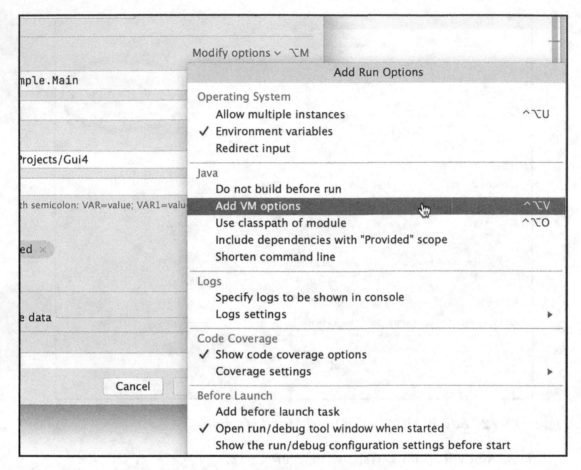

Figure 12-13. *Edit Run Configuration | Modify Options | Add VM options*

On the VM options text field (Figure 12-14), type the following:

```
--module-path /path/to/javafx-sdk-16/lib --add-modules
javafx.controls,javafx.fxml
```

Don't forget to replace **/path/to/javafx-sdk-16** with the actual directory path where you unzipped JavaFX.

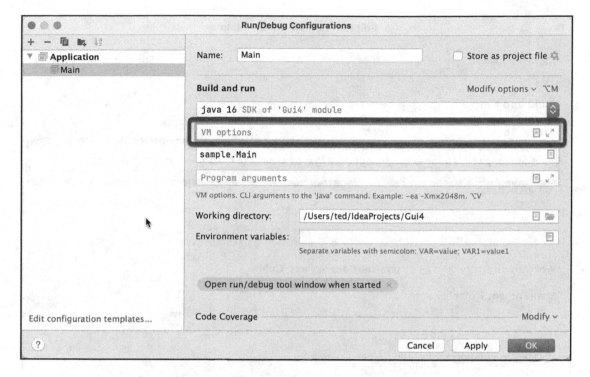

Figure 12-14. Run/Debug Configurations | VM options

In my case, I installed JavaFX in /Users/ted/progtools/javafx-sdk-16, so that's what I used in my VM options (shown in Figure 12-15).

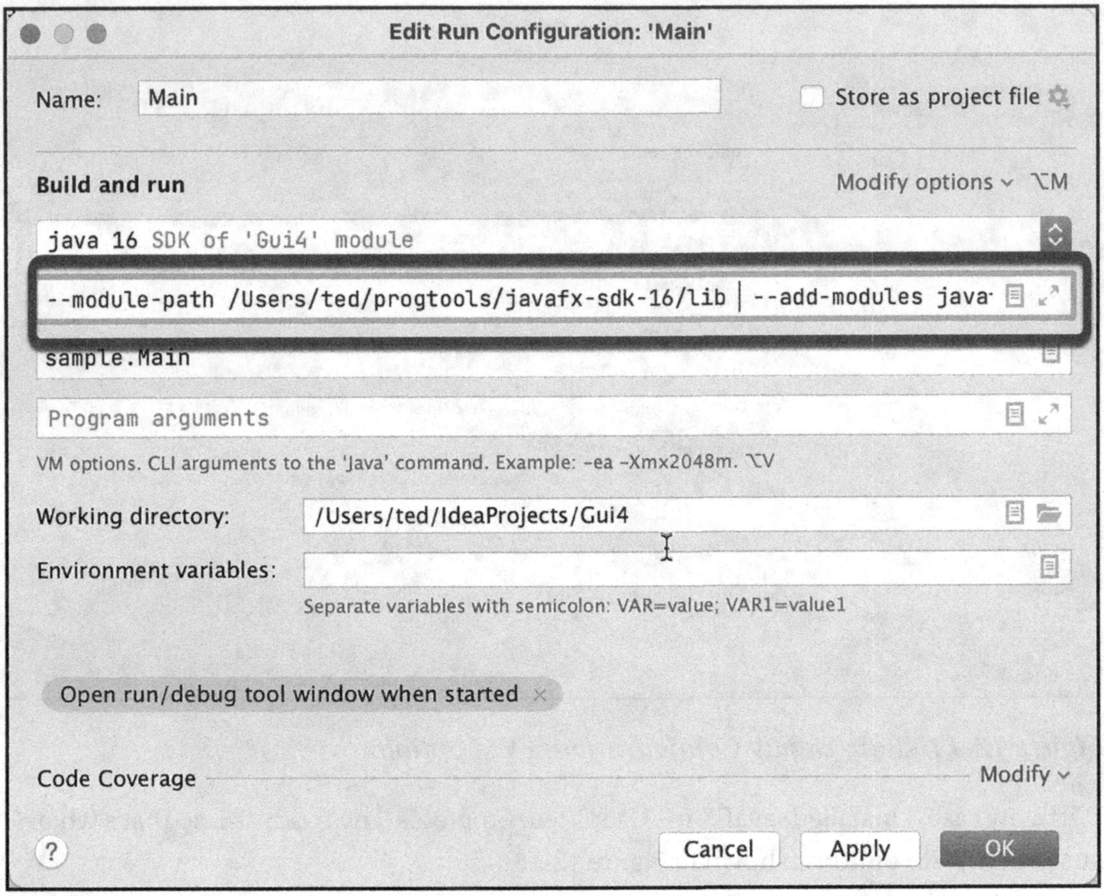

Figure 12-15. *Edit Run Configuration | VM options*

Click the OK button to complete the action.

Figure 12-16 shows our first JavaFX app in runtime.

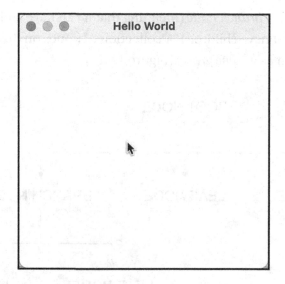

Figure 12-16. *JavaFX app running*

Stages, Scenes, and Nodes

JavaFX uses terminologies such as stage, scenes, and nodes.

Think of a stage object like an actual stage — where people perform plays, as in a theater stage. A stage is where all scenes (we're still on theater analogy) will be performed; each scene will contain a different setting and is intended for performing a specific act. Each scene will have a different set of props — one may have fake trees, another may have fake waves, etc.

It's helpful to think of a JavaFX app this way (using the theater stage analogy) because it actually is kind of like that. A scene belongs to only one stage; each scene will have a different set of props.

I'll stop using the theater analogy now, which means from this point forward, when I say stage, I mean JavaFX stage, and when I say scene, I mean JavaFX scene.

A stage object is a top-level container. It encloses the whole app. A scene belongs to only one stage. We can say that a stage is a container for scenes.

A scene typically contains child components; in JavaFX terminologies, these components are called nodes. We can say that a scene is a container for nodes. Nodes are elements placed in a scene. These nodes are the GUI elements, for example, Textbox, checkboxes, buttons, etc.

Each node is either a *branch node* (meaning that it can have children) or a *leaf node* (meaning that it cannot have children). A collection of nodes on the scene forms a tree structure and is known as a *scene graph* (Figure 12-17).

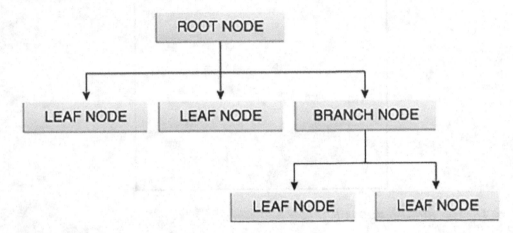

Figure 12-17. *Scene graph*

In the graph, the first node on the tree is known as the *root node*. It doesn't have a parent. Each element you will use in JavaFX is an instance of a Node (Node is a class).

The JavaFX API defines several classes that can act as root, branch, or leaf nodes. Examples of branch nodes could be HBox, StackPane, BorderPane, Group, Region, GridPane, etc. — these classes are typically the layout classes. Some samples of leaf nodes are Textbox, Rectangle, Slider, RadioButton, PasswordField, Separator, ToolTip, etc.

When substituted with actual class names, this same figure might resemble something in an actual application.

On an actual app, a scene graph might look like the one in Figure 12-18.

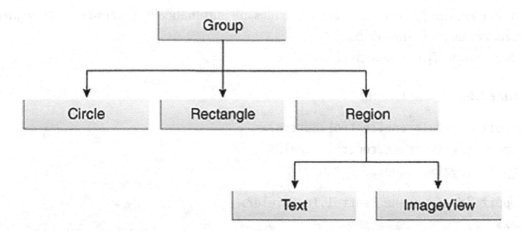

Figure 12-18. Scene graph for an app

Hello World

Let's go back to our "Hello World" sample project.

Select the *sample.fxml* file in the main editor's tab (Figure 12-19).

```
C Main.java ×    C Controller.java ×    sample.fxml ×
1       <?import javafx.geometry.Insets?>
2       <?import javafx.scene.layout.GridPane?>
3
4       <?import javafx.scene.control.Button?>
5       <?import javafx.scene.control.Label?>
6     <GridPane fx:controller="sample.Controller"
7           xmlns:fx="http://javafx.com/fxml" alignment="center" hgap="10"
8     </GridPane>
```

Figure 12-19. sample.fxml

An FXML file is an XML-based user interface markup language (created by Oracle Corp) for defining user interfaces for JavaFX. While it's possible to build JavaFX apps by programmatically defining all the nodes in a scene, it's a tedious exercise. The resulting code can also be difficult (and a chore) to maintain. FXML is the preferred alternative for building UIs for JavaFX.

When creating a JavaFX project, three files are automatically generated — *Main.java, Controller.java, and sample.fxml.*

Edit sample.fxml to match Listing 12-1.

Listing 12-1. sample.fxml

```
<?import javafx.scene.control.Button?>
<?import javafx.scene.control.Label?>
<?import javafx.scene.layout.HBox?>

<?import javafx.scene.control.TextField?>
<HBox>
  <Label text="User name"></Label>
  <TextField></TextField>
  <Button text="Login"></Button>
</HBox>
```

Even without further explanation, you can probably understand what's going on with the preceding code.

The first three lines are import statements. They function pretty much the same way as they do in our Java source files. The syntax is a bit weird because each statement is enclosed within a pair of angle brackets and question marks — but that's just how FXML files are.

We know that the HBox is a branch or parent container, so Label, TextField, and Button nodes are enclosed within HBox, which instinctively tells us that these three leaf nodes are children of HBox.

Rerunning the project gives us the results shown in Figure 12-20.

Figure 12-20. *Hello World*

Life Cycle of a JavaFX App

All JavaFX apps should extend the class **javafx.application.Application** class. When instantiated, the JavaFX Application object goes through the following life cycle:

1. Constructs an instance of the specified application class. If you defined a constructor of your own, any code within it would be called at this point.

2. The runtime calls the application's init() method. If your app makes any HTTP, database, or I/O calls, this might be a good place to put your initialization codes.

3. The runtime calls the start() method. This method is typically generated for you when you create a JavaFX project. This is where the FXML is flattened to Java objects to form the scene graph, where the scene is set for stage, and where the Stage.show() method is called.

4. Runtime waits for the application to finish, which happens when either one of the following occurs:

    a. The application calls Platform.exit().

    b. The last window was closed and the implicitExit attribute on the Platform is true — which usually happens when you click the close button on the window.

5. The runtime calls the stop() method. If you opened any I/O resources like network, database, or file resources, this is an excellent time to make sure they're closed.

Main.java

Now that we have some idea about the makeup of a JavaFX app, let's revisit the *Main. java* source file. Listing 12-2 shows an annotated explanation of *Main.java*.

Listing 12-2. Main.java

```
import javafx.application.Application;
import javafx.fxml.FXMLLoader;
import javafx.scene.Parent;
import javafx.scene.Scene;
import javafx.stage.Stage;

public class Main extends Application { ❶

    @Override
    public void start(Stage primaryStage) throws Exception{ ❷
        Parent root = FXMLLoader.load(getClass().getResource("sample.fxml")); ❸
        primaryStage.setTitle("Hello World");
        primaryStage.setScene(new Scene(root, 300, 275)); ❹
        primaryStage.show(); ❺
    }

    public static void main(String[] args) { ❻
        launch(args);
    }
}
```

❶   We extend `javafx.application.Application` class. All JavaFX apps inherit from
    this class.

❻   At runtime, the VM still uses static `main()` as the entry point. From `main()`, we invoke the
    `launch()`method, passing any command-line args to it (if we got any).

❷   The runtime calls the `start()` method and passes a stage object as an argument.

❸   A parent node object is created (this is the root variable). It gets populated by flattening the
    contents of *sample.fxml* into a scene graph.

❹   The scene object is attached to the stage.

❺   Finally, the runtime calls the `show()` method of the stage object. At this point, the app
    becomes visible.

Scene Builder

While it's easy — I should say "easier" — to define the UI elements using FXML rather
than via API, it can still be tedious, especially when the UI becomes more and more
complex. A visual editor that we can use to compose the UI element is still the ideal tool.
This is why we have the Scene Builder tool.

Scene Builder is a visual composition tool that we can use to build FXML files.
Oracle initially created it, but for some reason, they stopped supporting Scene Builder.
Fortunately, Scene Builder is open source, and so, another organization (Gluon) took
ownership.

You'll need to install Scene Builder separately if you want to use it; it's a handy tool to
compose FXML files visually. Like any visual composition tool, you can simply drag and
drop elements to construct UIs, edit its properties, and see a visual preview of how the
elements might look at runtime. By the way, Scene Builder was built using JavaFX itself;
that's why it works on all platforms.

To use Scene Builder, we'll need to download it from `https://gluonhq.com/`
`pDownload Scene Builderroducts/scene-builder/` (Figure 12-21).

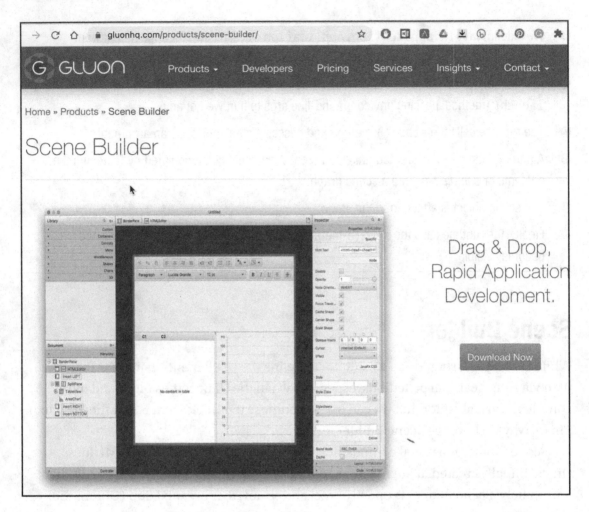

Figure 12-21. *Scene Builder download page*

Choose the installer for your platform (Figure 12-22), and then click the Download button to complete the action.

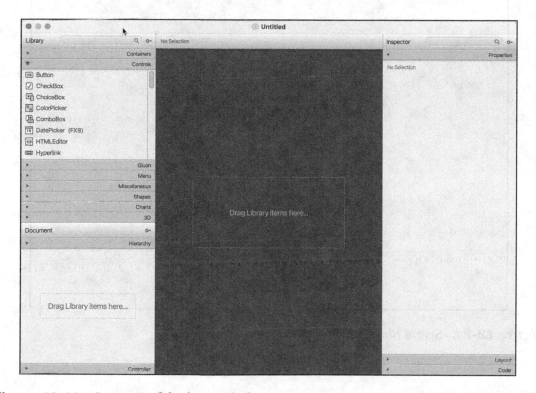

Download Scene Builder		

Scene Builder **16.0.0** was released on **Mar 26, 2021**.

*You can use this Scene Builder version together with **Java 11 and higher**.*

Product	Platform	Download
Scene Builder	Windows Installer	Download
Scene Builder	Mac OS X dmg	Download
Scene Builder	Linux RPM	Download
Scene Builder	Linux Deb	Download
Scene Builder Kit (info)	Jar File	Download

Figure 12-22. *Scene Builder download links*

Run the installer and follow the prompts to completion. Launch the Scene Builder application; Figure 12-23 shows the Scene Builder app with an Untitled project.

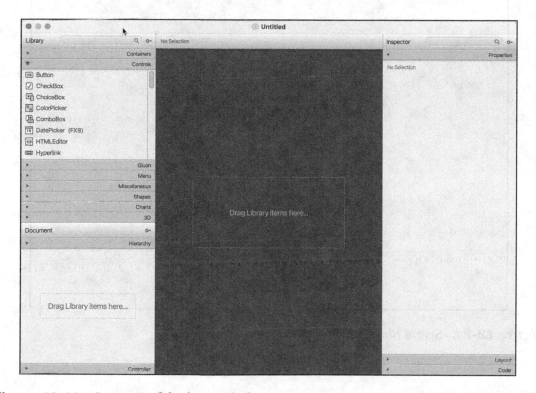

Figure 12-23. *Scene Builder | Untitled project*

Building FXML Files

Let's build a simple UI using Scene Builder.

Scene Builder has some great starter templates for UI. If you click on Scene Builder's main menu bar and then go to File ➤ New From Template, you'll get to choose from one of the pre-built UI templates (shown in Figure 12-24). This is a great way to get started. You can simply edit or delete UI components that you don't need and proceed from there.

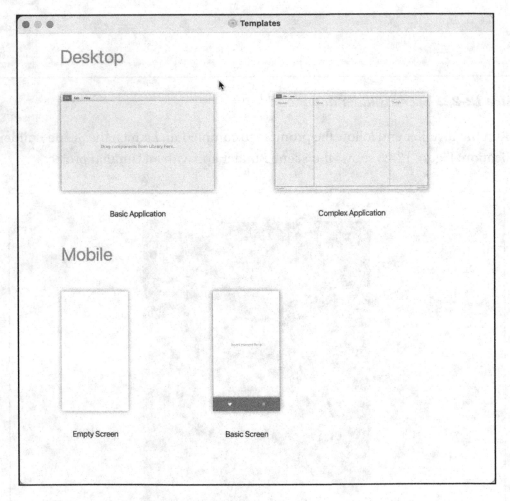

Figure 12-24. *Scene Builder templates*

But we won't go that route. We'll start from scratch.

In Figure 12-23, the middle panel of Scene Builder is our canvas. We simply drag and drop the UI components in this area.

The first thing we need is a container. So, open the accordion (left panel, shown in Figure 12-25) to **Containers**, and then click on VBox.

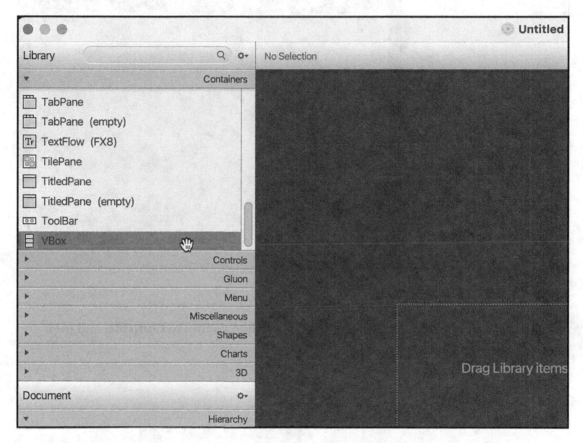

Figure 12-25. *Drag VBox to the canvas*

While still pressing the mouse on VBox, drag it onto the canvas (where it says "Drag Library items here"). You should see the VBox widget in the visual editor (Figure 12-26).

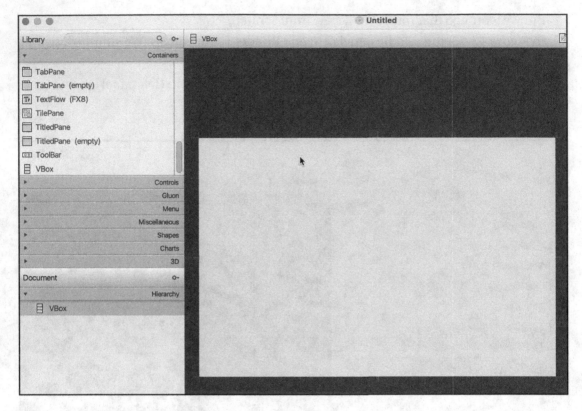

Figure 12-26. *VBox added*

Next, add a Label to the VBox. Open the accordion control to **Controls**, and then choose **Label** (as shown in Figure 12-27).

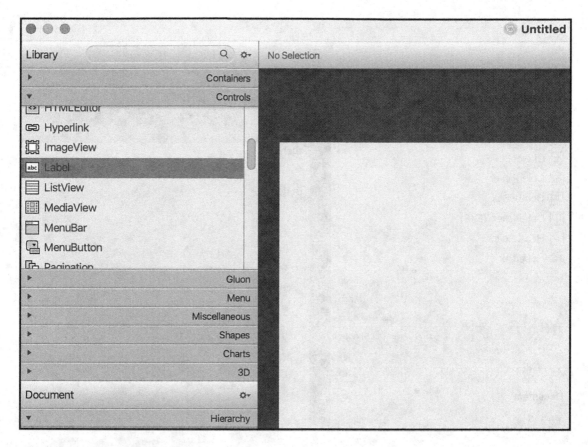

Figure 12-27. *Add a Label*

Using the same technique you used to add the VBox to the canvas, drag and drop the Label into the VBox.

Then, add a TextField and then a Button. You should have something that looks like Figure 12-28.

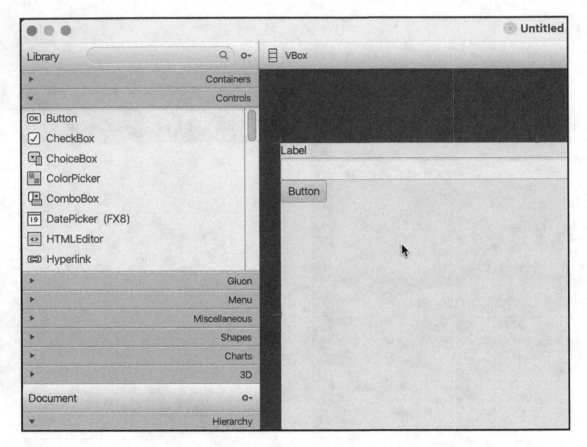

Figure 12-28. *Label, TextField, and a Button*

If you want to change specific attributes of the UI elements, you can select them in the editor and then go to the Properties section. You can change the attributes such as alignment, font, color, or the text property — as in my case, as you can see in Figure 12-29.

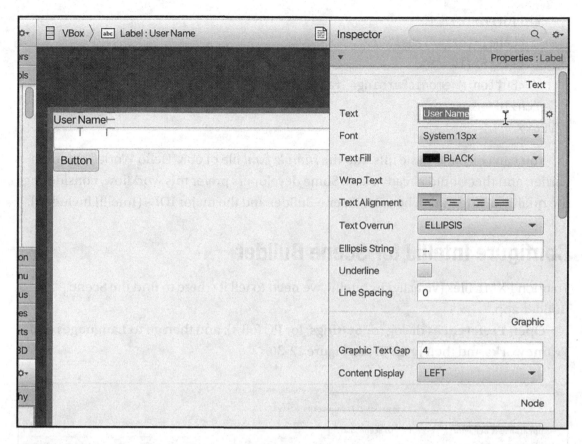

Figure 12-29. *How to edit properties*

If you save this file now and open it using a plain text editor, you'll see something like the one in Listing 12-3.

Listing 12-3. sample.fxml

```
<?xml version="1.0" encoding="UTF-8"?>

<?import javafx.scene.control.Button?>
<?import javafx.scene.control.Label?>
<?import javafx.scene.control.TextField?>
<?import javafx.scene.layout.VBox?>

<VBox maxHeight="-Infinity" maxWidth="-Infinity" minHeight="-Infinity"
minWidth="-Infinity" prefHeight="400.0" prefWidth="600.0" xmlns="http://
javafx.com/javafx/16" xmlns:fx="http://javafx.com/fxml/1">
```

```
<children>
    <Label text="Label" />
    <TextField />
    <Button mnemonicParsing="false" text="Button" />
</children>
</VBox>
```

You can copy and paste this into the *sample.fxml* file of our "Hello World" app from earlier, and that would already work. Some developers prefer this workflow, considering the quality of integration between Scene Builder and the major IDEs (IntelliJ included).

Configure IntelliJ for Scene Builder

To open FXML files (visually) in IntelliJ, we need to tell it where to find the Scene Builder app.

Open **Preferences** dialog (or **Settings**, for PC folks), and then go to **Languages and Frameworks** and then **JavaFX**. See Figure 12-30.

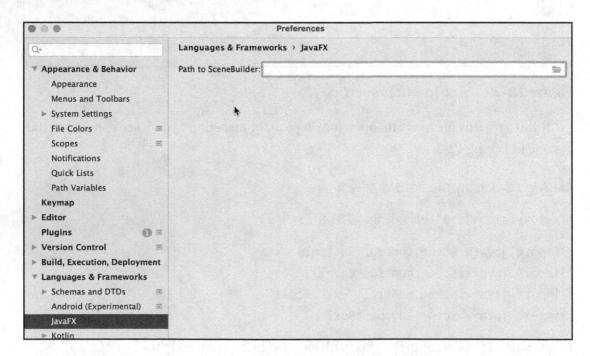

Figure 12-30.   *Preferences | Languages & Frameworks | JavaFX*

You need to point to where the Scene Builder app is installed. In macOS, this location is typically **/Applications/SceneBuilder.app**; in Windows 10, the default location is **C:\Users\user\AppData\Local\SceneBuilder.exe**.

Figure 12-31 shows the Scene Builder app, pointing to its location in the /Applications folder.

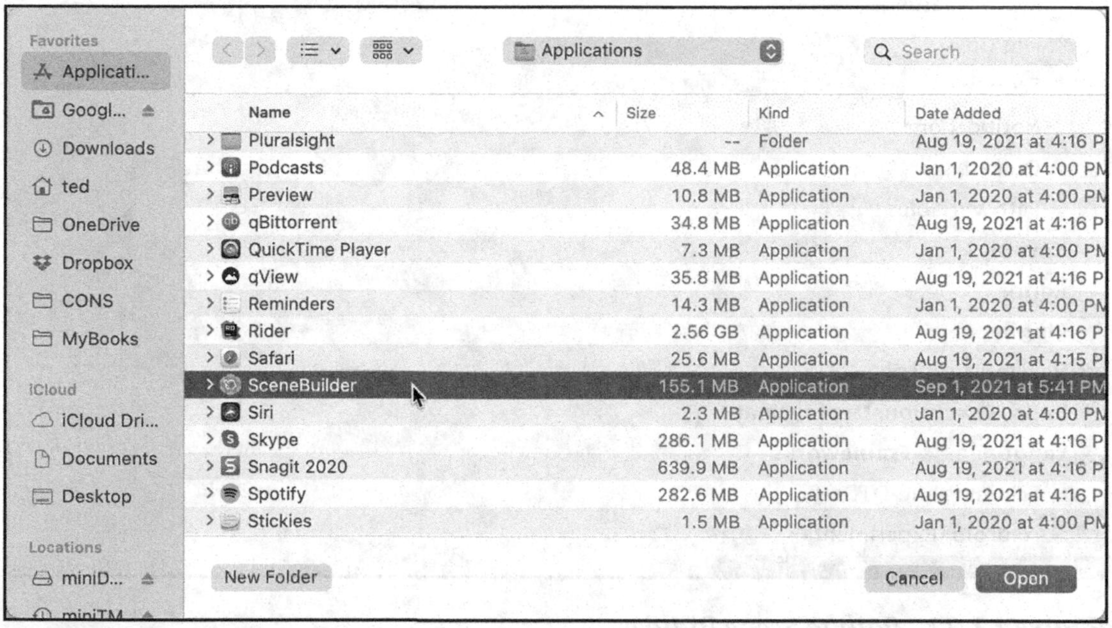

Figure 12-31. *Find the location of the Scene Builder application*

Click the Open button to confirm the selection.

You should be back to the Preferences dialog with the Scene Builder path filled up, as shown in Figure 12-32.

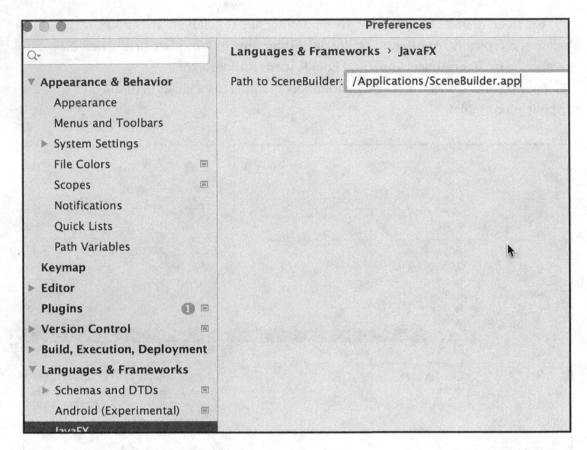

Figure 12-32.   Path to Scene Builder

Click the OK button to complete the action.

Opening Files in Scene Builder

When you open an **.fxml** file in the editor, there are two tabs underneath the editing area (shown in Figure 12-33).

The **Text** area lets you edit the markup in code.

```
 1    <?xml version="1.0" encoding="UTF-8"?>
 2
 3    <?import javafx.scene.control.Button?>
 4    <?import javafx.scene.control.Label?>
 5    <?import javafx.scene.control.TextField?>
 6    <?import javafx.scene.layout.VBox?>
 7
 8
 9    <VBox maxHeight="-Infinity" maxWidth="-Infinity" minHeight="-Infinity" min
10        <children>
11            <Label text="Label" />
12            <TextField />
13            <Button mnemonicParsing="false" text="Button" />
14        </children>
15    </VBox>
16
17
```

Figure 12-33. *FXML editor tabs*

The **Scene Builder** tab opens the .fxml in Scene Builder (Figure 12-34).

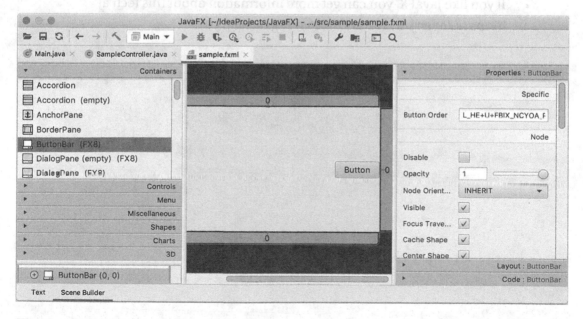

Figure 12-34. *Scene Builder in IntelliJ*

With that, we conclude this chapter; but let me leave with a word of caution. You need to set your expectations with how Scene Builder works with IntelliJ. At the time of writing, IntelliJ's support for Scene Builder is a bit spotty — most of the time, it works, but there are times that it doesn't; I've experienced both.

Mostly, the issue with Scene Builder's integration with IntelliJ is that the GUI editor doesn't show up in IntelliJ, but the Text markup works just fine. I've been tracking this problem using JetBrains' issue tracking (`https://youtrack.jetbrains.com`), and the issue still isn't closed (at the time of writing). Hopefully, this gets fixed in the future releases and updates of Scene Builder and IntelliJ.

Key Takeaways

- JavaFX is a good choice of tech if you need to build cross-platform desktop apps.

- You can build a JavaFX app via API, but that's tedious. Use FXML files to define the UI instead.

- You can build FXML by hand, but that too is tedious; use a visual tool like Scene Builder instead.

- If you like JavaFX, you can get more information about this tech at `https://openjfx.io/` and `https://gluonhq.com/`.

Index

A, B, C

Code navigation
  actions, 60, 61
  changes/files
    changes, 67
    locations, 66, 67
    recent files dialog, 66
  class dialog, 64, 65
  code generator
    class programmer, 78
    field selections, 77
    getters/setters, 76, 77
    programmer class, 79
    style program, 78, 79
    wizard screen, 75, 76
  coding process, 57, 58
  collapsed src folder, 64
  non-project items, 59
  opening files, 61–64
  project tool window, 62
  search everywhere shortcut, 58, 59
  searching files, 63
  symbols dialog, 65
  target type
    employee source file, 68, 69
    MainProgram, 69, 70
    member variables, 73, 74
    methods, 71
    peeking-definition, 72
    programmer source file, 68
    structure window, 74
    thread class definition, 71
    view class hierarchy, 74, 75
  terminal session, 60
Community *vs.* ultimate editions, 1–5
Compatibility testing, 200
Compliance/conformance testing, 200

D, E

Debugging, 147
  addName()/removeName()
    methods, 152
  breakpoints, 161–163
  checked exceptions, 148
  context menu, 154
  createNames()/printNames()
    methods, 152
  DebugSample class, 151, 152
  errors, types, 147
  FileInputStream class, 158, 159
  gutter, 152, 153
  logic errors, 150
  main method, 156
  output window, 154, 155
  pause button, 157, 158
  program execution, 156, 157
  runtime errors, 148–150
  sender class, 150
  stack trace, 160
  step actions, 160, 161
  syntax error indicator, 147, 148
Developer testing, 201

T. Hagos, *Beginning IntelliJ IDEA*, https://doi.org/10.1007/978-1-4842-7446-0

F

Functional testing, 199

G, H

Git
  branches dialog, 177, 178
  changelist, 178–180
  commit tool window, 175–179
  diff dialog, 180
  distributed system, 165
  git-scm.com website, 168
  ignore files
    add file, 182
    gitignore files, 181, 184–187
    gitignore project folder, 181
    new file dialog, 182
    source code, 183
  local repository
    contents, 174
    JetBrains, 171
    MainProgram lit, 173
    plugin process, 168, 169
    preferences, 169
    project configuration files, 170, 172
    project structure, 173
    toolbar strip, 172
    version control integration, 169, 170
  terminal window, 166, 167
  version, 167
  working process, 166
GitHub integration
  authorization, 188, 189
  commit/push repo, 194, 195
  confirmation page, 190, 191
  gist creation, 195–198
  JetBrains IDE integration, 189, 190
  preferences/setting, 187

share project, 192, 193, 194
version control, 191

I

Inspection
  addressing
    actions, 83
    AnotherMethod(), 84, 85
    import, 86
    options, 84
    println() statement, 83
    resulting code, 85
    unreachable statement, 83
  error message, 82
  IDE features, 81
  IntelliJ flagging, 82
  red light bulb, 82
  source code
    context menu, 89
    errors/warnings, 86
    icons, 87
    main editor, 88
    quick fixes option, 89, 90
    scroll bar, 92
    split pane, 91
    stripes, 91
    unreachable statement, 89
    widget, 92
  whole project
    code action, 93
    list, 94
    resolutions, 95
    scope specification, 94
Integrated developer tools, 4
Integrated development
    environment (IDE), 39
  main editor
    Android project, 54, 55

code folding, 53

editor gutter, 53, 54

JavaFX scene builder, 55

warning icons, 54

navigation bar

class level, 46

glorified bread crumb, 45

package level, 46

project level, 45

problem tool window, 50, 51

project creation, 39–41

project tool window

options, 44

packages view, 42, 43

project view, 41

tool window bar, 42

scratch files

compilation, 48, 49

context menu, 47

project creation, 47

structure window, 44

terminal tool, 51, 52

TODO window, 49, 50

warning message, 51

IntelliJ IDEA

configuration, 10–12

customization, 11

installation options, 9

Java (*see* Java project)

JetBrains, 8

large project, 27–29

Linux, 10

macOS, 9

refactoring, 106–112

requirements, 8

Scene Builder tool, 264–266

Windows, 8, 9

Intention actions

edit settings, 97

keyboard shortcut, 97

println, 95, 96

split declaration, 96, 98

J, K

Java Development Kit (JDK)

download page, 6

installation, 6

IntelliJ IDEA (*see* IntelliJ IDEA)

Linux, 7, 8

macOS, 7

Windows, 7

Java Foundation Classes

(JFC), 236

JavaFX project

app running, 249

directory path, 246

Hello World

life cycle, 253, 254

Main.java, 254, 255

results, 252

sample.fxml file, 251, 252

history, 235–237

javafx-fxml library, 238

lib folder, 242

libraries, 240, 241, 243

modify configuration, 244, 245

modules, 242

project creation, 239

runtime error, 243

Scene Builder (*see* Scene Builder tool)

setup project dialog, 237

stage, scenes, and nodes, 249–251

structure, 239, 240

user-friendly apps, 235

VM options, 245–248

Java project
  build project, 22, 23
  Hello World output, 26, 27
  keyboard shortcuts, 20
  Main.java file, 18–20
  mark directory, 24, 25
  name/location/package, 18
  options, 14
  preference/autosave, 21, 22
  project creation, 15
  running program, 25, 26
  saving files, 20
  SDK project, 16
  search projects, 14
  template, 17
  tool window, 23, 24
  welcome window, 13, 14
JUnit plugin
  actual class
    classpath, 216
    download library, 213
    existing class, 211
    lib folder, 215
    MainProgramTest, 215, 217–220
    root folder, 211
    sayYourName()/addTwoNumbers()
      method, 214
    setUp() method, 217
    test creation, 212, 213
  assertEquals()
    method, 205, 209
  assertion class, 208
  classpath, 205, 206
  download library, 206
  failing test method, 209, 210
  lib folder, 207
  parameter hinting, 205
  preferences, 203

SampleTest.java, 204
shouldShowSimpleAssertion()
  method, 208

L, M, N, O

Large project, build
  download ZIP, 28
  GitHub, 28
  Hello World project, 29
  nontrivial projects, 27
  zipped file, 29
Live templates
  abbreviation/description, 141
  boiler-plate codes, 123
  context, 141, 142
  declaration, 142
  details, 140
  ENTER/TAB, 125
  export settings, 144
  fori template, 127–130
  group, 138, 139
  insert option, 124
  Java language, 136, 137
  loop structure, 126
  love-and-hate relationship, 123
  main() method, 124
  name creation, 139, 140
  parameterized templates, 126–128
  preferences dialog, 135, 136
  psvm template, 125
  publicmethod template, 143
  share templates, 143–145
  for statement, 127
  surround code template
    control structure, 131, 132
    getTree(), 131
    MainProgram, 135

null (ifn) template, 133, 134
printStackTrace() statement, 133
TreeFactory/Tree/MainProgram
classes, 130, 131
try-catch, 132, 133
variables, 134
System.out.println(), 126
TAB expression, 127
template text, 137, 138
text template, 141
Localization testing, 201

P, Q

Penetration/security testing, 201
Performance testing, 200
Project files, 31
external libraries folder, 36, 37
.idea folder, 33, 34
iml file, 31, 32
JetBrains decompiler, 35
Main.class file, 35
out folder, 34–36
src folder, 33, 34

R

Recovery testing, 201
Refactoring
code fragment, 105
code smells, 104, 105
coding phase, 101
extract method, 103
preview mode, 112
printDetails() method, 113
printSomething() method, 111
separate method, 111
extreme programming, 104

IntelliJ
getters and setters, 108, 109
person class, 110
rename operation, 110
selection, 106
source code dialog, 107
variable, 108
move members
class member, 113, 114
destination class, 116
static members, 115, 117
printDetails() method, 118
printSomeDetails() method, 120
printSomething() method, 102
rename variable search, 103
signature, 117–121
spaghetti code, 102

S

Scene Builder tool
download page, 255, 256
FXML files
containers, 259
editor tabs, 267
edit properties, 263
label, 261
sample.fxml file, 263, 264
templates, 258
TextField/button/label, 262
VBox controls, 260
IntelliJ configuration, 264–266
languages/frameworks, 264
links, 257
opening file, 266–268
untitled project, 257
visual composition, 255
Soak/endurance testing, 200

Sound testing, 201
Source control systems, 165
    Git (*see* Git)
    GitHub, 187–197
Spike/scalability testing, 200

T

Testing, 199
    create Test dialog, 226
    directory, 221–223
    failing process, 231
    generate keyboard, 224
    JUnit plugin, 203–220
    passing results, 232, 233
    PosNeg class, 224
    posNeg() method, 228, 230
    posNegNegativeOneOneFalse()
        method, 230
    PosNegTest class, 227–229

project creation, 220, 221
source code, 231, 232
test sources root, 223
types of, 199–201
unit testing, 201–203

U

Unit testing
    codebase, 202
    input fields, 201
    regression testing
        framework, 202
    running process, 203
    writing process, 202

V, W, X, Y, Z

Volume testing, 200
Vulnerability testing, 199, 201

Printed in the United States
by Baker & Taylor Publisher Services

Printed in the United States
by Baker & Taylor Publisher Services